The Catholic University as Promise and Project

Reflections in a Jesuit Idiom

The Catholic University as Promise and Project
Reflections in a Jesuit Idiom

MICHAEL J. BUCKLEY, S.J.

GEORGETOWN UNIVERSITY PRESS/WASHINGTON, D.C.

Georgetown University Press, Washington, D.C. 20007
© 1998 by Georgetown University Press. All rights reserved.
Printed in the United States of America.
10 9 8 7 6 5 4 3 2 1 1998
THIS VOLUME IS PRINTED ON ACID-FREE OFFSET BOOKPAPER.

Library of Congress Cataloging-in-Publication Data

Buckley, Michael J.
    The Catholic University as promise and project : reflections in a
Jesuit idiom / Michael J. Buckley.
        p. cm.
    Includes bibliographical references and index.
    1. Catholic universities and colleges—United States. 2. Jesuits—
Education (Higher)—United States. I. Title.
LC501.B627 1998
378'.0712'73—DC21
    ISBN 0-87840-711-1 (cloth)
    ISBN 0-87840-710-3 (pbk.)   98-16019

To
the Community of Holy Cross
and
the Department of Theology
at the
University of Notre Dame

in gratitude, admiration, and friendship

And what you thought you came for
Is only a shell, a husk of meaning
From which the purpose breaks only when it is fulfilled
If at all. Either you had no purpose
Or the purpose is beyond the end you figured
And is altered in fulfilment

—T. S. Eliot,
"Little Gidding"

Contents

Preface

Antinomies in Higher Education

Two events gave the fall of 1854 peculiar promise. August had seen the young Henry Adams, led by "custom, social ties, convenience and, above all, economy," cross the Charles River to enter upon his freshman year at Harvard College.[1] Harvard already figured among his earliest memories from childhood. One of the "singularly gloomy winter afternoons" had brought him and his mother to call upon his formidable aunt, Mrs. Edward Everett, whose husband served solemnly as President of the College.[2] But the autumn of 1854 had a different purpose. It was to initiate the four years of collegiate education Adams would one day remember and measure in his masterpiece, *The Education of Henry Adams*. Two months later in Dublin, John Henry Newman with some twenty residential students inaugurated the Catholic University of Ireland, proposing to advance into institutional practice theories already framed and published as the *Discourses on Scope and Nature of University Education*.[3]

Adams and Newman were to tower over the world of education through works remarkable for their disciplined sensibility and perception, the cogency of their prolonged argumentation, and the suppleness of their language. Both men were prodigious in their range of interests and exigent in the standards by which they evaluated human achievements. They diverged profoundly, however, in academic histories and ecclesial commitments. As students and as teachers, both engaged the university education of their times, but what they found or hoped to form in these institutions of 1854 marks off even for the university of today many of its questions and antinomies.

"The chief wonder of education," wrote Adams, "is that it does not ruin everybody concerned in it, teachers and taught." He softened the harshness of this pronouncement with the concession that the Harvard of the mid-nineteenth century proved "probably less hurtful than any other university then in existence." Admittedly during his four years, the content of the teaching was little and the manner of teaching poor, but "it left the mind open, free from bias, ignorant of facts, but docile. The graduate had few strong prejudices. He knew little, but his mind remained supple, ready to receive knowledge" like an empty sheet of stationery—blank, writes Adams, before the impressions it would receive, imprinted only with the Harvard watermark upon it.[4] Collegiate years fashioned an intellectual character more negative than positive, cleansing the mind from partisan narrowness and political—not to say, religious—enthusiasms.

The Calvinism for which previous generations once claimed Harvard had long since faded into a pale Unitarianism. This doctrinal evanescence did not turn Adams towards Concord and its Transcendentalists. For this young student, the material world was both too real for him to adopt Emerson's *Nature*, and at the same time too demanding to leave him satisfied with the education offered by the College. Theological education would not figure among the courses and conversations to be remembered. With a prose steeped in weariness, Adams judged that neither the president of the College nor the students took collegiate education all that seriously. "For them all, the college offered chiefly advantages vulgarly called social, rather than mental."[5]

The spring of 1859 came and with it graduation. Adams spoke as Class Day Orator. A distinguished relative protested that "as the work of so young a man, the oration was singularly wanting in enthusiasm." This young man wondered to himself whether "this absence of enthusiasm was a defect or a merit, since, in either case, it was all that Harvard College taught, and all that the hundred young men, whom he was trying to represent, expressed."[6] This was the calm, dispassionate, and, above all, critical habit of mind, one distant from inflamed convictions and "slipping away from fixed principles."[7] There is a paradox here. His was a generation, taught by the lecture system to question, but not to profess. Within the decade its graduates would be felling one another over the murderous fields of the Civil War, but even their fierce commitments, tested by the horror of those years, issued more from a Southern social instinct and a Northern moral judgment that were, if "beyond appeal, not an act either of intellect or emotion or of will, but a sort of gravitation."[8]

Before such a cultivated reserve, Newman's Catholic university with its articulate Catholic commitments could seem little more than vulgar, like the immigrant Irish roughs playing before their betters in the streets of Cambridge. To prepare for this short-lived institution, Newman had delivered, between 10 May and 7 June 1852, the first five of his lectures on the idea of the university. The next five were destined never to be presented as lectures but to appear that autumn initially as pamphlets. The complex of these lectures and pamphlets was published as a single volume in the subsequent year.[9] If Adams' great work was to display and weigh one form of higher education as it actually existed and had been experienced, Newman's was to argue the university as it was defined in theory and desired in intention. However attenuated Christian commitments might be found at Harvard, they were the source of the integrity of the university for Newman.[10] He could speak of the university as the product of the Church and of this in its turn as the issue of faith, but for Adams that could not be. "If he were obliged to insist on a Universe, he seemed driven to the Church," wrote Adams about himself, for "the Church alone had asserted unity with any conviction . . . but the only honest alternative to affirming unity was to deny it; and the denial would require a new education."[11] For Newman that sense of unity found its embodiment in the university, in its *circulus artium*, and was realized in the product of university education, the philosophic habit of mind.

Newman held as axiomatic that the Catholic university, like any university, bore as its determining goal this "cultivation of the intellect." It was a cultivation that made "discriminating convictions" possible. Students graduating from universities without this liberal education and the unity of mind it imparted were forever impoverished: they possess "no principles laid down within them as a foundation for the intellect to build upon; they have no discriminating convictions and no grasp of consequence." This was to be another great divide between description and desire. Both Adams and Newman raised the question about the purpose and character of a university education. If Adams reluctantly found that the social de facto predominated over the mental development of the student, Newman framed the purpose of the university emphatically in terms of the latter:

Our desideratum is, not the manners and habits of gentlemen;—these can be, and are, acquired in various other ways, by good society, by foreign travel, by the innate grace and dignity of the Catholic mind;—but the force, the steadiness, the comprehensiveness and the versatility of intellect, the command over our own powers, the instinctive just estimate of things as they pass before us, which sometimes indeed is a natural gift, but commonly is not gained without much effort and the exercise of years. This is real cultivation of mind.[12]

Affixed to the Georgian mansion opening onto St. Stephen's Green that once served as the new university's first home, a modest plaque still recalls Newman's government as rector—as well as the later presence of Gerard Manley Hopkins as professor of Greek and of James Joyce as student in the Jesuit remnant of what Newman had established, University College, Dublin. For unlike Adams' Harvard, Newman's Catholic University could not perdure. Too much counted against it even from its birth: the intractable narrowness of its episcopal supporters, the inability to grant civil degrees, the incapacity to communicate its nature and its purpose, the lack of sufficient secondary schools from which to draw an adequate student body. Some twenty-eight years later, in 1882, it would give way, assimilated as University College into the newly founded Royal University of Ireland. In properties that ranged from ecclesial commitments to intellectual development to cultural supports—the contrast between the two institutions was marked.

Harvard College flourished over the centuries, growing to number among the finest universities in the world. Newman's Dublin enterprise was soon to perish. But from its originating genius came much of the understanding and inspiration of what a university, a Catholic university, could become. For the dream of a Catholic university within the great centuries of enlightenment and modernity did not initially germinate nor did it die with Newman's institution on St. Stephen's Green, and as these universities passed into or out of history, they raised repeatedly the same questions about ecclesial character, unified purpose, concrete possibilities, and intellectual culture.

Over that same nineteenth century, comparable if inchoative Catholic institutions, beginning with Georgetown University in the last decades of the previous century, were launched in the United States, convoked under various auspices and writing very different histories. Universally strapped for funds in their feeble moments of foundation and similarly narrowed by the intellectual culture that was to surround and to support them, they emerged as major institutions of higher learning only some two hundred years after the great private universities of the East Coast and were defensively slow to recognize that, in Newman's words, "as to the range of University teaching, certainly the very name of University is inconsistent with restrictions of any kind."[13] Their initial years of threatened beginnings gave way to those of much greater development and progress, however one reads that development or weighs that progress.

Concomitantly, the antinomies posed in such different ways by Newman and by Adams have arisen anew for these institutions of higher learning. With mounting urgency, Catholic universities within the United States are asked or must ask themselves about their ecclesial identity and their academic purposes—whether they will repeat the religious and curricular histories of their peer institutions in the United States, whether they will become less religious in their commitments and character as they became better universities in the competence of their instruction, the range of their research, and the pluralism of their student bodies and faculties. Will they realize in their relationship between the church and the academy, between the academic institution and American culture, something of the possibilities suggested by the history and practice of Adams' college or by the theory of Newman's university? Unique to this century, perhaps even to this continent, may be the specific character given to these questions of the identity and the purpose of a Catholic university; but perennial are discussions, however specified by place and time, about the nature and character of higher learning within the institutions that foster such an education.

Questions of Character and Purpose

Such discussions are inevitable. They dictate the life of a university. For those who give or receive instruction within a university, who advance knowledge by discovery or inculcate the habits of mental culture, who govern, lead and deliberate about such an institution, are continually faced with this problem—whether they choose to pursue it or to ignore it—of determining the nature and the value of what they are doing. This relentless problem is, of course, both perennial challenge and opportunity for such an institution. A university is often only a composite of vastly divergent departments, multiple perspectives, and even insulating specialties. But it can be drawn beyond these separations into that vital interchange that constitutes an academic community by a common question native to its life: What are we doing together? A community exists when human beings share something in common. An academic community exists when what they share are the goods of knowledge in instruction, conversation, development, personal research, and collaborative inquiry.

Such a common, pervasive problem can evoke the discussions that inform and strengthen an academic community, i.e., the question about the identity, about the purpose and direction of a university. It only appears to simplify if confined to a single discipline or, more comfortably, to a single research project or an individual course. In isolated study, such questions can be pursued without touching the university as a whole. This appropriation to a single course or department of issues central to an entire university, however, does not address these questions. It actually represses them. For the questions and their resolution are by their very nature common to all the members of the university.

This isolation does not mean that the great questions of purpose and identity will go unanswered; it means that the answers will not come from the faculty and students. The questions will be answered by drift and default, by economic pressures and the unchallenged attitudes of minds formed by advertisement, social mobility, and television. When faculty and students fail to sustain a continual conversation about the nature and value of the education they offer and receive, when they abdicate their collective responsibilities, university education degenerates under alien influences into premature specialization, into the destruction of the college of the liberal arts, into an undergraduate instruction that is really not much more than a vocational honing, and into a paradoxically pervasive anti-intellectualism of unawakened minds restless with any discussion of the aims and contents of the academic institution itself.

Without serious academic damage, no university can escape the continuous question of what it is about—even if one concludes with the pessimistic reading of Professor Steven Muller, the former president of Johns Hopkins University, "that universities are turning out potentially highly skilled barbarians."[14] This judgment bears heavily and minatorially upon the future of this nation as a republic. Barbarians do not compose a free and responsible citizenry. As early as 1835, Alexis de Tocqueville wrote that "it cannot be doubted that in the United States the instruction of the people powerfully contributes to the support of the democratic republic; and such must always be the case."[15] Those without an educated ability to discern among incentives and arguments are easily manipulated, as their appetites are dominated by media hype, sophistic politics, and regressive appeals to sensationalism, money, race, power, and individualistic self-interest. It is no exaggeration to assert that the future of the democratic vitality of the United States depends upon the decisions it makes about education. Not the least of these determinations is that of the character and purpose of its universities.

These pages attempt to explore one province in the massive realm of American higher education: the Catholic university. Within this still very general subject of some two hundred and fifty colleges and universities, the following essays concentrate particularly upon questions and options that confront the twenty-eight Jesuit colleges and universities within the United States. This focus need not indicate a narrow or sectarian selection among the Catholic universities. One hopes that such a concentration can engage issues, promises, and possibilities that challenge other Catholic universities as well, that these explorations of problematic situations within Jesuit experience and institutions can evoke commensurate reflections from others engaged in Catholic higher education, and, finally, that the reflections of both can enrich the common inquiry into the aims, values, and disciplines that give direction and structure to American higher education in general.

For example, at a Jesuit university, the inherent and perennial call that a university discuss its collective meaning and the worth of its common achievements has been heightened both by the challenges that any new period carries and also by a significant recent development within the orientation of the Jesuit Order: the call that all of its academic commitments have as an essential dimension a concern for justice within this ravaged world, that somehow or other the education of its students engage the misery that is the lot of the vast majority of human beings. Though this summons has come from the Society of Jesus to the Society of Jesus, it is not a challenge unique to Jesuit higher education. It bears upon Catholic universities as such, and indeed—as will be argued in chapter 6—upon all universities. But this commitment raises profound questions of free inquiry and ideology, of social propaganda and humanistic education, of disinterested research and seemingly useless studies. As these questions are discussed here, occasioned by recent public commitments of the Jesuit Order, one trusts that they are not confined to so limited a sphere, but that they engage colleagues in Catholic and non-Catholic higher education.

For whom have these reflections been written? The question about audience is a legitimate question. The author has no particular professional group in mind, e.g., instructors, students, and staffs at universities, administrators, professors within American schools of education, concerned students of culture and religion, clerics, Jesuits, etc. The book is not aimed at a class or profession. It is aimed at those who for a million different reasons question the character or the future of the Catholic university and who possess a certain habit of mind, a capacity for a dogged willingness to commit oneself to what Hegel coined as *"die Anstrengung des Begriffs,"* the exertion of the concept.[16] What matters is not genius or much background or cleverness, but the burning issue and surrender to the demands of "patient, laborious, and at times tedious reflection."[17] It is hoped that this book will furnish some address to the questions about the Catholic university. One even hopes that the reader will not be too surprised to find in the following pages references to such classic texts as the *Contemplatio ad amorem* or to such concepts as instrumental cause. They appear because, as will be repeated throughout this book, the author is convinced that much of Catholic higher education takes its originating genius not so much from an antecedent philosophy of education as from one form or another of Christian spirituality.

Essays and Fragments

The following reflections do not pretend to a fullness of treatment, a comprehensive investigation of all the topics they engage. This book is more a collection of essays, each bearing upon a cognate question, than a steady and single argument. Its unity is thematic rather than systematic. Its subtitle attempts to signal this fragmentary character with "reflections." It comes out of a theological tradition that celebrates such fragmentation in intellectual reflections, whether these fragments form *stromateis* or *quaestiones quodlibetales*. Perhaps a word about this tradition to situate these essays.

Those committed to Catholic higher education, if they appropriate its history in some depth, are inevitably brought before the extant works of Titus Flavius Clemens, known to theological posterity as Clement of Alexandria. Born in the middle of the second century and educated in wandering fashion by scholars and thinkers in Greece, Magna Graecia, Syria, and Palestine, he finally settled in Egypt. Egypt gave him Pantaenus, educator and founder of the great catechetical school of Alexandria. Towards the end of the century, Clement succeeded to the direction of that center of Christian education or, at least—for the records are unclear—devoted the remainder of his life to lectures, instruction, and writing within it. Three major books remain from these efforts: the first, a work of apologetics addressed to pagans (*Protrepticus*), the second a treatise on the moral education of Christians (*Paedagogus*), and the last on ... practically everything. While the first two are systematic, Clement called this final volume of what is taken to be "his great trilogy" *Stromateis*, literally "tapestries," or a patchwork, pieces of cloth of different kinds. This title suggested a series of concentrated essays, written in a deliberately elliptical style, miscellanies if you will—a form that allowed him greater freedom of thought than the systematic cast of his previous books.[18] Subsequent theological education is indebted to Clement on so many scores, not the least of which is the legitimacy of reflection in fragments.

The Middle Ages continued this piecemeal tradition, albeit transposed into controversies. Together with the *lectio* or examination of "great books," the classic *quaestio disputata* constituted the heart of medieval university instruction: the problem stated, variant resolutions or objections proposed, elements of the resolution advanced and explored, the controversy engaged, and the *disputatio* closing with the *determinatio* by the master. Less well known are the *quaestiones quodlibetales*, those twice a year public disputations, done in the manner of a disputed question, in which any student or master or bachelor in the audience could propose any subject for a question and demand a response from the master. M.-D. Chenu notes that these lacked all unity in subject and entailed absolutely unforeseeable conflicts and consequences, so much so that many masters would not take the risk of such a public exposure. "This explains why we have so few large collections of *quodlibeta*."[19] Thomas Aquinas, however, apparently entered into this chaotic arrangement with gusto. Indeed, he may have pioneered this potentially embarrassing form of academic controversy, and this together with the boisterous students of Paris explains why we have *determinationes* from so grave a doctor on such questions as "whether a man can be a father and a virgin" and "which is more powerful, wine, women, the king or the truth?"[20] However unexpectedly topics emerged, the form in which they came into academic consideration continued the tradition of fragments in Catholic intellectual history.

From that tradition of reflections outside of systems, the following chapters draw their justification. These essays do not introduce and carry through to its resolution a single problem. Rather they deal with a variety of elements within a set of problems around a central topic: the character and issues of the Catholic, Jesuit university. As the variety of questions suggests, remembrance of the *stromateis* and *quodlibets* of the past, so the career of the central topic exhibits a thematic if not systematic unity.

The initial chapters consider the Catholic university in general; the subsequent ones specify this to the Jesuit university. This latter raises two problems, two "signs of contradiction" in the contemporary world: its commitment to open, free discussion and academic pluralism—to the objections of some in the church; and its commitment to the promotion of justice—to the objections of some in the academy. Finally, attention turns to the two architectonic wisdoms whose pursuit has been emphasized in the history of Jesuit higher education—indeed, in Catholic higher education in general—and which particularly need to be strengthened if that education is to flourish: philosophical and theological studies. Suggestions are made for the advancement of each of these disciplines: the first, in its emergence from all the forms of disciplined human inquiry and knowledge; the second, in its assimilation of the liberal arts as general skills specialized to theology. The thematic development, then, of this very general topic of Catholic, Jesuit higher education proceeds from issues of identity to those of recent growth to those of constitutive components.

Many more subjects could have been introduced—professional schools, disciplines of undergraduate education, research and learning in the graduate departments. Indeed, these should have been introduced if the attempt had been made to treat this topic comprehensively. This is not the effort of this book. Rather it proposes only to consider some of the questions or possibilities that arise almost spontaneously from the present crisis in growth and identity of the Catholic, Jesuit university in the United States.

Finally, one who writes of purpose and ideals, of hopes and promise for great growth must continually counter the charge that his essays ask for an ideal order that has never existed nor will ever be realized, that he dreams rather than perceives. But this charge confuses descriptive with prescriptive discourse, as if ideals are to be taken as descriptive of a place attained rather than as directives for a journey engaged. One does not realize ideals; one guides one's life by them. They are essential for significant decisions and development. Purposes and ideals do not require or request or expect completion; they do require or request or expect serious choices about a course of actions toward their increased attainment. It is a counsel of madness to describe a utopia in theory and demand it in practice; such dreams have proven themselves demonic. But it is a counsel of despair to condemn ideals because they are essentially regulative and always pervasively imperfect in their realization.

But there is a second reason for rejecting the counsel to write descriptions rather than discuss purpose and ideals. Quite simply, what has occurred in Catholic and Jesuit higher education could never have been antecedently described. One hundred years ago, one could never have predicted that these inchoative institutions would have developed in this fashion. Ideals and purposes drove their founders to create something new. Only as it was emerging has the Catholic university understood what its initial promise was to become, as it bore formatively in its history the achievements and the mistakes that enter into any human project. The university can enrich that future history by learning from both. Such a lesson constitutes part of its project. It explains the epigraph to this book. The purposes and the programs of the great Catholic educators were altered and will continually be altered as they approached further stages in their fulfillment.

MICHAEL J. BUCKLEY, S.J.
Boston College
October 12, 1998

Acknowledgments

Ungrateful is the person, wrote the Stoic Seneca, who denies a benefit previously accepted or pretends not to have been given one or fails to return the favor. But the most ungrateful of all is the one who has forgotten [*De beneficiis* III. 1.3]. The author of this book cannot forget that this work owes a great debt to others. It is a joy to remember their kindness with gratitude.

Students and colleagues too numerous to mention have contributed so much over the years, but I am particularly grateful to those who took the time to review this manuscript as it was evolving. I must express my appreciation to Charles Hefling, Sunny Manuel, Dennis Parnell, Stephen Privett, Stephen Schloesser, Michael Connolly and the members of the *Ratio Nova* Seminar of the Jesuit Institute who read earlier drafts and offered helpful suggestions. For their extensive comments on various redactions of the manuscript, I am deeply indebted to Joseph Appleyard, Martin Cook, Paul Goda, Eric Hansen, David Hollenbach, Leon Hooper, James Le Grys, George Madaus, and John Mahoney. I want especially to thank my brother, Tom, for his reading this text, his considered advice and his unflagging encouragement. Finally, I am grateful beyond counting to Brian Daley and John O'Malley. Brian submitted the entire manuscript to an exhaustive review; John gave the same attention to several redactions of specific chapters. They were particularly generous in making their immense scholarship so available. The assistance of these benefactors has eliminated many errors that marred original pages of this work. Those that remain are mine.

Earlier drafts of the reflections that follow have been published previously as papers in different contexts, and I am grateful to the publishers for their permission to adapt that material for use here. Chapter 1 in an earlier version appeared as "The Catholic University and the Promise Inherent in Its Identity," in *Catholic Universities in Church and Society: A Dialogue on Ex Corde Ecclesiae*, edited by John P. Langan, S.J. (Washington, D.C.: Georgetown University Press, 1993), pp. 74–89. Chapter 2 may be found as "The Church and Its Responsibility to Foster Knowledge," in *Current Issues in Catholic Higher Education* (volume 12, Summer, 1991), pp. 41–46. Chapter 3 was published as "A Collegiate Conversation," in the September 1993 issue of *America* magazine, pp.

18–19; I am also grateful to David O'Brien for permission to include his comments. Chapter 4 in a much different guise first appeared as "Theology and Critical Reasoning: Ignatius' Understanding of the Jesuit University," in *Critical Reasoning in Contemporary Culture*, edited by Richard A. Talaska (New York: State University of New York Press, 1992), pp. 333–349. Chapter 6 takes its origins from "The University and the Concern for Justice: The Search for a New Humanism," in *Thought* (volume 57, 1982), pp. 219–233. Chapter 7 derives from "The Catholic University as Pluralistic Forum," in *Thought* (volume 46, 1971), pp. 200–212. Much of Chapter 8 appeared as "Philosophy and the Liberal Arts," in *Perspectives* (Western Michigan University), volume 3 (1971), pp. 18–31. Finally, Chapter 9 may be found as "Toward the Construction of Theology: Response to Richard McKeon," in the *Journal of Religion*, University of Chicago Press (volume 58, Supplement, 1978) © 1978 by the University of Chicago. All rights reserved. pp. S52–S63.

I am indebted to John Samples, my editor at Georgetown University Press and to Patricia Rayner, production manager, for their patience, good humor, and diligence in shepherding this volume through the stages of publication. I am also grateful to the copy editors at Georgetown for their painstaking review of the manuscript.

My debt extends heavily to the Jesuit Institute at Boston College and its Manager, Susan Humphrey, as well as to my research assistants. Without Susan Humphrey's efficient management of the Jesuit Institute at Boston College, the ensuing chaos would inhibit the Director of the Institute from assuming such an undertaking as this book. Brian Hughes, my research assistant of five years standing, has been a part of this labor from its very beginning, and has worked diligently on both coasts to help bring it to completion. Joseph Curran and Michael Moreland have been indefatigable both in their research and in the final stages of preparing the manuscript for publication. For the generous and competent support offered continually by the Manager of the Jesuit Institute as well as by my research assistants, I am far more grateful than these few lines can convey.

I should like also to express my appreciation to the Jesuit communities in which these pages have been written: the Jesuits at Boston College, especially at Roberts House of which I am a member, and the Jesuits at Santa Clara University who have offered me their generous hospitality every summer of the past decade. For their brotherhood and support, I am deeply grateful.

Some ten years ago, Richard McBrien, the then Chairman of the Theology Department at the University of Notre Dame, graciously invited me to teach at Notre Dame. I did so, and for three years enjoyed the hospitality of that great University and the colleagueship of its exceptionally fine and friendly Department of Theology. Members of that department as well as members of the Holy Cross Community went out of their way to make me feel welcome. This book gives me the opportunity to express to the Holy Cross Fathers and Brothers and to the members of the Department of Theology my gratitude and great admiration. May they continue to prosper at doing what they have been doing so obviously well for so many years.

PART ONE

Crisis, Choice, and the Catholic University

CHAPTER ONE

The Catholic University and the Promise Inherent in its Identity

The problem of self-identity is not just a problem for the young. It is a problem all the time. Perhaps the problem. It should haunt old age, and when it no longer does it should tell you that you are dead.

—Norman Maclean, *Young Men and Fire*[1]

The Question and Its Urgency

At noon on 16 September 1992, Boston College, led by its president, was at prayer. The Mass of the Holy Spirit, celebrated on the steps of the O'Neill Library, was not a time for the president to address the faculty nor for administrators to make welcome incoming students nor for instructors to inaugurate their courses with information about semester requirements and contents. This had all been done at faculty convocation, over many meetings, and in initial classes. Now this complex of president and administrators, students, doctoral candidates and faculty—this university—turned formally and explicitly as a university to address God, to ask God's gracious guidance over the approaching year and over the directions of this university. Only custom and usage could blind one from seeing how singular, how strange it was that an academic institution in the United States would begin its year with the Eucharist. Perhaps it is here that the anomaly of the Catholic university becomes most palpable.

The great medieval universities out of which Boston College and all Catholic universities have historically arisen—Bologna and Paris, Prague and Oxford—initiated their year and inaugurated their government much as was done that day. In his magisterial history of the medieval universities, Hastings Rashdall records that in twelfth century Bologna, the greatest of university centers for Western law, "the scholastic year opened with a Mass of the Holy Ghost in the Dominican Church on the morrow of S. Luke, i.e. 19 October."[2] From Bologna to Boston College, the tradition and its commitments had held.

The prayers and readings that floated on the air of that brilliant autumn afternoon, now some seven centuries later, spoke repeatedly of the influence that is the heart of academic inquiry and learning, the Spirit of Truth. The Judeo-Christian Scriptures supported the petitions threading their way through the liturgy: that the Spirit of God would descend upon this university over the coming year, that this Spirit would mark its teaching, guide its inquiry and research, and permeate its collective life as a *collegium*, that this university as a Catholic university would realize the promise of the Gospel: "the Spirit of truth who will guide you into all truth" [Jn 16:13].

That the Mass of the Holy Spirit was being celebrated indicated a Catholic university, conscious of its past and faithful to its identity, possessed of the conviction that the religious and the academic belong in concert and that their union is to be celebrated in beauty and worship. That classes remained in session, that sundry students made their way indifferently through the congregation to reach the library, and that the university community—some thirteen thousand—attended only in the middle hundreds, bespoke disinterest among many as well as problems unresolved but pervasive in Catholic universities throughout the nation.

These numbers and the general recognition of the centrality of this religious moment would significantly augment in the years that followed, but I found myself wondering during the liturgy: What is this upon which we invoke the unspeakable mystery of God? What is this "we" who are at prayer? The question did not seem a distraction. It seemed central and pressing, with this kind of institution something of an unspoken enigma in American culture upon whose character and future one might well meditate as this community worshipped.

Many voices today state with increasing urgency that the Catholic university will disappear; that it is already disappearing as a specific reality in American higher education; that the Catholic university will repeat the secularizing history of so many of the great universities in the United States; that this evanescence of its religious character is inevitable, disclosing gradually the unfaced irrelevance of the religious to the intellectual; that as the university becomes more authentic, more academically distinguished, its Catholic character will proportionately become more muted, will incrementally dissipate and disappear. In a widely remarked article of several years ago, David R. Carlin wrote that the Catholic identity of such colleges and universities has since the 1960s "grown increasingly tenuous . . . Catholic colleges seem to be traveling the same road many Protestant colleges journeyed in the nineteenth and early twentieth centuries—a road leading to complete secularization, to complete loss of religious identity."[3] Distinguished thinkers in contemporary higher education have aligned themselves with such an interpretation of the present situation and urged that it be discussed before the question is overtaken by the threatened results. Despite countering reassurances from the insightful David O'Brien, Loyola Professor of Roman Catholic Studies at the College of the Holy Cross, and his more optimistic reading of the career of Catholic universities, it would seem ill-advised simply to dismiss these widespread concerns about the muting of their religious identity.[4]

Many of the greatest universities in the United States and Europe have already written such a history of religious atrophy.[5] One can wander about their campuses and remark the chapels and statues, the maxims on the gates or the portraits on the walls, and confront symbols that speak of a former religious intensity now long since dead. There one can paraphrase something of the cultural diagnosis of Friedrich Nietzsche: "What are these universities now if not the tombs of God—monuments to the death of God within an academic culture?"[6] It would be unwarranted to imagine that the Catholic university is not liable to the same influences, naïve to believe that it cannot repeat their history, albeit perhaps in a different mode.

As a matter of fact, Catholic universities have long since recapitulated much of the history of their secularized peers. One may recall the address of Robert Maynard Hutchins, then president of the University of Chicago, to Catholic educators as far back as 1937: "I find it necessary to level against you a scandalous accusation. . . . You have imitated the worst features of secular education. . . . What I say is that Catholic education is not Catholic enough." Hutchins directed this charge while recognizing that "the Catholic Church has the longest intellectual tradition of any institution in the contemporary world, the only uninterrupted tradition and the only explicit tradition; that is, it is the only institution which is conscious of its tradition. What I say is that this tradition must not be merely an idea, but must be practiced." In contradiction to this rich intellectual tradition, Hutchins found Catholic higher education adopting the worst of secular education: athleticism, collegiatism, vocationalism and anti-intellectualism. In these four areas, he stated: "I believe Catholic education is as bad as, maybe worse than, secular education."[7] Years have past since that judgment was leveled, but in continuity with it one may advance an additional question: whether this imitation will or has already reached into the Catholic identity of these institutions as well.

For the Catholic university is not a stable fact, not simply a here-and-now-and-always reality, not complete in itself. The nature and possibilities of anything human are disclosed only if its temporality is taken seriously. So the university must necessarily understand in itself—whatever its traditions and its promise, whatever the variant realizations that historical circumstances evoke or encourage—the possibilities of its own demise. "Human creations," wrote Sigmund Freud, "are easily destroyed."[8] Both the liabilities inherent in any human project and contemporary readings of the Catholic university, then, should make one peculiarly sensitive to the threat inescapably native to such a life-form: the Catholic university can be destroyed. It can admit its own dissolution as gradually and as imperceptibly as a sponge is permeated by silent drops of water.[9]

If this is true, then, one can only read the mission statements of some Catholic universities with a sinking sense of regret. The very vagueness of their language and the indeterminacy of their acknowledged commitments can leave one with the sense that the decline in some institutions may be already advanced, that the conjunction between a vibrant Catholicism or a Catholic culture and these universities appears increasingly faint, that the vision is fading. Presumably the mission statement is the document in which the university expresses its self-understanding, its character, its mission, and its dreams—to be confirmed or attenuated concretely through its subsequent allocation of resources and its policies in hiring. The mission statement should be the product of the university's thinking about itself: what it is, what it wants to do. It should be the public statements of its identity. The recent Apostolic Constitution, *Ex corde Ecclesiae*, is not alone in its expectation that there, or in some similar document, "every Catholic university is to make known its Catholic identity."[10]

One can select, almost at random, three mission statements that have come out of Catholic colleges and universities, each of them Jesuit, during these last decades. With obvious variations, they represent well one group of such documents from Catholic universities, and they raise the question—at least, the question—about the vitality of their Catholic identity.

All three frame general statements about education within the Jesuit or Judeo-Christian or Catholic tradition or identify the university as Jesuit or Catholic. They embrace the service of faith and the promotion of justice, the generic focus given to all Jesuit apostolic commitments by its Thirty-Second General Congregation.[11] However, there is not much beyond this level of formulaic generality, bland prose, and second-hand slogans. When one has left deference and set phrases behind, they do not indicate how this Catholic tradition and Jesuit orientation tell significantly and uniquely upon the educational core of these institutions, upon the content of its curriculum, its priorities in research, and its academic atmosphere. "Faith and justice" are not translated to play out concretely as an ideal for higher learning or for an academic integration of gospel and culture. Even further, the faith of Christianity—what constitutes the content and richness of the creed and inspired two thousand years of Catholic reflection and intellectual life—seems reduced to a general social ethic or morality. It is not what is contained in these documents that suggests decline. On the contrary, they comprise a number of valuable and important concerns. The problem is what is left out or reduced to faded, unchallenging generalities. It might be helpful to look at each of these three mission statements in more detail.

i. Contextualized by its religious tradition and wishing that the students develop their "full range of human qualities: intellectual, personal, social, moral, and spiritual," University X will afford students "the opportunity to have meaningful contact with art, music, history, philosophy, literature, and the religions of the world." This is the only mention of "religion" in the statement in a page devoid of reference to anything as stark as the self-disclosure of God or to Christ or to the Catholic Church. The term "church" appears only to recall the history of "service to church and state" that has characterized Jesuit colleges since the founding of Georgetown. Occidental or Smith could and would be willing to say almost as much, i.e., to speak respectfully of their religious traditions, however attenuated, to espouse "spiritual" development, and to include with their commitment to the liberal arts the study of "the religions of the world." The "Goals" coupled with this statement do not advance much beyond this pale picture. The only implication drawn explicitly from the Jesuit tradition in education is that this institution "aims to emphasize the importance of moral and spiritual values; to offer religious studies on an academic, ecumenical, professional basis; and to provide opportunities for religious worship and activities." Once again, it is hard to see any real difference between this and the goals set by many serious liberal arts colleges once identified with a particular religious tradition.

ii. In the prologue to its statement of identity, University Y also acknowledges the tradition out of which it comes, a religious heritage that comprises "compassionate service of persons in need, commitment to quality education, the service of faith and the promotion of justice." When one comes to the mission statement itself and how these charisms tell upon the academic community, it is stated that "the University takes its mission from its educational traditions which emphasize concern for the dignity of the person and for the common good of the world community. This education seeks to integrate intellectual, spiritual, moral and social development." Later in the document, "religious" will be added to this list, and the university is said "to provide a value-based holistic education of exceptional quality."

Whatever its rich tradition and whatever the quality of its offerings, this university's mission statement frames a vision lacking in anything specifically Christian. Granted its emphasis upon social leadership and responsibilities, the statement does not progress much beyond American civil religion and a committed social ethics. A secular university could locate itself comfortably within its rubrics with very few changes. One looks in vain for anything that needs or demands as inescapably appropriate to its mission the study of the influence of God, of Christ, of church, and of theology or indeed for anything uniquely Christian or Catholic in the paragraphs that speak of the core curriculum. They do not appear. The Catholic, Christian character is shaded off into a vacuity that offers neither challenge nor direction to the education given.

iii. One could take University Z as a final example, an institution whose "primary objectives are to develop the creative intellectual potential of its students and to foster in them ethical and religious values and a sense of social responsibility. Jesuit Education, which began in 1547, is committed today to the service of faith, of which the promotion of justice is an absolute requirement. [University Z] is Catholic in both tradition and spirit. It celebrates the God-given dignity of every human person." The University is satisfied to give this generic orientation of the Society of Jesus and to offer as the only academic specifications of the Catholic tradition and spirit the celebration "of the God-given dignity of every human person" and the welcome given to diversity. Beyond this, nothing is provided in the paragraphs that follow about the vision that Catholicism carries or about the unique character that such a Catholic, Jesuit concentration effects within the institution. Nothing specifically religious or theological figures in the descriptions of the liberal arts and professional schools, nothing about the interchange between culture and gospel. Nothing in this statement indicates how the genius of Catholicism tells upon the kind of student that the University hopes to produce. Any cultivated intellect, however innocent of religious engagements or persuasions, could subscribe to the educational ideals concretely enumerated to guide this Jesuit university.

The blandness in these documents, I suspect, emerges from several conjoined factors, the first two of which paradoxically constitute the liabilities of an overall change for the better. First, Catholic educators can remember the parochial narrowness that too often marked pre-conciliar Catholic higher education and the language that covered while it promoted that narrowness. One cannot forget the stultifying arrogance encased in such statement as "we have the truth," nor the restraint upon open discussion occasionally attempted or effected by ecclesial authority while citing a doctrinal understanding of the church. There the appeal to the specifically "Catholic" had become sectarian and confining. It served to undermine the credibility of Catholic higher education.

No one wishes to return to the constrictions of those days. Indeed any contemporary efforts—however abortive—to impose that kind of control over the faculty or the speech of the campus have proven counterproductive: they generate or encourage the very tendencies towards secularity they were enlisted to oppose, as if "secularity" were the only effective defense against unwarranted and crippling inhibitions upon the academic freedom of the university. The vagueness in so many mission statements may be attempts to join the Catholic with the credibly academic, presenting the identity of the institution in terms vague enough to dampen any disparagement of its academic life or to inhibit any temptations for outside interference. The bland has been formulated as a defense of credibility and freedom.

Second, over recent years, the Catholic university has progressively added more and more faculty from traditions other than its parent culture. These additions and the resultant pluralism within the university spell out significant institutional progress. It is commonly admitted as an axiom that all reasonable discourse should find its place within a university. A university is to include the variant forms of human culture. But when one attempts, then, to write a common statement of mission or purpose for the institution and to pass this document through the faculty, the very diversity within the faculty can discourage anything much beyond religious banalities. "No faculty member should be excluded or made to feel second class; none should be imposed upon" becomes the measuring axiom according to which the foundational concerns of the university are to be described. And the articulation of a strong Catholic vision for the university can be taken as relegating those of other faiths and traditions to a secondary status. What emerges, then, in the self-statements of the university, is the lowest common denominator, offending no one and subsuming the Catholic character of the university under general phrases about tradition and slogans about social concern that have become unobjectionable because they are politically correct.

But this is ultimately self-defeating. Such a settlement does not appreciate a crucial point: that the Catholic identity of the university is not to counter or exclude the fundamental humane and religious values of other traditions, but to support and endorse their presence. The Catholic university essentially presupposes that serious religious and humane commitments constitute a crucially important focus of human life and belong in a university that is to comprise all human culture. The very Catholic character of the university, then, offers still another reason, besides the comprehensive nature of the university, to treasure the profound values of other religions and intellectual traditions. It should support these traditions and find support within them as religious and as humane. The Jew and the Protestant and the secular humanist should find in this Catholic academic community a greater respect and encouragement for so much they hold dear than they would experience in a university ostensibly free of all confessional affiliations and indifferent to religious interests. The Catholic university should provide still another encouragement for the pursuit of so many of their values, support them out of its own religious genius as well as theirs, and become a more authentic university as it sponsors those open religious discussions that are an ultimate indication that these traditions are taken seriously. Such a common academic life offers both a significant contribution to each religious or academic tradition and a strengthening of the vitality of the exchange that is a university.

Third, the featureless character of some mission statements may also result from the need to garner funds from state and federal agencies or from those foundations or benefactors that are suspicious of religion and Christianity. But here the history of the nineteenth century may be repeating itself:

> Philanthropic foundations also figured in the secularization of higher education. The Carnegie Foundation before World War I specifically excluded church-related schools from receiving grants, holding that such institutions by definition put limits on intellectual freedom and could not meet the test of a true college or university. In 1905, it offered to fund pensions for faculty but restricted eligibility to nonsectarian higher education. Anxious for financial support, Bowdoin, Wesleyan, Rochester, Drake, Coe, Hanover, Occidental, and other schools cut their already tenuous denominational ties. In the century following the Civil War, several hundred colleges, once strongly Protestant, became officially nonsectarian.[12]

Other examples could have been selected from the identity or mission statements of Catholic universities in the United States, but these should suffice. These are cited not to disparage academic institutions that have served the church and society well and continue to do so today. They are not deprecated in any way. It is common knowledge that their accomplishments are far greater than the contents of their mission statements. But it is precisely when such significant institutions are satisfied to allow the Catholic character of their education to fade into blandness, to be subsumed by vague contextual references to a religious heritage, to be described by moralisms that any mildly enlightened figure would applaud, then one who admires such institutions and hopes for great things from them cannot but suspect some decline, at least in collective vision. It presents a situation that merits reflection.

Extrinsicism

In response to the threat or in anticipation of such a decline, many Catholic educators have attempted to articulate for our own time the meaning of such a distinct academic institution as the American Catholic university. Some have defined it through the activities of campus ministry and the presence of religious and Catholic lay faculty and requirements in religious studies or in theology. This definition-through-its-elements resembles the strategy of the Protestant universities of the nineteenth century: "There were three defining characteristics of the leading nineteenth- and twentieth-century Protestant colleges and universities: chapel service, parietal rules, and a capstone course in moral philosophy."[13] This history of this definitional procedure has not been a happy one.

Others have described the Catholic university as one in which there is a strong Catholic presence. It is a university in which the church has a pronounced presence. A single example might suffice. In his annual report for the academic year 1980–81, the late Timothy Healy, S.J., an influential as well as much loved and admired Jesuit educator, framed the question in this manner: "How does the Church live within a university? How do the two institutions interact on common ground? Indeed how do they share in the minds and hearts of faculty and students? In more local terms, what is it that makes and keeps Georgetown Catholic?" In response, Father Healy suggested a vision in which the church and the university are cast as two distinct, interacting institutions: "The Church also lives here [in a Catholic university] in two distinct ways: first, it leads *its own life* on our grounds; secondly, the church *joins in, shares and influences the life and the work of the university* itself."[14] In explaining the latter, Father Healy maintained that at Georgetown, "education remains principally a *secular* business, and the university is a *secular entity* with a clear secular job to do. The Church can deeply influence how that secular job is done."[15] Presumably the Catholic university is a secular reality modified by the presence and the influence of the sacred—without ceasing to be its secular self.

This seems seriously inadequate. At best, it presents a vision of the Catholic university in which the religious and the academic, however interrelating and intersecting, are fundamentally extrinsic to one another. In no way does either bring the other to its own intrinsic or inherent completion. They do not constitute a cultural unity. The religious has its distinctive life and set of functions; the university has its own set of functions. Father Healy's "two distinct ways" in which the church is to share in an institution could describe the presence of the church within any major secular society, as the church "joins in, shares, and influences the life and work" of the City of San Francisco, the deliberations of the federal government, and the University of Massachusetts. In each, the essentially secular (to use Father Healy's distinctions) is somewhat directed and shaped by the religious, which exists as a separate entity within. Theologically, such an understanding of the Catholic university reads like dated theories of "pure nature" and "the supernatural."

To understand the genius and the unique academic promise of the Catholic university, however, one cannot frame the relationship between knowledge and faith, nature and supernature, the "secular" and the "sacred" as extrinsic to one another—two distinct entities related to one another only additionally or influentially. The failure of so many *apologiae* for the Catholic university may well issue from a heritage of the neoscholastic misunderstanding and miscasting of the relationship between nature and grace, an extrinsicism carried for centuries by the manualist tradition in school theology. In this tradition, "nature" was treated as a unit, entire unto itself, with "grace" taken as an addition to nature for which nature had no intrinsic orientation. Grace was, in that sense, "extrinsic" to nature.

One should not think that this extrinsicism in education is a recent compromise, a contemporary concession to secular respectability. From 1894 through 1952, the annual catalog of Boston College carried a four-page statement of the educational system of this Catholic institution, informing its readers that "education is understood by the Fathers of the Society in its completest sense, as the full and harmonious development of all those faculties that are distinctive of man. . . . Learning is an instrument of education, not its end. The end is culture, and mental and moral development." There follows a detailed exposition of the academic training of the student, defended in terms of the training of the human faculties.

Religion, let alone theology, is not mentioned until the last paragraphs:

> Lastly, the system does not share the illusion of those who seem to imagine that education, understood as an enriching and stimulating of the intellectual faculties, has a morally elevating influence in human life. While conceding the effects of education in energizing and refining imagination, taste, understanding and powers of observation, it has always held that knowledge and intellectual development of themselves have no moral efficacy. *Religion* only can purify the heart, and guide and strengthen the will.
>
> The Jesuit system of education, then, aims at developing, side by side, the moral and intellectual faculties of the student, and sending forth to the world men of sound judgment, of acute and rounded intellect, of upright and manly conscience. And since men are not made better citizens by the mere accumulation of knowledge, without a guiding and controlling force, the principal faculties to be developed are the moral faculties.[16]

The catalog is quite clear. The secular subjects develop the intellect in habits and knowledge; the teaching of religion develops the student morally. By the most ironic of paradoxes, this is not too distant from the current secularist distinction: science deals with facts; religion deals with values. What is even more remarkable is that this statement "was embodied in whole or in part in the catalogs of a number of other Jesuit colleges from coast to coast."[17] The reduction of religion to morality has a long history.

Did the prose of the catalog simply fail to do justice to the Catholic character of the college? Yes and no. The Catholic colleges of those years—many a combination of what is now the four-year high school and three years of college—were custodial institutions: Catholic because their components were by-and-large Catholic—students, faculty, administrators—with courses that excluded alien influences and with libraries and textbooks ecclesiastically censored. These institutions were to safeguard the faith and morals of their students and to defend Catholic truth against contemporary error. Much of the "Catholic character" of these institutions came out of this custodial focus and penetrated the discipline, the round of studies, the conversations, and the expectations of the campus. The Catholic culture of these institutions sustained much of their Catholic character, e.g., daily mass, First Friday devotions, and monthly confession. So often when contemporary concerns about

Catholic identity mount to threnody, what is mourned is the decline of the custodial institution.

But that being said, the catalog was more a mirror than a distortion. Theology was not taught; religion was. Neoscholastic philosophy was taken as the culmination of the curriculum. The courses in religion were catechetical and apologetic, and were not infrequently taught by the more inept members of the faculty. What is important to notice even during these years is the separation of serious studies and professional education from an inherent relationship with theological reflection. Religion was for propositional orthodoxy and Christian morality. In no way did it organically integrate with the other disciplines, bringing the dynamism of the mind to its native completion in the self-revelation of God. One can legitimately explore not so much how Catholic such an institution was, but how much of a university the institution was, whether Catholic or otherwise.

Thus, it is critically important to note, if only by way of contrast, that the contemporary problematic does not present only a single vector within the history of the Catholic university, that of inevitable or threatened decline from a past that was golden. This would be to "romanticize the Catholic past," a sentimentalism that David O'Brien justly censures.[18] Like most historical phenomena, the situation emerges as far more pluriform and complicated than such an oversimplification expresses. The Catholic character of the universities has been strengthened academically over the past thirty years, for example, by the establishment of theology as a significant academic discipline within undergraduate education and as an area of scholary inquiry within graduate education. There can be found in the United States something unprecedented in the history of the church: thousands of women and men studying theology in their early adult years with the intellectual care and seriousness that higher education demands. In addition, Catholic theology itself is becoming no longer a clerical preserve, but a lay discipline as well. Hundreds of young lay women and men are majoring in theology as an undergraduate concentration, taking advanced degrees in theology, and assuming professorial positions in departments of theology—again, an unprecedented development. Both of these phenomena bespeak a radical advance in the religious identity of these institutions and in the execution of their responsibilities to the life of the contemporary church.[19]

Such positive indicators counterbalance but do not settle the question about the vitality in religious identity and the muting of a Catholic character. Single courses or programs do not provide the intellectual formation that only a vital Catholic culture can provide, although such courses may well suggest that the issue can be addressed more effectively. One must further admit that the current lack of a structured relationship among the disciplines within the university continues to foster an extrinsicism between the academic and the religious. Theology remains one more course among others. Fragmentation lives, and many celebrate it as culture come of age.

The Integrity of the Academic and the Religious

The fundamental proposition that grounds the Catholic university is that the academic and the religious are intrinsically related, that they form an inherent unity, that one is incomplete without the other. What does this foundational conviction mean? It means that each term of this dyad and the realities to which they refer—the academic and the religious—do not simply exist juxtaposed to one another in influential contiguity. It means, rather, that one dynamically involves the other. This proposition, then, stands in need of some explanation.

Any academic movement towards meaning or coherence or truth, whether in the humanities, the sciences, or the professions, is inchoatively religious. This provocative statement obviously does not mean that quantum mechanics or geography is religion or theology. It does mean that the intellectual dynamism inherent in all inquiry initiates processes or habits of questioning that—if not inhibited—inevitably bear upon the ultimate questions that engage religion.

Any inquiry moves to the satisfaction of questions. Any satisfaction of questions sets in motion further questions, which in their turn open up further inquiry. Questioning keeps "going on" because the drive to know is not satisfied. It is looking for something else. The drive of the human mind is towards an ultimacy, i.e., towards a completion or a whole, in which it can obtain comprehensive sense. The human intellect moves asymptotically towards the satisfaction of inquiry in this completion. One keeps asking questions—unless this natural drive is repressed—until they lead to questions about ultimate explanation or intelligibility, about the truth of the finite itself, "which all human beings call God."[20] This relentless inquiry constitutes the natural career of the academic mind unless the culture arrests its progress by dictating the despair of its fulfillment.

Similarly, the commitments and the instincts of faith are inescapably towards the academic. This again and obviously does not suggest that all serious religion is scholarship and academic inquiry. It does mean that the dynamism inherent in the experience of faith—if not inhibited by fideism—is towards the understanding both of itself and of its relationship to every other dimension of human life. Faith moves towards its own self-possession in comprehension. The experience of faith becomes the source of questions that lead naturally into the sciences and arts, questions that bear upon the meaning and truth of the commitments of faith and upon the relationship of so universal a stance towards everything else that falls within human experience.

If allowed their full development, then, the religious intrinsically engages the academic, and the academic intrinsically engages the religious—granted that this development is de facto always imperfectly realized at best or often seriously frustrated. One leads into the other. To assert this fundamental proposition is not to guarantee the realization of this dynamism, but to speak about its direction. Any ideal such as this will at best remain as much aspiration as accomplishment.

To grasp the character and promise of the Catholic university, then, one must understand it as a unique institution, dedicated to the organic fulfillment of these two desires for knowledge. The inherent integrity both of the full faith-experience moving towards intelligence and of finite intelligence moving towards its satisfaction in transcendent completion—this mutual entailment—is what a Catholic university must affirm and embody, however halting and imperfect its attempts.

Thus, it is no accident that historically the university issued out of the church—not out of the hierarchy alone, but out of the people of God, the community that is the sacrament of human salvation. John Paul II has stated that

> such an ecclesial origin of the university cannot have been fortuitous. Rather, it expresses something more profound. But why does the church need the university? ... The reason for this need should be sought in the very mission of the church. In fact, the faith which the church announces, is to be a *"fides quaerens intellectum"*: a faith that demands to penetrate human intelligence, to be *thought out* by the intellect of the human person.[21]

The Catholic university is that academic community of higher education which issues out of the church and in which the church, in the words of the Second Vatican Council, "strives to relate all human culture to the announcement of salvation."[22] This is "all human culture," comprising whatever passes for significant discourse, for philosophic, scientific, and humanistic inquiry, etc. What the Catholic university proposes is a union between the human and the divine, a union between culture and faith. Perhaps it is here, above all, that the paradox of the Catholic university emerges into evidence—the tradition out of which it comes touches jarringly upon the understanding of higher education in contemporary America.

Christ as Paradigm

Why this paradox? Because if one would understand the Catholic university, certainly also in its Jesuit character, one must understand it in terms of Christ—and not Christ simply as a sapiential teacher out of the history of religion, but as the one in whom God worked the personal union of the divine and the human, the final purpose of all things. For the Catholic theological imagination, any unity between the divine and the human, even as this comprises faith and human culture, finds its paradigmatic realization in Christ.

But isn't that all rather speculative, rather tediously abstract? Not really; ideally, just the opposite. The doctrinal vocabulary may ring abstract and the long history of the dogmatic debates run into a badly remembered past, but the basic point is bread-and-butter Christian belief and piety. Jesus is the union of God and humanity. So also—similar, but also very dissimilar—the Catholic university is a union of faith and all human culture. God becomes incarnate in humanity; faith becomes incarnate in human culture. Divinity does not become humanity; faith does not become culture. But if they are not identified, neither are they separate. The reality of Christ lies in the union of divinity and humanity; the reality of the Catholic university lies in the union of faith and human culture. In this sense, one can say that Christ is the model of the Catholic university. But this needs to be clarified.

For the Christian, the wisdom and the revelation of God is above all in Christ. What does this mean? It means that if one wants to apprehend something of the incomprehensible mystery that is God—what God thinks and judges and directs, one can find this revealed above all in Christ—even allowing for the infinite difference between the divine Word and the finite humanity of Jesus. If one wants to determine what is a completely human life—even, what it means to be a human being—one will find that above all in Christ. Christ is the revelation of God; Christ is the revelation of the human being. It was for Blaise Pascal, mathematician and philosopher, scientist and contemplative to put this Christian conviction so starkly: "Not only do we understand God only through Jesus Christ, but we understand ourselves only through Jesus Christ. We understand life and death only through Jesus Christ. Outside of Jesus Christ we do not know what life is, nor death, nor God, nor ourselves."[23]

But what is more: Christ is not only the disclosure, he is the union of the divine and the human—a union classically called "hypostatic" or "personal" in Catholic theology. In this union, each of the constituents remains. The human is not destroyed nor absorbed into the divine. Jesus does not cease to be fully human. Just the contrary. He becomes more completely human in this unity. The divine does not annihilate the human, but in this union brings the human to its perfection. The humanity remains human; the divinity remains divine. One nature is not transposed into the other. They are united, not identified. They are united in the person that is Jesus of Nazareth.

Something analogous to the hypostatic unity is true of the Catholic university. The Catholic university knows that religion does not substitute for the sciences and arts. Physics does not become theology and business is not piety; law remains forever itself and mathematics has its own autonomy. Faith and culture are distinct, but not separate. In the university, they are united but not identified. What the Council of Chalcedon said of the humanity and divinity of Christ can be said of faith and human culture as components of the Catholic university in a highly analogous fashion: one is not to be confused with another; one is not to be changed into the other; they are not to be divided off from one another; they are not to be separated from one another.[24] It is their unity that constitutes the university. It is their individual integrity that allows for them to be united rather than identified. And this union—not identity or confusion—is finally between faith and all forms of human culture.

The Christian believes that Christ, the personal union between the human and the divine, is the disclosure of the meaning of all things. It is in Christ that one comes to apprehend something of that unity which is the completion of human life. So, if one looks at the origins of the Jesuit university for an example of one kind of Catholic university, one will discover that it emerges not so much from a philosophy of education as from a spirituality that moves to the union of all things in Christ. It is the urgency of this spirituality that lies at the basis of the Jesuit university, and its character cannot be captured without reference to Christ. As Gerard Manley Hopkins asked:

Wording it how but by him that present and past,
Heaven and earth are word of, worded by?[25]

Other phrases may be more culturally intelligible, but they cannot substitute. Jesuits have used "men and women for others" as a true, even gallant phrase from their previous Superior General, and it captures much of the orientation of the university, but there is nothing particularly Christian about it. The phrase occurs in Porphyry's description of the consciousness of the neo-Platonic philosopher, Plotinus: "He was able to live at the same time both within himself and for others."26 "Educating the whole person" is invoked by educators at every graduation; "well rounded" goes back to Horace's "*in se ipso totus, teres atque rotundus*"; while it is from Juvenal that one obtains "a sound mind in a sound body." Even the motto of Boston College, "ever to excel," comes from the Sixth and Eleventh Books of the *Iliad*.27 All of these are appropriate; none of these is adequate. If one would understand the unique character of the Catholic university, it must be explicitly in terms of Christ, Christ reaching out to all things to unite them in his disclosure of God—to Horace and Plotinus and Homer and Juvenal.

The Catholic university takes its historical beginnings and its articulated purpose, then, in the unity of all things with God, a unity whose principal instantiation and pattern is found in Christ. The university embodies this unity in the intersection of faith and culture, the divine self-disclosure and the great achievements of human beings in knowledge, practice, and the arts, in the cultivation of the mind in all of its ranges. This intrinsic union is its fundamental identity.

What could that mean concretely? Perhaps a very small example: We learn something about the meaning of human life and death from Tolstoy—the great stretches of its promise and beauty, the pathos of its young loves and misunderstandings, the sorrows of its partings and betrayals. We also learn something about our life and death from courses in human anatomy and physiology, in human genetics and neurophysiology; we see something of ourselves in the self-replication of DNA and the evolution of the species through natural selection. We learn also about human life and death from political science and economics—the study of the interaction of nation states, the massive issues of war and peace, the relationship between interest rates and inflation, a free market economy, welfare and the possibilities of a humane life for the poor. Schools of nursing, social work, education, law and business immerse their students in so much of what it is to be human.

But we finally understand human life in terms of Christ. As the Catholic university is coherent in its education, we bring all of that human promise and beauty, pathos and sorrow, intricate structures and biological drives, massive disagreements and debates about political interactions and economic forces to a theological inquiry into what it means to hear the great promise of the Gospel: "I have come that they might have life and have it more abundantly" [Jn 10:10]. Without the density that all the human disciplines and human experiences impart to the word "life," ecclesial statements about more abundant life in Christ could become the empty recitation of catechetical formulae; but, on the other hand, without the serious appropriation of the promise of Christ, we could look upon all of the human richness that the disciplines impart as provisional moments before the final word that is death. In their union, human culture and faith are brought to a new depth and a reflective enhancement.

The Catholic University and Its Definition

The Catholic university is to realize this intrinsic relationship of culture and gospel in the many ways in which it is a university: in the research and instruction and conversations that give a peculiar expression to its spirit; in the service and symbols and collective life and richness of an ecumenical Catholic culture; in the intellectual growth of its students and faculty and in the sharing of the diverse traditions out of which they come; in the passion for a just society that must characterize its graduates and that will in turn measure the religious and humane quality of their education.

How is such a university Catholic? The university is Catholic, above all, in its deliberate determination to render the church and the broader world this unique service: to be an intellectual community where in utter academic freedom the variant lines of Catholic tradition and thought can intersect with all forms of human culture, with the most complex resources, challenges, contradictions, and reinforcements of contemporary thought, and can move towards a reflective unity—in the knowledge and habits of the students, in the directions of faculty research, and in the vital interchange of the academic community—between human culture and the self-revelation of God.[28]

These do not simply intersect; one brings the other to its completion. The experience and practices of faith reach a new completion as faith advances into human understanding; the human dynamic to understand, found in whatever field of inquiry, reaches a new completion in the ultimacies of the self-disclosure of God.

It is not that the Catholic university is an institution in which the church—almost as a foreign body—is present and has an influence as extrinsicism would have it. The Catholic university exists to deepen the unity between Christian faith and all the forms of knowledge. No other institution within human culture can render this unique and critically important contribution to the church and to the contemporary world.

The university's reach must be towards all things, towards anything that bespeaks human experience and serious discourse—so that members of traditions other than Catholic should find themselves more at home here than elsewhere, experiencing that the high human and religious values, the humane achievements and concerns, to which they have given their own lives, are treasured, affirmed, and fostered here with an intensity and concern that comes out of the Catholic character of the university. Here, in its purpose, lies its meaning and its urgency.

This unique purpose gives or should give a particular cast to the internal academic structure of the university—to the priority of questions that its research will entertain, to its evaluation of the knowledge most worth having, to the habits it inculcates as part of the education of its students, and to the common life, spirit and atmosphere it fosters. It is the order of questions for inquiry, of knowledge for instruction, and of intellectual habits for assimilation that gives each institution of higher learning its formal identity and integrating spirit. In a Catholic university, this organic integrity of the several disciplines and sciences should be embodied finally in a theological wisdom in which all of the sciences and arts, professions and forms of human achievement are integrated (united, not identified) both in the structure of the curriculum and in the habits of mind that such an education should elicit.

It is here that so many of the component elements become critically important. They become the internal agencies through which the purpose and the structure of the Catholic university are to be realized. It is not that this university is made either religious or Catholic simply by the presence of a vital campus ministry, required courses in theology, or the significant presence both of Catholic intellectuals within its faculty and of professors from other traditions who understand and contribute to its mission. But these are indispensable if the university is to be sustained actively in its Catholic identity. It is hard to imagine the university's continuing to exist without deliberate policies of hiring and encouragement that would insure the presence and the strength of these vital sources of its life. All of them enter in with the students, staff, faculty, and administrators to form and effect the community that is concretely this university, a community defined by its governing purpose: the unity of the gospel with all human culture. Such a community must also include within itself all that passes for knowledge, all human traditions and cultures as well as the academic freedom which makes open discussion possible. Without the active presence of all of these various traditions, it would be neither a university nor of service to the church in promoting the relationship of the gospel "to all human culture."[29] The fullness of intellectual culture is essential if the gospel is to achieve both its reflective depth and union with all that is human; and the presence of Catholic intellectuals and of others committed to the identity and mission of the university is essential if the pursuit of knowledge is to be encouraged in its own reach towards ultimacy and final meaning, if the university is to be formed into what it is.

The multiple components of the Catholic university can be subsumed under "faith" and "human culture"—however various and multiple the instantiations of either—and the purpose of the university is to
realize in so many different ways their unity. This inherent unity bespeaks the character and the purpose of the Catholic university: to allow
the dynamism native to each to reach its completion in the other. Rather
than truncate the dynamism of knowing through interdicting the religious dimensions of life or isolating the religious from the academic, the
Catholic university has the resources and the charge to integrate them
by allowing each its full development. The university strives for a coherence that for the Christian reaches its paradigmatic expression in Jesus
Christ and extends to all forms of human culture and knowledge.

Something of this purpose occurs in the Catholic universities of the
United States, however partial and halting. These universities will realize
their own unique identity to the degree that this integrity is their
achievement. No other institution in the church can promote the full
development and embody the inherent unity between the academic and
the religious nor offer the church a place where steady and serious
reflection can be brought to bear upon issues that arise at the intersection of faith and human culture.

This constitutes the major challenge for the contemporary Catholic
universities: to become gradually what they are, to realize their identity,
to allow what is prescriptive discourse to become valid description. In
this identity is their promise; in this promise is their identity.

Ex corde Ecclesiae

In the very recent past, the Holy See, out of its concern for the integrity
of the Catholic university, has issued the Apostolic Constitution, Ex
corde Ecclesiae, which explores this issue of identity and which constituted the initial occasion for the reflections of this chapter.[30]

This Apostolic Constitution insisted upon the organic integrity of
faith and knowledge, not so emphatically in the document itself and its
norms as in the papal introduction.[31] These first eleven paragraphs take
up precisely the point presented here as crucial: the inherent and dynamic integration of the academic and the religious. The Pope phrases
this unity as that of a "universal humanism," which conjoins reflectively
all "aspects of the truth in their essential connection with the supreme
Truth, who is God" [4]. The components that are brought to their natural
integrity are variously described as "faith and reason" [5] or "the riches
of Revelation and of nature" [5] or "Gospel and the variety and immensity of the fields of knowledge" [6] or the church together with science

and world cultures [10]. The Pope envisages in the university "the united endeavor of intelligence and faith that will enable people to come to the full measure of their humanity, created in the image and likeness of God, renewed even more marvelously after sin, in Christ, and called to shine forth in the light of the Spirit" [5].

Such an integrity issues out of an "encounter . . . between the unfathomable richness of the salvific message of the Gospel and the variety and immensity of the fields of knowledge"[6]. The "encounter" with a clear determination of its components brings the discussion of the specificity of the Catholic university into a relief that seems absent from a number of mission statements of the American Catholic universities. The papal introduction does not speak explicitly of the native dynamism of the intellect for the ultimacies of the religious or of the religious for its self-possession in knowledge, but it does suggest this organic unity of desire by speaking of the Catholic university as "distinguished by its free search for the whole truth about nature, the human person and God" [4 (m)]. And it strengthens this dynamic orientation with its appeal to Augustine and Anselm: "Intellege ut credas; crede ut intellegas"[5].

The initial section of the Apostolic Constitution takes up the Catholic university as described by the final document of the Second International Congress of Delegates of Catholic Universities, and here the theory seems less satisfactory. The list of four characteristics is neither clear nor is its adequacy self-evident [13]; and the university is unfortunately distinguished into the community of scholars conceptually distinct from "an academic institution in which Catholicism is vitally present and operative" [14]. But in this section also, the unitive functions of the university are given an important emphasis: the integration of the disciplines with the aid of philosophy and theology; the dialogic integration between faith and reason, both bearing witness to the unity of truth; the unity of the ethical and scientific; and the synthetic function of theology [16–19].

What is critical to note is that these forms of the unity between the academic and the religious are placed within the elaboration of the identity of the Catholic university. What the norms will later legislate must be seen as instrumental to this finality, as subservient to it and to be judged accordingly. The Apostolic Constitution allows such judgments, permitting modification of their incorporation into the statutes of Catholic universities through the phrase "as far as possible" ["General Norms," Art. 1, #3]. The immense variety of institutions bearing the name "university" would necessitate this flexibility.

What are the implications, then, of the Apostolic Constitution, *Ex corde Ecclesiae*, for the American Catholic universities? It calls for a much stronger, much more concrete affirmation or articulation of the Catholic character of these universities, the grasp of the promise inherent in such an identity, and the direction that its character or identity be found in its purpose, an organic unity between the gospel and culture. In this, *Ex corde Ecclesiae* performs a valuable, needed service. The Apostolic Constitution can be received as an opportune summons by the church for these universities to move towards a deeper, more articulate sense of what they are. Such calls are always helpful; at the present time, they seem particularly needed. William P. Leahy, S.J. concludes his recent study of Catholic higher education with this judgment: "Catholic postsecondary schools suffer from a lack of vision; and as Proverbs 29:18 proclaims, 'Where there is no vision, the people perish.'"[32]

American Catholic universities will not likely receive a more authoritative summons to articulate their identity, to develop a deeper sense of what they are—however appropriate or inappropriate one finds particular statements or norms by which this identity is to be fostered. Maladroit were the initial attempts by the Implementation Committee of the National Conference of Catholic Bishops to frame regional "ordinances" or norms, ending with a bitterly contested document that was not submitted to the Episcopal Conference or to the Holy See. This committee of bishops, together with its consultative representatives of the Catholic colleges and universities, returned to prolonged discussions and subsequently formulated a new document, as a result of these exchanges, for application in the United States. This document won the general approval of Catholic educators and was formally approved by the American bishops by an astonishing majority of 224 to 6. It was then submitted to the Holy See in November 1996 for a *recognitio*. Unfortunately, it was not completely acceptable to the Vatican Congregation for Catholic Education and subsequent conversations are now under way to frame a second draft—a process whose outcome it is impossible to predict completely.

The situation is far more serious than its surface observation would indicate. It is important that the American church confront it with utter realism. Ill-conceived ordinances could fortify a dangerously growing disaffection from the Holy See within the United States, especially perhaps within the academic community. To a degree unprecedented in the church in the United States, many in the Catholic academy have been profoundly alienated by what they perceive as an unwarranted centralization of power by Roman curial authorities and by those who represent that power in the United States. More particularly in the field of education, many have perceived as demeaning or unwarranted the employment of this power in imposing mandates, professions of faith and oaths of fidelity, in prohibiting within pontifical faculties academic appointments or promotions or awards of honorary degrees, and even in intervening at least once in those same faculties to prevent a distinguished theologian from lecturing.

This admittedly indicates a situation for the church in the United States that is quite troubling, one that grows more serious by the month and feeds into some of the most insistent attacks on the very possibility of a Catholic university. But to cite it as grounds for denying a sympathetic hearing to the central summons of *Ex corde Ecclesiae* would be tragic. This voice and this summons to a more definitive understanding of the Catholic university deserve to be heard.

CHAPTER TWO

The Church and its Responsibility to Foster Knowledge

M'illumino d'immenso

—Giuseppe Ungaretti, "Mattina"

Since the Enlightenment, the rhetoric of human advancement has taken as almost axiomatic the privatization of religion and religious convictions, and this has worked a destructive influence upon what was once an intrinsic conjunction between church and university. The Catholic university increasingly appeared an anachronism in Europe, perhaps even an offensive anachronism. Let the church do its job, if you will, but let it stay out of the academy, the classroom and the laboratory, as it does out of the law courts, the federal government, and the stock exchange. In the heady centuries of the absolute nation-state and the identification of the body politic or the whole complexus of public society with the state, this could only mean the separation of the church as such from all public life; and even in the contemporary, more modified versions of this tradition, it has usually meant its isolation from the university.

Paradoxically, even from within the Catholic Church, arguments also mount against this conjunction. The last decade of the twentieth century is one of dwindling resources and declining numbers of religious and clergy. Should the church, then, bend its efforts to foster learning that is on the face of it secular? For the church is charged to preach and reflect upon the gospel of the crucified and risen Christ, to foster sacramental life and the evolution of the Spirit of God within human interiority and human history, to become that community in which the presence of Christ is continued in time and space and through which the mystery of God approaches each succeeding generation of human beings. What part does such a religious community have with the world of the university except in the pastoral care of those within it and the development of those reflections that are intrinsically theological? Should the church, to be much more concrete, encourage—even nurture—as specifically part of its unique mission research into the physical and biological sciences? Such questions can and must obviously be extended further into the social sciences, the professions of law, business, and medicine, even the humanities; but perhaps it is stated most vigorously, most effectively, in the case of the natural sciences and can be framed in terms of them as the discipline in which this question about secular knowledge is best instantiated. All of these tell upon the church's extensive commitments to higher education. Should the church, to be itself, field universities in which massive consignments of time, money, and human energy, of scholarship and instruction, bear upon knowledge that is not immediately evangelical or theological?

This is not to ask if the church should encourage all forms of human development; it obviously should. The church should and must encourage all those forms in which the human being develops and flourishes. But this question reaches beyond encouragement into engagement. Should the church, as part of its own responsibilities for evangelization and sanctification, be vitally engaged in the assimilation and growth of that knowledge which is neither intrinsically Catholic nor immediately religious? This question lies at the heart of the Catholic university.

To Specify the Question

This question is not asking if the Catholic university precisely as a university should foster the physical and biological sciences. The answer would be obvious—if the institution wishes to be a university at all. Rather, the issue is whether the church, precisely as such, should foster these sciences and, consequently, foster universities. Is there something about the nature and mission of the Christian community that underscores those obligations incumbent upon the university, as such, something about the church that uniquely supports the common responsibilities and undertakings of higher education and which would give added meaning and warrant to the remarkable proposition of John Paul II, cited in the previous chapter, that the church needs the university?[1]

But is not the answer to such a question on the face of it a banality? Has not the teaching of the church for two thousand years emphasized that creation is a divine gift? Does this conviction of gift not mean that we should pay attention—even in the most disciplined and serious manner—to what God has entrusted to us?[2] Has not the church in its dogmas and in the struggles of Augustine insisted against Manichaeanism that the world is good and that matter and history are the stuff of salvation? Does not creation give obvious importance and even a religious dimension to the work of science? And has all of this not been repeated a thousand times!

There is something generically true about such a response—but that constitutes its fatal flaw or easy deceptiveness. It offers us a comfortable journey down what R.S. Crane called "the high priori road," i.e., assuming the relevance and authority of theoretic doctrines prior to the examination of concrete issues and evidence.[3] It does explain why Christianity has exhibited a pervasive sympathy for nature and for the disciplines with which it is explored. But this explanation remains at so abstract a level that it does not touch the actual issue as it has emerged in the crises within history, nor does it reach the level of practical obligation—"*should* the church"—at which the question has been posed. To be satisfied with it is to be informed by neither recent history nor current concrete Catholic practice.

Can any Catholic recall without blushing Pius IX's enthusiastic letter to the anti-Darwinian, Dr. Constantin James, dated 17 May 1877 and published by James in 1888? The Pope denounced evolution:

> a system which is repudiated by history, by the traditions of all peoples, by exact science, by observation of facts, and even by reason itself, would seem to have no need at all of refutation, if alienation from God and the penchant for materialism, both stemming from corruption, were not avidly searching for support in this fabric of fables . . . But the corruption of this century, the guile of the depraved, the danger of oversimplification demand that such dreamings, absurd as they are, since they wear the mask of science, be refuted by true science.[4]

Does not the same shame rise when one recalls that the works of Copernicus and Galileo remained on the *Index of Forbidden Books* into the eighteenth and nineteenth centuries?[5] Can we not remember that the volumes of Teilhard de Chardin were ordered removed in the summer of 1962 from the shelves of the libraries of Catholic seminaries, this coming after a *monitum* of the Holy Office that these works contained such ambiguities and grave errors as to offend against Catholic doctrine? The Holy Office admonished religious superiors, rectors of seminaries, and presidents of universities that should safeguard "the souls, especially of the young" against these dangers.[6] All of this is common knowledge, so common that it undermines something of the credibility of the church and feeds the extravagant myth of a constant and even inherent antagonism between science and religion. Each year freshmen courses in Western Civilization retrace something of this path laid by benighted religious leadership. But not just scandalized freshmen! Are Catholic university presidents in the United States unaware that at the very end of the last century, the first president of Cornell University, Andrew Dickson White (1832–1918) compiled case after case of such repression in his massive 1896 work, *A History of the Warfare of Science with Theology in Christendom*, a book leveled quite explicitly at Roman Catholicism?

Science *in abstracto* and science in the day-by-day—the church has a long history of positive affirmations ranging from benignity to significant assistance, most recently under John Paul II. It is true that the great revolutionary changes in science have sometimes met misunderstanding, resistance, and even repression—not just by church leaders, but by theologians and manualists. Perhaps the key here is "misunderstanding." These moments were often the result not of viciousness or politics—though this moral acquittal could not be extended to the Galileo fiasco—but to an intractable narrowness, an ignorant misreading, a positive paranoia before novelties equated with threat. "*Nihil innovetur nisi quod traditum est*" was easily extended to the constitution of the world and the nature of its origins. But here the paradox becomes more acute. The heliocentric universe was condemned by some theologians and ecclesiastical authorities not because they failed to understand Copernicus, Kepler, or Newton, but because they failed to understand the Book of Joshua or the accommodation principles of Thomas Aquinas.[7] Fear arose about evolution because ecclesiastics such as Henry Edward Cardinal Manning judged it "'a brutal philosophy'—to wit, there is no God, and the ape is our Adam."[8] It was often a decadent theology and barren philosophy that constructed these artificial antinomies or that failed to mediate between the gospel and the developing culture. Here, as often as not, the problem in mediation lay not so much with the new sciences as with a theologically inept understanding of the intellectual patrimony of the church that could make novelties welcome and mediation possible. Where this theological sophistication was present, the story was quite different. Newman wrote to Pusey, for example, that he saw no theological difficulties with Darwinism, judging that it contradicted neither "the distinct teaching of the inspired text" or promoted atheism—whatever the fuss among some divines about Oxford's awarding Darwin academic honors in 1870.[9]

So the question—if it is not to be a banality—can be honed more precisely. Should the church, as such, foster science, science even at its most inventive moments, science when its conclusions seem raw or when it opens a frontier that seems to contradict what has been accepted even as dogma, when a synthesis has not been made between faith and science in this new area of inquiry? It is not simply obvious that the church should foster such knowledge. Nor is it simply regressive to see the possibility of some theories to undermine the faith of simple or ill-instructed Catholics. In the third century, Clement of Alexandria registered with humor that some Christians "are scared of Greek philosophy, as children are of masks, fearing that it will lead them astray."[10] In pursuit of their responsibilities, church authorities have occasionally looked at the concrete effects of scientific knowledge and disparaged such research and teaching as "confusing the faithful." Over this latter caution, one can evoke Madame Roland before the monument to freedom: "what crimes are committed in thy name!"[11]

But one need not become unfair or hysterical over this history. The church has contributed enough encouragement to science in general during these centuries, and the oppression or excessive caution ecclesiastics have exhibited can find its secular counterparts in the efforts of American universities to deny a hearing to the dangerous doctrines of Professor Shockley, in the prolonged resistance even to entertain the original theories of Alfred Wegener about plate tectonics, in unspoken expectations for politically correct opinions on some university campuses, and in the establishment as departmental orthodoxies of a particular version of philosophy or literary criticism. The problem is a profoundly human one, not exclusively an ecclesial one. But ecclesial history does furnish added weight to our question: Should the church, as such, encourage and foster all genuine and ethical scientific inquiry, no matter where it seems to be tending? "Ethical" is used deliberately because these remarks are concerned with dogmatic compatibility, not with the more technological uses or experimental inquiries of science that raise serious questions of morality and ethics.

This issue is sharpened still further if one considers the present attacks on science within American higher education—attacks that issue from the challenge of deconstructionism or that are mounted in the name of egalitarian leveling of all "logocentric hierarchies" or that are embodied in the heated discussions over a canon of appropriate texts or the content of a core curriculum.[12] All of this makes this question more real: Why should the church, even before pockets of academic indifference or hostility, encourage and support a passion for scientific inquiry as well as those institutions in which this passion is fostered?

A response might be advanced in two theses: (1) In one way or another, contemporary scientific inquiry raises serious questions about ultimacies and so constitutes part of the present religious problematic itself; (2) The scientific passion for the truth about the world is a part of that general passion for truth that makes faith—any vital faith—possible. One of these theses deals with science as a body of knowledge, as a content; the other deals with it as a method or procedure and a habit of mind.

Thesis 1

Over the past thirty years, the relationship between the physical sciences and the religious dimensions of life has radically altered. One can better assess this sea change if it is seen in contrast with the settlements between science and religion since the dawn of modernity. To draw the lines of these intellectual covenants very broadly, these centuries may be said to have emphasized four significantly different relationships: subsumption, separation or isolation, alienation, and correlation.

Subsumption:

In the seventeenth and eighteenth centuries, natural philosophy or physics or experimental science was subsumed as the foundation for religion, most specifically for the assertion of the existence of God. Certainly this was the interest that motivated much of the work of Isaac Newton, but one can also find it as the concern of such scientific giants as Robert Boyle and John Ray and in the resultant physicotheologies of William Derham and William Paley. The evidence from physics became those of geometrical design and functional subservience, and the mathematics embedded in the universe pointed to a universal geometer. Foundational religious reflection often looked to science for its warrant to assert its fundamental assertions about God.

Separation:

Under Laplace and Lagrange and the great revolutions of the Enlightenment, physics and astronomy freed themselves from furnishing the foundations for religious assertions. William Herschel recorded the conversation between Napoleon, then first consul of France, with M. de Laplace on 8 August 1802. The subject was the sidereal heavens, and Napoleon asked in a tone of admiration: "And who is the author of all of this?" Laplace maintained that a series of natural causes could account for this phenomenon. "This, the First Consul rather opposed." The story has been simplified by having Laplace respond to Napoleon's suggestion of God with the celebrated retort: "I have no need of that hypothesis," and then by having Laplace misunderstood over subsequent years, as if it indicated that his astronomy was atheistic. That interpretation is false. Laplace is simply saying, in opposition to Newton's *System of the World* and to the "Queries" at the end of Newton's *Optics*, that science was self-contained, that it would not furnish the basis for religion.[13] The new settlement was to be between two distinct, isolated fields methodologically indifferent to one another.

Alienation:

In the nineteenth century, the evolutionary theories of Darwin and Wallace were read as eliminating both the classic argument from design as well as a special place for human consciousness, a consciousness that both philosophers and theologians had made integral for the establishment of the existence of God. Many religious leaders and scientists read this development as a fundamental change in the relationship between science and religion, i.e., as attack and contradiction. With such rare exceptions as John Henry Newman, they understood it basically as threat. Cardinal Wiseman received permission from the Holy See to found an academia, one to which he summoned the faithful of England in these words: "Now it is for the Church, which alone possesses divine certainty and divine discernment, to place itself at once in the front of a movement which threatens even the fragmentary remains of Christian belief in England."[14] In his Terry Lectures, John Dewey in the United States announced that religious belief with any supernatural content could not survive before the surge in the empirical sciences. During the important Solvay Conference of 1927, Dirac and Pauli expressed amazement to Heisenberg that Einstein could evince any respect for religious consciousness.[15] Recent generations grew up in that atmosphere of hostility and alienation and—because of its ignorance of history—were indoctrinated easily to talk about the "ancient" battle between science and religion.

Correlation:

But within this century, this settlement has itself begun to give way before an unexpected development. Increasingly, scientists such as P.W. Atkins, Robert K. Adair, and Harald Fritzsch find themselves in basic agreement with the theoretical physicist, Paul W. Davies: "Right or wrong, the fact that science has actually advanced to the point where what were formerly religious questions can be seriously tackled itself indicates the far-reaching consequences of the new physics." In fact, Davies claims quite flatly: "It may seem bizarre, but in my opinion science offers a surer path to God than religion."[16]

This is no place to survey the evidence that Davies and others mount, but this much must be said. The way the contemporary world reveals itself in its fundamental constitution and origins poses or suggests enormous questions of ultimacy, even if (*pace* Davies) the questions are not answered. This is neither unprecedented nor extraordinary. What is extraordinary is the growing recognition that this is the case. Any human situation, explored with careful discipline and examined in depth, raises questions of ultimacy for which the methodology at hand is unequipped.

This can occur in two ways. First, it discloses problems about its own foundations, about the validity of its own presuppositions, the reference claims that can be made for its axiomatic sets, its postulates, and finally its relationship to other kinds of knowledge. Second, a thorough scientific inquiry may well establish conclusions which themselves raise further questions or hint toward further knowledge which its own methodology cannot responsibly treat. Such an inquiry may suggest possibilities about the universe which it cannot responsibly explore. It has classically been the function of metaphysics to deal with the first of these sets of problems, i.e., to inquire into the foundations of science and of mathematics and into the relationship of one area of knowledge with another. But is it the second, i.e., the inevitable development of scientific knowledge and the questions about ultimacy and about receding horizons that it raises, that inevitably involves the interest of religion. For religion, or the disciplined reflection upon religious experience that can be called theology, is essentially about the ultimacies, the absolutes that impinge upon human existence and that elicit a possibility of the world embodying mysteriously the personal interchange between the divine and human.

One example: one can look at the fundamental constants of nature and come to see the universe as breathtakingly, unimaginably finely tuned. Stephen Hawking has written that if "the rate of expansion one second after the Big Bang had been smaller by even one part in a hundred thousand million million, the universe would have recollapsed before it ever reached its present size." If, on the other hand, the rate of expansion had been ever so slightly greater, the expansion would have been too great for stars and planets to form. The universe would have been impossible.[17] That fine-tuning can be found in such fundamentals as the mass of the electron, the strength of the strong nuclear force, and the relationship between matter and antimatter. This number of such "remarkable coincidences" can admittedly be advanced indefinitely.

Some are using these data, as did Boyle and Newton, to establish an argument for the existence of God. This seems finally misguided. But what does appear legitimate—not to say hypnotizing—is that at the very minimum the data raise questions about purpose and even personality in the universe. Such evidence inevitably evokes the wonder as to whether there is mind and purpose, even a care for human beings, at the basis of our existence. And although the data that help raise this question are unable to settle it, such data do give the question a new basis, a new plausibility.

The reaction to this kind of knowledge or recognition among theologians and thinkers within the church has been threefold. The vast majority, knowing little about science, kept themselves wary, suspicious, at best respecting this knowledge at a great remove. Unfortunately, they are ignorant of these scientific developments or of their enormous importance in the contemporary understanding of the world. Consequently, they cannot appropriate the character or the contours of this problematic situation that contemporary culture frames for religious inquiry and responses. The second group, enthusiastic about this new knowledge, join those scientists who enlist these data to ground religious affirmations about the existence and nature of God. This appears to be a category mistake, one that mingles different kinds of knowledge and repeats the errors of the seventeenth century. But the third reaction has been to treat this new knowledge in one field as constituting a set of problems, suggestions, or questions opening up to religion. The fundamental constants—the emergence of life, the appearance of consciousness, expansive if not directional evolution—raise the question of profound purpose in this universe of some eighteen billion years.

This opens up in a very different way to the question of God—in a new and very plausible way. Does not the church, which talks about God and Christ, even the cosmic Christ, about providence and salvation, have a way of taking up these findings with their suggestions or issues, transposing them into properly theological questions, and, in terms of theological methodologies and evidence, dealing with these in a way that the physical sciences cannot? It is consequent upon the mission of the church that it foster, encourage, and be in vital contact with scientific inquiry, not because science will answer the questions of religion, but because it poses some of them.

In scientific inquiry, the world progressively discloses itself. Theological research, investigation, and instruction will only be as vital as the questions they address. Their questions will possess vitality to the degree that they emerge out of life. Science easily constitutes one of the greatest and most continual efforts of the human intellect to push to its ultimate what we know about our world and about our lives. The church can and must encourage the advance of this knowledge, confident that the reach of the mind will extend into a profoundly religious dimension—that questions will be elicited which the science or the discipline itself cannot resolve. For science in so many different ways mediates the world to religious consciousness. As that world becomes progressively engaged—whether in molecular biology or astrophysics or cosmology or quantum mechanics—it will raise issues not merely about the social and ethical implications of what is discovered (matters of enormous moral interest to the church), but about the meaning or purpose in the universe, the pervasiveness of matter, the final destiny of all that is known.

The church must foster science as a body of knowledge because it must engage the religious dimensions of this self-disclosure of the world. Through the questions that it raises, such a disclosure evokes new insights into the significance of the gospel and the concrete meaning of the one in whom and through whom and for whom all things were made.[18] The church advances in its understanding of the unique christological significance of salvation as it understands the world to which Christ is the immeasurable response—as he is seen to respond to the issues or hints that the physical universe and human life pose about existence and meaning or even to bring to its fulfillment the continual self-transcendence of physical and spiritual reality that constituted the evolutionary history of the cosmos.

Understood in this way, science forms part of the problematic situation for contemporary theology. If the church wants the mystery that it bears to be engaged by those to whom it is addressed and if it wants to come to deeper understandings of this mystery itself, then the church must foster all those human engagements in which ultimate questions are uncovered in-depth and presented with urgency and cry out for a religious transposition and theological reflection. If, on the other hand, the church ignores these developments—and how many members of the Catholic Theological Society of America or of Catholic theology departments have anything that could qualify as scientific literacy?—then theology loses the vitality that this contact with culture can uniquely offer.

One can advance this first thesis slightly farther. It is arguable that the human mind only understands the dimensions of its question as the answer itself begins to emerge. One understands the question in the answer. Conversely, one understands an answer only if it is seen as within the horizon of the problem to which it is a response. Fundamental questions and answers are mutually clarifying. Then one can ask the church and its theologians: how much do they understand about Christian hope—and specifically, about the recapitulation of all things in Christ—when they do not see or understand so much of the world to which it is a response and good news and which is available to them in a continually developing awareness through contemporary science?

That is the first thesis this chapter wishes to propose: the church must encourage or foster science because science done with integrity constitutes something of the problematic situation which confronts the reflection and even the self-understanding of the church.

Thesis 2

This second thesis does not deal with science as an expanding body of knowledge, but as a habit of mind issuing in a methodologically self-conscious, exact and demanding exploration of the world in order to determine what is true about it. This can be taken as the generic purpose of science, no matter how different or how instrumental may be its best available conclusions. This is where the almost hypnotic appeal of the scientific enterprise lies, whether its efforts bend on solving problems of tensor calculus or building a multibillion-dollar superconducting supercollider, whether it be purely theoretic in its interests in subatomic physics or technologically oriented towards global warming and space stations. There can be an almost addictive appeal in learning what is the case, what is the solution to a problem, what is the truth about things. This dedication constitutes the scientific mind at its finest—not just the scientific mind, of course, but the scientific habit as one form of this dedication, one of its strongest forms in contemporary culture.

No one is unaware, to forestall an objection, of the vanity and the vicious competition, of the ego-investments and financial greed that can and have entered into this world. But at its best—a best which the church must encourage and reverence—there is a grandeur that the scientific mind calls for, a purity of heart, a self-transcendence, a profound orientation towards truth. In this orientation, one encounters the absolute, i.e., that which is directive and normative of all life and is itself not governed by or subject to or relative to or dependent upon anything else. One tells the truth simply because it is the truth. Its value and its claim is itself. This may not necessarily emerge in the conclusions of the work of scientists, but the decencies of their calling dictate that it be always operative in the uncompromising claim that truth makes upon them.

Truth is both the horizon towards which the scientist moves and the imperative that directs her or his choices. The scientist, as a scientist, is called upon to explore what is the case in as imaginative and as disciplined a form as possible and to tell the truth that his or her research discloses with a certain disciplined exactitude.

In order to focus the argument at this point, attention should be directed to what may seem a very dry and inconsequential proposition in Thomistic theology. It is the very first issue that Aquinas raises when he deals with Christian faith. He asks this question: What is the formal object of faith? In other words, what is the indispensable aspect under which human beings must see what they are asked to believe, that aspect by which something becomes credible and which entails the inescapable commitment for making an act of faith?

Aquinas answers this very simply. The formal object of faith is the primary, i.e., the absolute truth.[19] Christian faith for Aquinas is not a blind leap in the dark; it is not opposed to cognoscitive rigor, nor does it constitute a voluntaristic *sacrificium intellectus.* "One would not believe if she or he did not see that these things should be believed."[20] Human beings believe something because they believe someone; and they believe someone because they come to trust that he or she speaks the truth. The grace of faith, Aquinas says, "makes one see the things that are believed."[21] The content of faith and the source of faith are conditioned by this absolute or primary commitment—an uncompromising, nonnegotiable commitment to the truth: "Nothing can fall under faith except so far as it stands under the first truth."[22] In this way, faith does not contradict intellectual activity, but "brings the intellect to its completion."[23] Only this commitment to truth can make authentic faith possible: both the commitment of God to its revelation and the surrender of a human being to its absolute primacy.

Under that seemingly dry proposition, Aquinas is proposing an understanding of Catholic faith that makes the church's encouragement of zealous, self-sacrificing science a matter of crucial moment. To evoke authentic faith, the church must foster in every possible way an uncompromising commitment to truth, in whatever way it discloses itself. The Christian community must give itself to build a world in which truth is explored, disclosed, and spoken. The church itself must be understood or come to be more vitally the place where truth is reverenced and demanded and spoken. For this openness to the real—whether one of physical nature or of mathematical coherence or of biological and human nature—this acceptance of what is, simply because it is, constitutes a fundamental condition for the possibility of Christian faith. As this disposition dominates the scientific mind—and the church must encourage it to be faithful to itself—as it governs and directs a person's entire career, as it permeates teaching and drives research through difficult, discouraging, and dogged moments, as it works against the vices and the narrowness that make for dishonesty and pretense, as it counters a defensive unwillingness to face up to the way things are—such a disposition develops in the mind those habits that are essential if faith is to be authentic. For the finest reaches of the scientific mind lie in an undeviating determination towards the truth; and from the time of Paul it has been said that the failure in faith is basically a "failure to love the truth and be saved."[24]

St. Thomas is not alone in giving this sacred, religious character to such a commitment to truth. William James, in defending however successfully his description of personal religion, insisted that "a man's religion might thus be identified with his attitude, whatever it might be, towards what he felt to be the primal truth."[25] In her autobiography, Simone Weil summarizes what gave meaning to her life: "It seemed to me certain, and I still think so today, that one can never wrestle enough with God if one does so out of pure regard for the truth. Christ likes us to prefer truth to him because, before being Christ, he is truth. If one turns aside from him to go toward the truth, one will not go far before falling into his arms."[26]

It is of vital importance that the church encourage, demand, propose, and foster every serious engagement by which human dedication and its consequent effort engage itself with an enterprise whose purpose is truth and whose natural climate and institution is the university.

And what must the church ask at those crisis-moments when scientific inquiry and dogmatic assertion seem to clash, when they even appear to contradict each other? That both continue their inquiries or experiments, their discussions and reconsiderations without impediment or mutual condemnation, as Cardinal Newman wrote, "with full faith in the consistency of that multiform truth, which they share between them, in a generous confidence that they will be ultimately consistent, one and all, in their combined results, though there may be momentary collisions, awkward appearances, and many forebodings and prophecies of contrariety."[27]

One could, perhaps, argue even further that this costly love for truth is not only a disposition for faith, but as it becomes absolute constitutes that universal surrender which Karl Rahner has signaled as transcendental faith: the obedient acceptance of God revealing himself as the all-guiding, all-governing truth, permeating all things, giving meaning and urgency to its smallest participation and confronting one continually in a relationship of absolute closeness and summons. The day-by-day

honest drudgery of science could well constitute the categorical mediation of such transcendental revelation and its responding faith.[28] And
what is said here of science, taken as physical science, must be expanded
and applied to science in any legitimate use of that word.

Conclusion

Each of these theses needs more development and nuance, but their
basic point is this: the church must encourage scientific inquiry as it must
care for the sources of its own vitality. It must both foster an undeviating
determination for the truth wherever this occurs as the only matrix out
of which Christian faith can emerge, and it must further those disciplined
inquiries whose natural dynamism develops into those profound questions or suggestions about ultimacy that constitute the religious dimensions of life and reach towards the unspeakable mystery that is God.
Both of these lie at the heart of the Catholic university.

CHAPTER THREE

A Conversation with a Friend

Cultural achievement is bound to be at once pervasive and precarious. It must be renewed from within each generation rather than passively inherited.

—Geoffrey H. Hartman, *The Fateful Question of Culture*[1]

[Author's note: In the *Future of an Illusion,* Sigmund Freud warns against an extended monologue that allows no opportunity to voice objections. This seems as good a place as any in this volume to allow disagreement to enter the lists, especially when that challenge comes from a scholar internationally recognized not only as a historian of the American Catholicism, but as a serious and insightful commentator on American Catholic higher education. The history behind this interchange runs as follows: On 29 May 1993, *America* published an article in which I summarized much of the argument of the first chapter of this book. This occasioned a response from Professor David O'Brien, the distinguished occupant of the Loyola Chair in Roman Catholic Studies at the College of the Holy Cross. His article appeared in *America* on 11 September 1993 together with my response. Professor O'Brien's article and my response are printed here both to broaden the discussion with the inclusion of another voice and to allow me the grateful chance to suggest additional precisions to what has been said already.]

Professor David O'Brien

No one describes "the inherent promise," and responsibility, of the Catholic university more eloquently than Michael J. Buckley, S.J., most recently in *America* (5/29). Still, even those of us who share Michael Buckley's hope for Catholic intellectual and academic life should take a second look before making his argument our own. For one thing, Father Buckley, along with many other recent commentators, sees U.S. Catholic higher education as caught in an almost suicidal (the Catholic university "can destroy itself") repetition of the "secularizing history" of other, once church-affiliated American universities. His reading of recent experience is decidedly negative, conveying a "sense that the *decline* in some Catholic institutions may be already advanced, that the conjunction of a vibrant Catholicism and these universities seems *increasingly* faint, that the vision is *fading*" (emphasis added). No one familiar with Catholic higher education can deny a measure of truth, though a small one, to these stock arguments. But Father Buckley knows very well that there was no golden age of "vibrant Catholicism" from which Catholic higher education has declined. Once upon a time, a few isolated idealists inspired by Christopher Dawson or Jacques Maritain may have run highly selective honors programs or discussion groups that manifested Catholic integration, but most of what passed for philosophy and religion (theology was rarely taught before Vatican II) was by general admission awful. Students may at some point (this is far from proven) have been more Catholic, but they were probably no more Christian than today's undergraduates. And it would not take long to persuade Father Buckley that the education dispensed when Catholic colleges and universities were supposedly most Catholic seemed quite well suited to the economic, political and social integration (could this be secularization?) of Catholics into American society. No decline there.

The sister- and priest-president reformers who changed these schools, almost single-handedly, were driven by a vision at least as noble as any now available: to enable the faith to renew itself and the church to reform itself at the center of—which means with shared responsibility for—U.S. society and culture. What the presidents and the religious orders of the last generation, in men's and women's colleges alike, did that almost no one else dared to do was to trust the church and its people. They took the risk of turning their colleges over to lay boards of trustees (it is worth repeating: they gave them the schools!) and turning their academic work over to faculties and staffs that were increasingly lay, professional and religiously diverse. To make this move to real shared responsibility, so different from the options in most Catholic parishes, dioceses and parochial schools, they had to affirm academic freedom, and, with some pain, they did. Eventually, in most places, they also learned to accept academic self-government as well, with the faculty ordinarily dominating matters of curriculum and academic personnel and sharing responsibility for overall institutional policy.

What this came to mean, of course, is that the Catholic intellectual ideal, if it is to remain a vital part of the self-identification of an institution, will have to enjoy the support of trustees, administrators, benefactors and especially faculty. Some of us who believe in that ideal occasionally get frustrated and demand that "the institution" or "the administration" fulfill its Catholic responsibilities—say, by hiring more Catholic theologians (with emphasis on Catholic). But, when pushed, we admit that we will have to do a better job of selling the Catholic idea to our colleagues, usually as hard a sell with Catholic as with non-Catholic faculty and staff.

So that brings us to the second problem, the image of integration that measures change as secularization and therefore decline. Anyone who has served on a faculty committee charged with reforming the core curriculum could only smile at Father Buckley's eloquent summary of the Newmanesque ideals of John Paul II's Apostolic Constitution, *Ex Corde Ecclesiae*: "the integration of the disciplines with the aid of philosophy and theology; the dialogical integration between faith and reason, both bearing witness to the unity of truth; the unity of the ethical and the scientific, and the synthetic function of theology." More cynical professors might say: "Good luck!" Others, not unsympathetic to the yearnings of Catholic colleagues, might wonder what one does with such aspirations. They seem so removed, so detached, from American intellectual life, with its hyperspecialization among and within disciplines and its clashing plurality of voices on every element of metaphysics and epistemology, and on the content and methods of general education. Perhaps contemporary debates about the canon are perverse, as many Catholic commentators believe, but organizing and implementing a core curriculum, much less a theologically grounded core curriculum, was problematic long before deconstruction and multiculturalism became academic buzzwords.

Father Buckley would probably say that this chaotic fragmentation makes it even more important to hold up the wondrously unifying Catholic banner, and that sounds right. But is it? Will we privilege—in budgets and symbols—theology, Catholic theology (not religious studies)? What else? Required Catholic theology courses? Hiring more Catholics? In all departments? How decide who's Catholic? Will we develop graduate programs in theology that will produce identifiably Catholic theologians? Will all or any of this do the trick? And even if it will, how is it to be done? By persuading colleagues of all its wisdom, or by persuading administrators and trustees to mandate integration, with or without faculty consent? The fact that many readers might well tell the dwindling number of religious who still hold high office on many campuses to do their duty, is one reason I suspect that Michael Buckley's appeal to raise the banner is not quite right. For it is simply not that easy.

The problem of disintegration, the absence of meaning and common ground, is not a problem caused by the Catholic pursuit of false gods, secularization, to be solved simply by an act of will: recommitment to the authentically Catholic. As University of Michigan historian James Turner insisted at an important Notre Dame conference last fall, Newman's ideal of philosophy relating the disciplines to one another and to some common core of knowledge was once everyone's ideal, and its loss is everyone's problem; indeed, it is the problem of contemporary academic life. For us Catholics it is now our problem because John XXIII and Vatican II in a big way, and those reforming academics of the last generation in small ways, helped us move out of the Catholic subculture and relocate ourselves out there in contemporary culture with everyone else. I am sure that's where Michael Buckley wants us to be, but his argument, with its disdain for secularization and its insistence on the really Catholic, might not keep us there.

Let me put the issue sharply. Separate incorporation, professionalization, internal diversity, all make it difficult to articulate a compelling Catholic position for the Catholic university as a whole. To the extent one disdains the loss of control (and the bland mission statement) that comes with the increased numbers of non-Catholic faculty and staff, and demands that explicit Catholic ideals be placed at the center and in possession of the institution, then the problem of Catholic identity leads to a solution which can only sound sectarian and restorationist, whatever the intention. It is quite another thing to attempt, as Father Buckley is attempting through the Jesuit Institute at Boston College, to build a vibrant Catholic intellectual community within a school, hoping first of all to bring a Catholic voice to the common problems of meaning and value in our culture and in every serious academic community, only then hoping that such dialogue will sustain a positive sense of Catholic identity for Boston College when the Jesuits are finally without power.

Like Peter Steinfels in a widely reported commencement address at Fordham this year, Father Buckley is understandably concerned that Catholics are losing their capacity to speak as Catholics. All of us need to do what we can to build a strong Catholic intellectual community. But I think we should worry even more if Catholics decide to solve the problem of pluralism, not by helping to define a common good, but by locating and reaffirming a supposedly distinctive Catholicism. The option for distinctiveness is what got us into trouble in the first place, but at least before Vatican II it reflected the outsider status of Catholics and their church. Now we occupy a very different social and cultural location, as the last generation's reformers knew we would. We are now too far inside this culture, and share too much responsibility for what it has become, to think we can solve its problem or ours, by symbolic options for Catholicism.

A few years ago people like Buckley and Steinfels and the readers of *America* thought distinctiveness was not such a hot idea unless it served wider human interests. They thought Catholic schools were called by their history to try to "do theology"—that is, to think through the meaning of experience with God in the midst of those wider communities within which we must live. For such schools, the most important thing to say about the world outside the church is not that it is secular, or that it is not the church, but that it is ours. Such schools might value Catholic theology tremendously and cherish a close association with the Catholic tradition. But even its Catholic faculty might argue that one must find ways to speak of God, and connect with the Catholic tradition, while standing outside church, in the various "killing fields" of our century, perhaps with the poor, as some friends elsewhere suggest, at least among this people, our people, with whom our fate is bound up.

Catholic colleges and universities should continue to seek a renewal of their historic effort to integrate faith and learning, not by reclaiming the institution, but by persuading colleagues and the public that this is a worthwhile thing to do together. That option would better guarantee the choice to stand at the heart of this conflicted and contentious culture, messy as that choice might be. In the end I think it a better choice for the schools, for the students and for the church.

Response

Professor David O'Brien has framed a forcible set of reflections, as stimulating as they are challenging—not to say eloquent! It is an honor to be in this conversation with the distinguished author of a recent, much admired biography of Isaac Hecker. Whatever our disagreements, the range of agreement stretches much farther.

I wonder, however, if a curious anomaly does not subvert something of David O'Brien's diagnosis. His initial paragraphs take to task those who read serious decline in the Catholic identity of some universities; "these stock arguments" are conceded only a small measure of truth. But in his concluding paragraphs, O'Brien argues that in these universities the distinctively Catholic presence has become so attenuated that it would "make it difficult to articulate a compelling Catholic position for the Catholic university as a whole"; this is judged acceptable because the demand (to which O'Brien joins a directive control) that "explicit

Catholic ideals be placed at the center leads to a solution which can only sound sectarian and restorationist." At the end, Professor O'Brien's paper actually seems to assume a more emphatic decline than I would. He does not refute the sense of a fading Catholic identity for these institutions as a whole; he seems to confirm it.

O'Brien's compass of topics and assertions is so capacious as to preclude their adequate review in a single response. Dealing with some of the matters he has introduced must be left to subsequent chapters. Further, distinct issues seem confusingly merged: decline in academic quality and in religious identity; Catholic ideals and the capacities or strategies to assert them; dangers and actualities, etc. To keep our conversation from becoming either miscast or scattered, let me try to sort out some of these and to isolate as clearly as I can what actually stands as disagreement between us.

First, what is not at issue between us: that the earlier Catholic colleges and universities successfully integrated their students into American society; that these institutions did not embody a golden age of Catholic higher education—"golden ages" in general are hard to come by; that Catholic institutions of higher learning have subsequently reached an intellectual development hitherto unobtained; that a great deal of credit for this academic progress goes to the generation of university presidents who courageously furnished the leadership and vision for so great an accomplishment; that turning these colleges and universities over to lay boards was an enormous act of trust in the laity which was itself richly rewarded both in the freedom gained from external and sometimes damaging controls and in the academic advance of these institutions; that the Catholic university essentially includes within itself the presence and unique contribution of all serious intellectual traditions as well as the academic freedom that makes open discussion possible; that religious and cultural pluralism are a necessity within a university; that the Catholic university should help to define a common ground for the common good within American culture; that the Catholic university should attempt to speak of God in the various "killing fields" of our century, especially among the poor, with whom we should be in solidarity, and stand "at the heart of this conflicted and contentious culture," etc. There is no need to delay on these and kindred propositions—let alone to marshal them as if they fell upon my thesis with stunning force. I have held these and written extensively on many of them over the past twenty years. These are not in disagreement between us.

Second, what could also be confusing: I find that O'Brien exaggerates some of my positions beyond recognition, while his reading of change in my past persuasions about distinctiveness is simply unwarranted. To assert, for example, that the Catholic university can destroy itself is not to say that it is "caught in an almost suicidal repetition of the 'secularizing history' of other once church-affiliated American universities." Rather it is to urge that attention be paid to what is a commonplace about human projects. It is to talk about a potentiality/liability ["can"] not an actuality—a liability that has been realized often enough to warrant concern. Further, the governing noun occasioned by some mission statements was deliberate: I spoke of "a sense" they convey "that decline in some Catholic institutions may be already advanced, etc." A bland, noncommittal mission statement can convey such a "sense," but only that—neither persuasion nor conviction. All that one can take from a mission statement is a suggestion of what may be the case or of what appears problematic.

Still further, a vocabulary of power and control threads its way through O'Brien's comments with the implication that I am advocating an enforced settlement. That is not the case nor did my article suggest that it might be the case. This language is intentionally absent from my article precisely because this is neither my conviction nor even the question I am addressing. The issue of my article was not about control and power; it is fundamentally about fidelity to a religious heritage and an educational mission. It is critically important to get that mission correctly. To introduce questions of control and power at this point would be to dissipate the focus of these efforts at understanding, as would be any attempt here to correct O'Brien's misunderstanding of the Jesuit Institute at Boston College. Moreover, to be concerned that the Catholic identity not yield to "the secularizing history of other once church-affiliated universities" is neither to identify secularization with cultural integration nor to measure "change as secularization and therefore decline." Finally, to suggest that one is asserting that "we can solve its [our culture's] problems, or ours, by symbolic options for Catholicism" is to erect a strawman in a field that already seems overcrowded.

Third, what may contextualize our disagreement and explain our different understandings of such words as "decline" is a view of human progress. I think that most human development moves dialectically, advancing through contradictions to its own completion. I think that Catholic universities have exhibited—to paint with shamefully broad brush strokes—such a pattern.

Their initial stage appeared in an undifferentiated simplicity: the conjunction between the Catholic and the academic was embodied in custodial institutions of the nineteenth and early twentieth centuries, in which the Catholic inhibited a good deal of the academic in a simplicity or uniformity that belied the nature of the university. They possessed a sense of their identity in a clear curriculum, a definite ethos, a faculty generally and explicitly committed to Catholic principles, links to a supportive surrounding Catholic culture, etc. They were not as bad as O'Brien's prose paints; in many places, for example, philosophy possessed a genuine and influential vitality. But they had serious and unfaced internal contradictions. It was again no "golden age." Some institutions have attempted to fixate at that stage or to return to it because of panic with the present. This seems to me misguided. You cannot repeat the past nor stay its course.

Progress consisted in moving to the negation of this simplicity, progressing into all of the differentiations that came out of a new emphasis on professionalism, separate incorporation, academic excellence, internal diversity, cultural location within the American situation, academic freedom, etc. This kind of growth can seem or may actually be a contradiction of much that has gone before—involving the rejection of many of the religious symbols, practices, and demands that characterized the initial period. But it can also constitute real advance as well, a dialectical development rather than a final disintegration. I think that this is the present moment of a number of Catholic institutions of higher learning.

The next stage indicated for the development of the Catholic university lies neither in an attempt to return to the previous stage (restorationist) nor in a fixation in this present stage, a settling for the status quo with a "steady-as-you-go," but in a synthesis of what has been achieved over these recent decades with a much more sophisticated retrieval of what was promising in the early inspiration, practices, faith and culture of these institutions, whether in the curriculum or the concerns or the atmospheric culture of the university. This is not an attempt to recover the provisions of the past nor is such a retrieval an essay in cultural nostalgia—an academic *Dances With Wolves*. It is a transposition of fundamental aspiration into a vastly different settlement, to "redeem the unread vision in the higher dream."[2]

If Catholic institutions of higher learning are to develop in what they are, the next stage must exhibit the increasing realization of the mutual and inherent unity between the religious and the academic. This was the point of my remarks at Georgetown and the article in *America*: that rather than inhibit each other, the religious inherently entails the academic and the academic inherently entails the religious; and that the Catholic university exists to promote this organic unity in the intrinsic completion of each. This is the university's finality and its promise.

The word "decline" was used to indicate that the movement toward the differentiations that have furthered academic excellence have been attended not infrequently by a concomitant fading of the characteristic expressions and even commitments of Catholic identity. If such an "argument" is "stock," it could be because its truth is so obvious. Certainly, O'Brien's paper does not lessen it, while his narrative of unalloyed progress cries out for a good, stiff shot of suspicion and a willingness to recognize with some mild deconstructionist openness the contradictory within all of this affirmation.

Fourth, what seems to constitute the precise issue between us: if an articulate and unapologetic vision of Catholic faith specifies expressly the mission of the university, does this militate against the pluralism and diversity essential for the university to be itself? Does the Catholic rule out the catholic?

The last four paragraphs of O'Brien's paper seem to suggest that it does. Blending this issue with the divergent issue of control and power, he judges that an emphasis upon Catholic ideals "can only sound sectarian and restorationist." Why? Because such an emphasis would make for distinctiveness, and O'Brien's attacks on distinctiveness are unequivocal. Historically: "distinctiveness is what got us into trouble in the first place." In general: Catholic thinkers should be principally concerned about any attempts at "locating and reaffirming a supposedly distinctive Catholicism." Read carefully, O'Brien rejects "distinctiveness" because it renders one "outside" the culture. We may excuse this acceptance of distinctiveness during that past in which the Catholics and their church were outside, he maintains, but it makes no sense now that Catholics are far "inside this culture, and share too much responsibility for what it has become." His argument seems to imply that a "really Catholic" university would bespeak a narrow, sectarian Catholic subculture and preclude pluralism in faculty, courses, and student-body by its insistence on distinctiveness. It is puzzling, however, to see distinctiveness ruled out in the name of pluralism. Pluralism is precisely the admission and celebration of distinctiveness and difference on every level of unity. Each distinct unit makes an irreplaceable contribution to the richness of the culture.

The Catholic university, precisely and self-consciously insisting upon its identity, gives to American society—as well as to the church—another voice, another criticism, service, and support, that are uniquely its own and enriches the community as a result. At the same time, the university gathers to itself that great diversity which is essential to its distinctive purpose. As Peter Steinfels has wisely written: "A pluralism that requires every institution within it to mirror the pluralism of the whole is a false pluralism. . . . Universities should not be closed to any reasoned point of view, but that should not prohibit some of them from deliberately fostering scholarship within a certain tradition."[3]

O'Brien's apparent inclination here to read the Catholic as sectarian because it is distinct lies at the heart of our disagreement. He has, for another set of examples, the students more Catholic in the past but "probably no more Christian" and he suggests that to stand with the poor or in the "killing fields" of our century or with the American people, could very well mean that we must stand "outside church."

For finally what we are touching upon is not simply a question of Catholic higher education. The question is larger than the academic one. It is "Catholicism" in the United States that after the past ten or fifteen years stands in serious danger of being read as a sect and even being taken as such by Catholic intellectuals. There are influences within the church that would make it narrow, with carefully monitored speech and inhibited public discussion, negative in so much of its focus, harshly critical of disagreement and of attempts at nuance, increasingly demanding public protestations of loyalty and right-thinking, etc. The church is losing in the popular mind something of its profound reality as church (to coopt Ernst Troeltsch's distinction between church and sect). Accept "Catholic" with this understanding and one will be ridden with the pervasive fear that being distinctively Catholic will inhibit pluralism. Leaning towards this purchase on the church, O'Brien's argument seems to frame the alternatives for Catholic higher education as either secularization or sectarianism.

Either of these would spell its death. It is no wonder that in his last few paragraphs the difficulty of articulating a compelling Catholic position for the Catholic university as a whole seems so overwhelming.

Fifth, let me say only a word about another approach. The purpose that defines a Catholic university is to be that intellectual community in which the church, in the words of Vatican II, "strives to relate all human culture to the gospel of salvation." That means, "all" human culture, everything that passes for serious discourse and human advancement—just as the cosmic Christ of Colossians is to bring into unity the massive pluralism of all creation. This conjunction specifies the Catholic university, a conjunction that is the fulfillment both of the academic and of the religious.

For the church by its very nature and at its historical best is inclusive and pluralistic—not unlike a great net that is cast into the sea and contains all sorts of different fish.[4] Its concerns range over all the fields of human care and achievement from science and art to social liberation and international community. That is why a university can incorporate these concerns and become not less but more of a university—the religious giving focus and priority to questions of urgent human concern, the academic catching up all forms of human inquiry and discourse, the unity of these both allowing for the most radical realization of Christ as the one "for whom all things were created," and the one in whom "all things hold together" [Col 1:17–18]. The university, with all of the pluralism that goes with the university, came organically out of the needs of the church and this meaning of Christ.

One university is distinguished from another—receives its unique character—not by freedom of inquiry or commitment to diversity. Without that freedom and without diversity, there is no university at all. But universities differ among themselves according to the questions to which they give priority and the knowledge they think most worth having. Much of this is derived from the parent culture out of which they come, upon which they depend, and whose ethos they bespeak. Much of the difference between Harvard and MIT, Chicago and Stanford lies precisely in the questions and the knowledge regarded as fundamental and the commensurate conversations, inquiries, instruction and atmosphere these foster within the university.

This is true also of the Catholic university. It will take on its particular cast from the questions which dominate its inquiry and from the knowledge it thinks most important for the student to acquire. Much of its collective life will thus emerge not only out of the American settlement for higher education, but also out of the richness, the concerns and the heritage of Christianity, given a focus and an emphasis honed by centuries of Catholic intellectual culture, contemporary interests and the incarnation of this Catholic spirit within American culture—which is both broader and more limited than Catholic culture.

But many of the same questions and much of this same knowledge fostered by these intersecting cultures can and do engage many who are not Catholics. If such scholars and students come to a Catholic university to teach or to learn, their reasons should include—one would hope—the recognition that their own questions and the subjects they love are fostered with peculiar efficacy by and within this intellectual community, that the Catholic university, precisely because it is Catholic, sustains and promotes what is profoundly human. To this single academic community, each makes her or his own specific and indispensable contribution, as the community only realizes itself to the degree that it engages, as Vatican II maintained, "all human culture."

But is such a Catholic university possible? Are its proponents only holding up "the wondrously unifying Catholic banner" so naively that the world-weary, battle-scarred veteran of faculty committees "could only smile," and the cynical whisper (cynically?): "Good luck," while from the chorus of the enlightened falls in cadence the mournful mantra: "It is simply not that easy"? I don't think so. Nor is it easy to ascribe a contrasting realism to O'Brien's multiple insistence upon the persuasion of colleagues as the single strategy to revivify those institutions that have lost their sense of Catholic mission.

The first chapter of this volume, in its earlier and abbreviated form as an article in *America*, did not attempt to blueprint how this integrity could be realized—that would have demanded a much more extensive discussion—but only to suggest that this was the purpose, the ideal and justification for a university's calling itself "Catholic" without apology, and that its religious origin and character should make it more of a university, not less. If this suggestion is true, then such an understanding can provide a measure with which we can consider the means by which its identity can be furthered. This further question "how one does it" requires an enormous amount of work, covering every aspect of the university. Perhaps one only approaches an answer by fragments. But if we are at the juncture that I suggest we are and if there is an intrinsic entailment between the religious and the academic, then at least the question can be posed correctly: How does a contemporary Catholic university foster such an integrity between the religious and the academic in its pluralism and diversity? This is not to answer the question, but to get it right—and that seems to offer much more promise than writing it off.

For the stakes are very high. No other institution in the Western world can offer this unique service to the church and to the world.

Let me close, thanking my friend, Professor O'Brien, for his learned and obviously provocative essay and hoping that my response has not done his comments any injustice. It is difficult to discuss an issue in this way. I should not be surprised to discover that what I have written needs further reflection, nuance or correction. But none of this should be impossible. It was, after all, St. Thomas who spoke about the value of those great "conversations in which friendship principally consists."[5]

PART TWO

"The Universities of the Society"

CHAPTER FOUR

Ignatius' Understanding of the Jesuit University

> Por la misma razón de charidad . . . se podrá ella estender a tomar assumpto de vniuersidades, en las quales se estienda más uniuersalmente este fructo . . .

> —Ignatius of Loyola, *Constitutiones*[1]

The Fusion of Horizons

At this juncture, it seems appropriate to move from general considerations of the characteristics of a university that is Catholic to the specification of this character in Jesuit universities, but first a word about method and discourse.

Any attempt to deal with the distinctive Jesuit character of a university entails a series of options. One can simply describe what is taking place: these institutions are determined to be Jesuit; so this is what a Jesuit university must be. Sociologists can do this with the present or historians with the past. Under this rubric, a Jesuit university can be called a university in which Jesuits teach—and this is presented as an effective rejoinder to any question about identity overly eager in its enthusiasms and naïve in its expectations. But these simply descriptive definitions provide little of the initial vision which was the originating dynamism of such institutions, of the educational goals that remain to be realized, and of the criteria by which growth or decline can be measured.

The alternative is a prescriptive definition. The determination of a Jesuit university is taken from normative documents, and these documents are used to indicate what a Jesuit university should be. If descriptive discourse indicates what is (with little attention to purposes, objectives or goals), prescriptive discourse fairly bristles with finality, goals, and objectives—and it can delineate an institution that never was and never will be. In the descriptive, the emphasis is upon the factual and the actual; in the prescriptive, it falls upon the theoretical and potential.

Hans-Georg Gadamer suggests a third possibility: that the present de facto situation and the canonical statements of origins and purpose can be combined in a "fusion of horizons"—as though a conversation were taking place, one in which classic statements of purpose, often from the past, are presented to the questions that emerge from the present; and at the same time the present situation is itself questioned and opened by the issues that these great and classic articulations of purpose pose.[2] The fusion of the past and the present in a continuous dialogue brings out virtualities in a text that its author may never have realized. Simultaneously, this "fusion of horizons" submits a contemporary practice and its unspoken assumptions to the searching examination of a classic. "This is just what the word 'classical' means: that the duration of a work's power to speak directly is fundamentally unlimited."[3] The present situation can unlock that power to speak, and an older text can make one look critically at the present situation. The influence or exchange here is mutual. The definitional inquiry this chapter intends, then, proposes to be neither descriptive nor prescriptive; it is dialogic—with the hope that a classic text may challenge and illumine a present reality. How can it be brought into present relevance, so that its richness becomes available to vastly different institutions in a vastly different age?

Now the text or the classic proposed here for conversation is a section from one of the greatest works of Ignatius of Loyola, the founder of the Jesuits, *The Constitutions of the Society of Jesus*. Among the documents in some way authored by Ignatius, this is the one upon which he spent the greater number of his years, and it uniquely specifies the character of the Society of Jesus. *The Spiritual Exercises* are for the entire church. The *Constitutions* were specifically and definitionally for the enterprises and life of the Society of Jesus, although they came in subsequent years to be taken as foundational for some other religious orders as well. The usual difficulties in this generative dialogue with the sixteenth century Ignatian text, a dialectic that engages both description and definition, are increased enormously by the widespread lack of knowledge of this central foundational document in the Jesuit tradition. As a matter of fact, even many Jesuit educators simply do not know the *Constitutions*—although this situation has bettered itself over the past thirty years.

A striking example of this was provided by an observation of George Ganss, a distinguished Jesuit scholar and educator, on the initial options posed by *Project 1*. *Project 1* was an attempt of the American Jesuits, initiated in 1973 and extending over the next four or five years, to identify and evaluate their goals and efforts in the work of education, and Ganss delivered this critique of it:

> The second feature of *Project 1*, Volume 1 which strikes this writer is the virtually total lack of references to or use of Part IV of Ignatius' *Constitutions*, the locus where he most succinctly, clearly, and authoritatively enshrined his educational theory or rationale. That theory is his own application of the dynamic and apostolic world view toward which God led him. . . . In Part IV of the *Constitutions* he applied it to the formation of Christian persons in the secondary schools and universities he founded and administered.[4]

In a subsequent discussion with Father Ganss, another prominent Jesuit educator remarked that Part Four of the *Constitutions* was not only absent from the written reports of *Project 1*, but from almost all of its discussions as well. It would be instructive, perhaps, to discover how many Jesuits today, some thirty years after *Project 1*, and how many educators in Jesuit universities and secondary schools, have some knowledge of the characteristic elements that Ignatius placed in Part Four of the *Constitutions*, as distinct from those which subsequent Jesuit educators, beginning in the second half of the sixteenth century, specified in the academic program known as the *Ratio studiorum*.[5] This is a critical question for anyone who studies Jesuit higher education because in Part Four of the *Constitutions*, Ignatius elaborated seminally the meaning and structure of Jesuit higher education during and for his time.

Universities and the More Universal Good

Ignatius of Loyola came to understand the importance of higher education only very late in his life, indeed just a few years before his death. Initially, the Jesuits had no intention of engaging in academic institutions. They were to be wandering missionaries and preachers, ministers of the Word of God who promoted its interior realization through such ministries as confession, spiritual direction, the *Spiritual Exercises*, and the Eucharist, and its social embodiment in the works of charity and of reconciliation. What residences there were for academic work initially were envisaged almost exclusively for the education of Jesuit students for the priesthood, various kinds of houses of studies attached to major universities. Originally, Ignatius and his companions established these "colleges" that were simple residences for scholastics in their studies at the greatest universities in Europe. By 1544 there were some seven of them. Then a series of significant shifts occurred. Colleges followed, as with Padua, in which the academic offerings of the local university were supplemented by exercises and lectures in the college, but the students still remained Jesuits. Two years later, colleges were begun in which secular students could be educated together with the Jesuit students.

In 1548 at Messina, a critically important development took place: a secondary school intended principally for young laymen from the ages of eleven to eighteen was established. This was the kind of institution—not to be confused with the American "college," but rather more like the German *Gymnasium* in the age of its students and in the formational character of its education—that Paul Grendler credits with changing "the educational landscape in the second half of the sixteenth century. In contrast to the medieval mendicant orders, several of the new orders devoted themselves to teaching lay children. Unlike the Companies of Christian Doctrine, they established formal schools that daily taught a Latin or vernacular curriculum."[6] These colleges were secondary institutions, teaching the *studia humanitatis* that constituted the Latin curriculum of the Renaissance. The Jesuit college differed from similar Italian secondary schools "only in that it elevated the study of Greek to a secure, important position in the syllabus."[7] Messina inaugurated a more radical change than the study of Greek. For the first time, a religious order took formal education in secondary schools as a religious ministry, and not only a religious ministry, but its principal one.[8] Later sections of this chapter will take up the content, character, and the purposes of the *studia humanitatis*.

One must not make this development in secondary education too linear, however. In 1543 the Jesuits in India were teaching non-Jesuits in Goa, "at a kind of 'seminary,'" for which in a few years the Order would take full responsibility. In 1546 Jesuits began a modest college at Gandia in Spain that the Pope proceeded to call a university, or *studium generale*, and whose student body would number both Jesuits and non-Jesuits.[9] This latter was not the last Jesuit instance of launching institutions bedecked with grand titles but sustained with slender resources. But it did introduce a new term into Jesuit education, the "university." On 22 February 1551, the Roman College came officially into existence as another college, but it was soon and eventually spectacularly to support those faculties that would constitute it a university.[10]

Here one must compare and contrast what had been programmed for the colleges with what was now being formulated for the universities.

In the previous provisions for the colleges for scholastics, these Jesuit students preparing for ordination were to study "the humane letters of different languages [*las letras de humanidad de diuersas lenguas*]," with humane letters covered by the umbrella terms of "grammar" and "rhetoric." Upon the completion of these studies, they were to proceed through logic, natural and moral philosophy, metaphysics, scholastic and positive theology, and Sacred Scripture.[11] No effort was made in these chapters of Part Four of the *Constitutions* on the colleges to justify or to assess the particular relation among these collegiate disciplines or their common relationship to theology nor to evaluate their relative importance. "*El fin de la doctrina*" was given in a standard Ignatian specification: "*ayudar con el diuino fauor las ánimas suyas y de sus próximos.*" This purpose was to determine both what the Jesuit students studied and the duration of this academic concentration.[12]

When these colleges were extended to the education of non-Jesuits—designated in the hardly elegant Spanish expression "*los de fuera*" or the Latin "*externi*"—humane letters and languages were given pride of place; no college could be without them.[13] To these were added instruction in Christian doctrine and, if necessary, in casuistry. The ministries of preaching and confession are also included as appropriate for these colleges for *externi*, but the directions are given that "all of this is to be done without extending the undertaking into the higher branches of knowledge. To learn these, those students who have studied human letters should be sent from these colleges to the universities of the Society."[14] For this reason, when the Roman College—as a college, not yet a university—announced its very modest beginnings, it did so with the legend hung over its entrance: "*Schola di Grammatica, d'Humanità e Dottrina Christiana, gratis.*"[15] Students came to spend something like six years in the colleges: the first three classes were designated "grammar"; the next two years' class, "humanities," and the fifth class (but sixth year of studies) entitled "rhetoric." "Classes" did not designate a period of time, but units of academic work. In the colleges, the full course of humanistic studies, grammar, humanities, and rhetoric, would be completed, sending their products to become "upright leaders of society."[16] For the universities, this humanistic curriculum was to constitute but its first faculty.

Ignatius began planning for universities as such only in the last years of his life. In fact, his provisions for the universities came as his final major addition to the *Constitutions*, 1553–54. He was to die two years later. Jesuit universities just made it in the last act! The earlier chapters of Part Four of the *Constitutions* had elaborated a structure of education for scholastics in the colleges of the Society. Now as his last major contribution to the *Constitutions*, Ignatius and his collaborators formulated two additions to this same Part Four: (1) a seventh chapter which dealt explicitly with colleges for non-Jesuits; (2) an additional fascicule that became chapters eleven to seventeen of Part Four, chapters that outlined the anatomy of *las universidades de la Compañía*.[17] This articulation of the character and content of these universities was originally composed as a separate document in 1553 or 1554—the very years when the Roman College was taking its first baby steps. Much that is in this fascicule had come out of the Jesuits' experiences, both with their own colleges and with the non-Jesuit universities of Europe. It should come as no surprise that Part Four is the only part of the *Constitutions* for which Ignatius signaled the contribution of other Jesuits: Juan Alfonso de Polanco, Diego Laínez, and André des Freux.

Aided by the indefatigable Polanco, appointed secretary of the Society in 1547, Ignatius had continued to work for the rest of his life on the *Constitutions*, often revising them with his own hand, until his death in 1556, but about the section dealing with higher education, there was this notable difference. Asked about the influence of Polanco on the *Constitutions*, "Ignatius said that there was nothing in the *Constitutions* from Polanco, as far as the substances of those matters was concerned, except in case of the colleges and the universities, which was however according to his mind."[18] This report seems to be given by Jerónimo Nadal. Independently, Olivier Mannaerts had specified the aid given to Ignatius on Part Four by Polanco in a somewhat similar fashion, but with important additions: "He himself [Ignatius] composed all of the *Constitutions* and its *Declarations*, with this single exception: that in Part Four, dealing with the university, the *studium generale* and the conferring of degrees, he received some light from Father Diego Laínez, Juan de Polanco, and André des Freux, who had been in different universities."[19] These early Jesuits could bring to bear upon this formative consideration of the universities of the Society the practices and the results of some of the most influential universities of that period. Juan de Polanco had spent thirteen years at the University of Paris, receiving from this most distinguished among European Renaissance universities, his literary and philosophical education. He had later studied theology at the University of Padua. Diego Laínez could have contributed from his student experiences of the universities of Alcalá and Paris. André des Freux, once a pastor in Chartres, had done theological studies at the University of Padua. Ignatius' student years had, of course, been spent at Alcalá, Salamanca, and, above all, Paris.

They were a talented and varied lot. One cannot pass over, for example, the strangely varied accomplishment of André des Freux, "*vir mirabilis . . . in omnibus versatissimus*," who translated the *Spiritual Exercises* from the dogged Spanish of Ignatius into a more elegant flowing Latin that would make it acceptable at the papal court, put out an expurgated edition of the *Epigrams* of Martial, authored such school-books as *De utraque copia verborum et rerum praecepta* and *Summa latinae syntaxeos* and turned the *Imitation of Christ* into classical verse! Besides these literary conquests, he was appointed first rector of the German College (1552), and first occupant of the chair of Sacred Scripture at the Roman College (1553–56), during part of which time he also doubled as professor of rhetoric (1553).[20]

Ignatius inaugurated this commitment to universities because the good that could be accomplished through such institutions was greater, "more universal," than what could be achieved through other, lesser academic institutions. Colleges, i.e., secondary schools, had already been initiated, driven by the spirit for moral renewal that permeated Italian Renaissance humanism. Pedro de Ribadeneira, writing under the directions of Ignatius and a few months before Ignatius was to die, voiced a central conviction behind the Jesuit commitment to secondary education: "All the well-being of Christianity and of the whole world depends on the proper education of youth."[21] The *Constitutions* compare these colleges with the newly proposed universities: "Through a motive of charity, colleges are accepted and schools open to the public are maintained in them for the improvement in learning [*doctrina*] and living [*vida*] not only of our own members, but even more especially of those from outside the Society. Through this same motive the Society can extend itself to undertaking the work of universities, that through them this product may be increased more universally [*más universalmente*]."[22] It was a fundamental persuasion of Ignatius—framed in a maxim received from Saint Thomas—that the more universal a good, the more divine it is.[23] In the universities, Ignatius thought his educational ideal of an integration of faith, learning, and living could be raised to a more universal plane and the possibilities of the good that could consequently be accomplished extended significantly, especially since the graduates of the university "may be able to teach with authority elsewhere what they have learned well in these universities of the Society."[24] This last phrase, "these universities of the Society," is what the *Constitutions* would call the institutions that resulted from these persuasions.

For Newman, a university comprises the universality of knowledge; for Ignatius, a university accomplishes more universally the "improvement in learning and in living" that is the function of education. In both Newman and in Ignatius, priority is given to teaching rather than research. But while Newman defended knowledge for its own sake and the philosophical habit of mind as the finality and integrating habit of education, Ignatius spoke of the preparation of teachers as the practical end of a university of the Society and of theology as the governing, paramount discipline. The universities were to serve human beings especially by preparing future *doctores*. Newman's university was to prepare refined minds for their own good and for that of society; Ignatius' university was especially to educate, as will be seen, theologians who would teach.

This purpose accounts for a curious hendiadys that recurs through the *Constitutions*. "Learning" as an educational ideal is often coupled with "a method of expounding it." Twice in the preamble to Part Four of the *Constitutions*, the goals of studies are expressed in this way: "It will be necessary to provide for the building of their learning and a manner of expounding it, that these may be aids towards better knowledge and service of God, our Creator and Lord."[25] This emphasis upon communication and its service easily explains the place accorded rhetoric in the colleges and in the early years of university studies within the first faculty of the university. Rhetoric was the art of public speaking. Rhetoric as a developed skill gave the speaker the possibility of acting in the public arena, of molding the decisions that emerged in the sphere, of effecting instruction, evaluation, and change. The importance of public service dictated the importance of rhetoric. The humanistic ideal was "to prepare the individual for the 'active life' of service to the common good of society, and, in a Christian context, of service to the church."[26]

Similarly, communication dominated the purposes of the university, but in a very specific manner. Now the comprehensive emphasis was upon teaching, as only a university could equip and certify a human being to teach. Secondary education trained men for an effective presence in the public forum; university education instructed men for the profession of teaching. The university's emphasis upon teaching will govern the purpose and the provisions of the Ignatian universities.

This conviction that the university accomplishes a more universal good gave a very different tone and urgency to the meaning of this word, "university." "Universal" enters into Ignatius' discussion of higher education, of university education, in a unique manner. It does not suggest the corporation of scholars as was the *universitas* that began Paris, nor the corporation of students that constituted the University of Bologna, nor the confluence of universal knowledge as in Newman—though each of these themes would tell within the significance and direction of the Ignatian ideal.[27] The "university of the Society" was that institution of higher learning, composed of faculties of knowledge and bodies of students whose intrinsic academic finality—i.e., the purpose engaged both in its advancement and diffusion of knowledge—was a more universal charity, a more universal good.

For experience taught the founder of the Jesuits what it had taught Plato before him and Max Weber and John Dewey afterwards: that all substantial or permanent changes in a culture result from institutions. Even the prophetic voice will perish unless it reaches institutional embodiment. And the most telling or influential institutions are educational.

The "Universities of the Society"

What confronts one in these chapters on higher education is a university radically different from the contemporary American university, one oriented to theology as a discipline and to teachers of theology as a product. So important did Ignatius judge theology that the entire university was formed and took its character for its study. With proper modifications and nuance, one could almost state that the *Constitutions* envisaged a university that was nearly professional in its orientation towards teaching and theology, and correspondingly preprofessional in its studies of humanities, sciences, and art. But that statement would be too narrow. If one looks at those chapters—not to copy them fundamentalistically today, which would be impossible, but to dialogue with them—one catches something of what an Ignatian university was to be. Even in its differences in composition and purpose, this vision of the crucial purpose of theology and of teaching can challenge the goals of Jesuit universities today.

The Ignatian university was to comprise at least three faculties: humanities and languages; arts (i.e., philosophy) or natural sciences; and theology.[28] An ideal student—say, Bellarmine or Corneille or Calderón—would study the humane letters from ages ten to thirteen; arts or sciences from fourteen to sixteen; and theology from seventeen to twenty-one, or twenty-three (one should add) if he were to take the doctorate.[29] Frequently the age was somewhat older. No set period of years was allotted to the more humane letters, as the basic abilities and initial knowledge of those beginning these studies differed so much among these students.[30] About three and a half years were given for the study of the natural sciences and to achieve the degree of *magister artium*.[31] But six additional years were necessary for the study of theology, four years for the basic curriculum and two subsequent years to obtain the doctorate.[32]

The humanities course, like that of the colleges, could be taken as complete in itself, the student leaving the Roman College upon its completion. Those pursuing science would remain for the additional years required. Those training for careers in theology would complete the full curriculum. The division of students in the early Collegio Romano is instructive here. In 1561–62, some five years after the death of Ignatius, the university was educating about nine hundred students. The breakdown of numbers is not precise, but of these, 530 were studying in the first faculty, that of humane letters; about three hundred were studying in the faculty of philosophy; and over eighty were attending theology.[33] Six years of theological studies were required to obtain the doctorate.

If so short a course of studies would have raised an eyebrow anywhere, it would have raised it at the University of Paris, the academic institution Ignatius considered supreme in Europe. It is startling to notice how Ignatius changed its procedures. At Paris, a student would begin rudimentary arts, grammar and rhetoric, between thirteen and fifteen, and finish the arts curriculum and its regency—teaching period—in some five years. Only after acquiring the M.A. at twenty-one or older could he begin the theological curriculum, a course which would demand between thirteen and fifteen additional years of studies, as he moved through the six successive stages in which he was *studens, cursor, baccalarius* or *sententiarius, baccalarius formatus, licentiatus*, to reach the giddy heights of *doctor* (or *magister*) sometime after his thirty-fifth birthday.[34]

Why such a difference with a university program that Ignatius esteemed as superior to all others he knew? At Paris, the *magistri* were licensed to "read, dispute, deliberate and teach," but the fact was that very few of them did much teaching. Teaching was assigned to bachelors as a stage of their theological education, so that Scripture and the *Liber sententiarum* were more than provided for. "While some doctors did continue to lecture regularly after taking their doctorate, it is nevertheless clear that most limited their teaching to the one mandatory lecture a year on September 16, the feast of Saint Euphemia."[35] These eminent gentlemen spent their time presiding over both the inaugural lectures (the *principia*) and the numerous *disputationes* of those students working their way through this thirteen-year course, the *cursores*, the *biblici ordinarii*, and the *sententiarii*.[36]

Even more celebrated was their custody of Catholic orthodoxy. For this, they met faithfully and sometimes frequently to consult over faith and morals, to defend Catholic faith against attacks, to pursue and condemn heresy, and to carry on their relationships with other institutions both in the church and the state, to say nothing of the concerns of such a corporation of masters with academic procedures, ceremonies, financial affairs, and legal concerns.[37] The Parisian theologians were spoken of in a manner more commonly associated throughout the church with major councils and bishops. Theirs it was

> to maintain surveillance over ideas, to cite them before its bench, to discover in propositions, even those seemingly quite harmless, the hidden venom of heresy, to determine truth and error, and in error the degrees of error, to separate the one from the other, as chaff from wheat, to guard thus the purity of the faith and the immutability of tradition amidst vicissitudinous opinions.[38]

With such a sense of its major mission, the faculty of theology of Paris could hear itself described to the Parlement of Paris in terms that might raise a blush even on the cheek of the papal magisterium. In August 1525, the lawyer Jean Bochard declared:

> The Faculty is famous and attested to by all the world, and many foreign princes and others have had recourse to it when there was a question of knowing the truth which touches on the faith. . . . We would indeed be abandoned by God if this light and its doctrine fell into error. And even though as men they can fail and err, nevertheless it is unthinkable that God would abandon in that way his people of France, who could have neither doctrine nor teaching nor theological truth without this Faculty.[39]

Ignatius had nothing so grand in mind. He wanted good theologians, and good theologians precisely as teachers. Hence he wanted a university that would educate for such a service to the church. There is a religiously practical, even moral, finality to universities which he was to outline. His restoration of teaching as the principal function of the theologians dictated that the period for their education be less than at Paris and that the *studia humanitatis* with the emphasis upon communication be incorporated into this education. It is perhaps instructive to note that the history of theology in the seventeenth century does not indicate that the contribution made by theologians from so foreshortened a curriculum took second place to those whose education in theology was almost three times as lengthy.

For if Ignatius cut the Parisian course down ruthlessly in his plans for the new Jesuit universities, he gave almost by counterpoint the premier place to theology. The university was seen as a necessity for the study of theology. Ignatian higher education was geared to form theologians who are teachers, in a manner almost analogous to a contemporary medical school if it were to include within itself all the undergraduate studies that constitute a premedical course. That being said, it is important that this statement be modified. For the Ignatian university was open to other graduate-professional fields. It is true that theology, then, became no longer one professional or graduate school, sharing this honor with those of medicine and law, but the one which dominates and justifies everything else in the university. Graduate or professional education in the Middle Ages and Renaissance included faculties of theology, medicine, and law. But the *Constitutions* make this change: "The study of medicine and laws, being more remote from our Institute, will not be treated in the universities of the Society, or at least the Society will not undertake this teaching through its own members."[40] These graduate-professional faculties were not absolutely ruled out from the universities of the Society, but "encouragement" is not the first word that leaps to mind. As George Ganss notes, faculties of law and medicine made their appearances only rarely in early Jesuit universities. Some twenty years after Ignatius' death, in 1574, a Jesuit university opened in Pont-à-Mousson in Lorraine. A layman offered a course in law in 1577, "and gradually a faculty of law formed under a lay dean. A similar faculty of medicine arose in 1592."[41] While Ignatius' provisions might tolerate such a development, they expressly forbade the teaching of that part of canon law, *de processibus*, so involved in ecclesiastical courts and their adjudication of benefices in those litigious centuries in the church.[42]

This elimination or at least demotion of other professional, graduate schools is balanced by the preeminence given theology. Theology not only possessed its unique value, but explained in the *Constitutions* the presence of the other studies in the curriculum. Theology constituted the governing criterion for the inclusion and the exclusion of particular subject matters and disciplines within the university.

As the first stage of university education, Ignatius provided a place for the *studia humanitatis* of the Renaissance humanists. In the earlier colleges, the *letras de humanidad* had been designated by the umbrella terms of "grammar and rhetoric," with dialectic or logic subsumed into the philosophical curriculum.[43] In the Ignatian universities, the full range of the Renaissance reformation of the liberal arts into the humanities also finds its place; but now it is made an essential preparation for theology. The learning of theology and the practice of it requires the knowledge of humane letters and of the Latin, Greek, and Hebrew languages, and "under the heading of humane letters is understood in addition to grammar, what pertains to rhetoric, poetry, and history."[44] Such disciplinary terms were very flexible. Theology will be seen as the governing discipline in the Ignatian universities, but theological competence demanded humanistic education.

The Ignatian canon of university humanities—grammar and rhetoric, poetry and history—are precisely the studies which the Italian Renaissance humanists established (together with moral philosophy) to take the place of the medieval trivium.[45] Grammar and rhetoric had been classically part of the Latin *artes liberales* since the writings of Varro, but both had been transformed by the Renaissance humanists in their battles with the dialecticians or logicians of the university schools. The Ignatian *Constitutions* incorporate the Renaissance *studia humanitatis* first in the Jesuit colleges, and then in the universities.[46] The focus was upon linguistic skills and literary texts, combined with the mastery of classical languages: Latin, Greek, and Hebrew—the formative languages of Western civilization. For some students, in place of these Western languages, Chaldaic, Arabic, and Indian were to be learned, indicating something of the movement of modernity towards a global horizon and a curious anticipation of the contemporary reserve about an exclusive focus upon Europe by those whose lives were to be lived elsewhere. The *studia humanitatis* in the colleges were both for the formation of character and for the "utility of the city" as the Jesuits argued at Tivoli, i.e., for public service. This ministry of humanistic education "had civic and societal dimensions that carried the Jesuits beyond the evangelical models that principally inspired them."[47] Ignatius believed that the good accomplished by the colleges could be more universally obtained by the universities. This would mean that the university would not be indifferent to the product of its humanistic curriculum in the upright character, the public servant, the effective Christian leader, but over and above this would add the teacher of theology.

Second, there were the arts or the natural sciences (*las artes o scientias naturales*). The Middle Ages had fielded not only the three liberal arts of words (grammar, rhetoric, and logic) but the four liberal arts brought to bear upon things (arithmetic, geometry, astronomy, and music). This quadrivium had opened up the faculty of arts to the natural philosophy and metaphysics of the High Middle Ages, and these moved in their time into the "arts or natural sciences" of the Renaissance. As the focus of the humane letters was linguistic—books or languages—so the objects of the arts or natural sciences were things. The subjects studied in the arts or natural sciences were logic, physics, metaphysics, and moral philosophy, and "mathematics in the measure appropriate to secure the end which is being sought[!]"[48]

Linguistic competence was obviously necessary for theology, but the relationship between theology and the arts or natural sciences was more complex. Competence here enters into theology in three ways. First, it develops the *ingenios* of the students, that is, their natural intellectual capacities, so that they can go on to study theology. Second, theology demands this kind of knowledge intrinsically, both for reaching its own completion and for its exercise. Third, this mathematical, scientific, and philosophic knowledge by itself contributes to the same finality as theology.[49] The relationship envisaged between mathematics or science or philosophy on the one hand and theology on the other, i.e., between those disciplines that investigated directly some aspect of nature and that whose subject matter was God, was not at any time or in any way posed antagonistically. These disciplines constituted together an academic culture and developed the critical reasoning necessary for theological study. They entered into that study to bring it to its completion and into practice. They supplemented that study with their own natural development and inherent purposes. Not a bad understanding of the relationship between science and theology! One must further note the remarkable reconciliation among disciplines that was affected here: between the Renaissance *studia humanitatis* and medieval philosophy and theology; between literary studies and scientific; between scholastic and positive theology.[50] And presiding over this unity was theology.

There is no question about the comprehensive importance of theology within the Ignatian provisions for the universities. It was this professional importance that dictated the character of the Ignatian university. The discussion of curriculum made that conviction absolutely clear: "Since the end of the Society and of its studies is to aid our fellowmen to the knowledge and love of God and to the salvation of their souls; and since the branch of theology is the means most suitable for this end, in the universities of the Society the principal emphasis ought to be put upon it [*in hanc potissimum Societatis Universitates incumbent*]."[51] Theology would explain, either in whole or in part, the presence within the universities of the other faculties. The justification of the study of humane letters begins: "Since both the learning of theology and the use of it require (especially in these times) knowledge of humane letters and of the Latin, Greek, and Hebrew languages. . . ."[52] The years given to philosophy and the sciences have a similar legitimization: "Likewise, since the arts or natural sciences dispose the intellectual powers for theology, and are useful for the perfect understanding and use of it, and also by their own nature help toward the same ends, they should be treated with fitting diligence and by learned professors."[53]

It is important to note what is being said and not being said in these critical paragraphs. Ignatius is not saying that a "university of the Society" is a university in which Jesuits teach or in which the majority of instructors are Jesuits or in which the *Spiritual Exercises* permeate the curriculum.[54] All of these assertions—so often heard in contemporary discussions about the Jesuit university—may be somewhat true or somewhat false, but they are not his point. Further, Ignatius is not saying that what characterizes the universities of the Society is something so vague and featureless as "value-centered education" (the same could be said of those in mainland China) or the active presence of a vital campus ministry or the interest taken by the faculty in the students. These do mark a Jesuit university, as they do many others, but they are not his point. What he is saying—and saying in some distinction to the practice of the great medieval universities and Newman's splendid *Idea of a University*, or even to the contemporary usages of Jesuit universities and houses of study—is this: that theology is essentially a university discipline; that it draws into itself—as the apex of a cone draws the lines of a cone—all of those studies which are designated as liberal or scientific or philosophic; and that it is theology which specifies the curriculum and its content within what Ignatius called the "universities of the Society." It is quite true that the Ignatian university was partial or limited or professional; it aimed at producing teachers of theology. But the reason that Ignatius wanted these universities was because of the importance given to theology.[55] Theology dictated that there would be a university and, for Ignatius and his collaborators, a university of this stamp and focus.

It is not merely that theology is present as one branch of knowledge among others. The bare presence of Catholic theology does not mean that a university is Catholic either for Ignatius or for contemporary educators. As Newman insisted, it simply means that it is that much more a *university*, an institution which embodies the universality of significant human discourse and knowledge. What characterizes a "university of the Society" for Ignatius is the organic relationship between the other disciplines and theology. (One should also notice that what is at issue here is theology, not simply the theology department.) In the *Constitutions*, theology constitutes the ultimate justification for the presence of other branches of learning within the university, as wisdom constitutes the ultimate justification for the arts and sciences. For Newman, what should emerge from any university education is that integration of knowledge which he called the "philosophic habit of mind." For Ignatius, what should emerge from a Catholic university was the integration of knowledge into a theological wisdom—the highest achievement of critical reasoning. These are not contradictory ideals, but neither are they simply identical. Their differences may indicate something intrinsic and important about the Catholic nature of Jesuit education.

One must recall how Ignatius understood theology. It included sacred Scripture, conciliar decrees, the canonical legislation governing Christian practice, the theology contained in the patristic tradition, and the more theoretical or synthetic scholastic theology.[56] In theology, the principal author among the great books was Thomas Aquinas, allowing also for the *Sentences (Liber sententiarium)* of Peter Lombard. This meant in practical terms a choice of the *Summa theologiae* for the Jesuit university, and this confirmed that theology would not be simply one discipline among others. The *Summa theologiae* is an enormously synthetic work, containing discussions that are cosmological and psychological, legal, philosophic, and humanistic—all within a theological setting. One can understand, then, that theological studies demand both a humanistic and a scientific education, capacities for critical reasoning in a variety of manners, if one also understands that the theology stipulated was a synthetic and thoroughly methodological discipline. All other disciplines did not simply prepare for theology and leave off once one had crossed into the temple. The temple was much more a town. Philosophy and science found their place within it—indeed, there is a constant discussion between them within such a theology. All contributed to the ongoing enterprise of theology itself and brought it to a completion that would have been otherwise unobtainable.

Ignatius, however, was not wildly wedded to the *Summa theologiae*; the work itself is not mentioned, though the "scholastic doctrine of St. Thomas" is explicitly given primacy. He allowed for lectures also on the *Liber sententiarium* of Peter Lombard and explicitly provided for someone to write another *summa* "better adapted to these times of ours"[!][57] Yet Saint Thomas's *Summa theologiae* represented the kind of theology that Ignatius wanted, a theology precise in its evidence and argument and in vital contact with the natural sciences and philosophy and the church's tradition. This kind of theology could draw other disciplines and habits of learning into integration and wisdom. A Jesuit university was to institutionalize the unity within its curriculum through theology. In this way, theology specified the Catholic university for Ignatius: "On this should the universities of the society put their principal emphasis [*in hanc potissimum Societatis Universitates incumbent*]."[58]

The Constitutions as Resource and Challenge

It bears repeating, perhaps, that the purpose of these reflections is not to copy the Ignatian formulations to a different time and different context, but to dialogue with his understanding of a "university of the Society," to mine this understanding for its resources, and to allow it to challenge, even with its "professional" focus upon theology, the contemporary settlements. If the *Constitutions* are allowed to question or challenge the contemporary Jesuit university, the results can appear paradoxical. Until recent decades, this emphasis of the *Constitutions* upon theology is pre-cisely what the modern American Jesuit universities had lacked. This focus was left to the pontifical faculties of theology, training students for the priesthood and situated outside the ambit of the universities. Reli-gion was taught in earlier Jesuit universities in the United States and was required of all the students, but rarely did the university follow the Ignatian strictures that theology should be treated by "highly capable professors," or that it would be a kind of theology which would presup-pose the other disciplines by its nature or integrate them by its influence and character.[59] It tended to be much more an apologetic catechesis than a demanding and rigorous academic discipline.

The question must be asked honestly: What contribution did Ameri-can Jesuit universities make to the theology that prepared for and finally influenced the Second Vatican Council? Virtually none. If one were to bring a parallel question to bear within more recent decades, how-ever—some thirty-five years after the Council—and ask about the con-temporary quality and consequent influence of theology in major Jesuit universities, the answer would be far more positive. Then in this critical and specific area, one can locate contemporary Jesuit universities much closer to the vision that directed Ignatius to form the "universities of the Society" than at anytime in the Jesuits' American history—perhaps in a good deal of Jesuit history in general. If a vital theology rather than ubiquitous Jesuit presence or control is what is *potissimum* in the speci-fication of such a university, then there is no doubt that in the last forty years some American Jesuit universities have developed more positively in the Ignatian direction than is commonly credited. There are obviously many other characteristics that make a university both Catholic and Jesuit, but here is the central one for Ignatius of Loyola, the *potissimum*.

The history of philosophy supplies a term that may be applied to the Ignatian understanding of the function of theology within a Catholic university, i.e., as its specifying and integrating wisdom. It is a term whose origins lie with the division of the sciences in Aristotle, but which achieved its modern prominence in Kant. The term is *architectonic*, and it designates a kind of knowledge that brings order into the vast assem-blage of human sciences and disciplines, subject matters and activities.[60] In the *Constitutions*, the order of these disciplines in the university emerges both as developing stages towards that theology for which they prepare and also as interlocutors with the same theology, in which they are vitally located while preserving their own integrity and autonomy.

The architectonic nature of theology does not lie—as does that of the philosophy of science and of education—in the analysis of the founda-tions, axioms, and methods of the various sciences or in the location and distinction among the subject matters of these various disciplines. This analysis of presuppositions is essentially the work of philosophy, as will be suggested in chapter 8. Theology does not so much analyze the presuppositions as it synthetically reflects upon the conclusions of the sciences. Theology, then, must not be seen as one science among others, self-contained in its own integrity and adjacent to the other forms of disciplined human knowledge. It is much more like a place, a place within which the critical thought and developed habits of reasoning in the arts and sciences are encouraged and their ineluctable movement toward questions of ultimacy taken seriously. Such questions of ultimacy are not simply about interlocking content, but are even about the absolute commitments entailed by serious teaching and inquiry themselves. This is theology as an architectonic wisdom rather than as a particular *Wissenschaft*, theology as one wisdom within which disciplines are distinct but not separate. They depend upon one another; one crucially influences the other. Theology is exploration into God's self-revelation and all other things in terms of God—*fides quaerens intellectum*—for which various areas such as Scripture, history, experience, and creedal affirmations function as evidence and for which moral theology, liturgy, spirituality, and social ethics function as consequences of what God has done for us in Christ. Howsoever one distinguishes various aspects of theology, it remains one wisdom.

Some Jesuit universities seem closer to the Ignatian vision than they were thirty years ago, but the claims of Part Four of the *Constitutions* can still leave one feeling "like some watcher of the skies / When a new planet swims into his ken," or with this question about such a programmatic in education: "Was it a vision, or a waking dream?"[61] Can theology function in any architectonic manner within the contemporary university, especially in institutions of higher education that are so different from those of the Renaissance?

One can perhaps best respond realistically to this question with a single concrete example, one that could be multiplied in many and various ways in other Jesuit universities. Santa Clara University has established an annual institute in the winter quarter that promotes courses to be formed in the arts and sciences and professional schools together around a single topic. The first such topic was suggested by the American bishops' pastoral letter on the challenge of peace, and it dealt with the issues of war and peace. Courses were offered in literature ranging from Homer to Hemingway, in history, in economics and political science, in biology and military science, in philosophic ethics and theology. More technical courses were offered by seminars in engineering and in international law. All of these courses were supplemented by a series of lectures, ranging from James Redfield's analysis of war in the

Homeric heroic ethos to Helen Caldicott's description of the medical horrors inherent in atomic war to the panel discussion of the ethical and Christian issues raised by American nuclear deterrence. Over a thousand students took at least one of these courses; all of them were responsible for the common lectures. Such an institute gave the university an interchange among its various schools that it had never experienced before.

The integrative function of theology here was twofold: to raise and press in critical Socratic fashion a question of common and urgent importance; and to contribute to a common effort that both traced something of war's pervasive presence within every aspect of human experience and moved to the resolution of some of its many issues. In this way, theology provided for common critical reflection among all the university disciplines, accomplishing a collaborative reflection unachievable by any of these disciplines taken separately.

So successful was this initial effort that Santa Clara continued this academic integrating institute in subsequent winters with great success. A few years ago, the common topic, again following the episcopal lead, was poverty. The following year, reflecting the influence of a location in Silicon Valley, the topic was technology in world culture. In 1995 the common theme was environmental concern. These common issues could have emerged from any number of disciplines. De facto, they came out of the Catholic university—a community whose self-reflection is theological. If theology is vital, it must engage the other disciplines, and this engagement will constitute the university both as Catholic and as a university. One way of doing this is the raising of a question or topic of common university interest, one that brings the various kinds of knowledge into a discussion with the inquiries that are properly theological.

The Ignatian idea of a Catholic or a Jesuit university is one in which theology functions as an integrating, an architectonic, wisdom. This vision will be realized today differently from its embodiment in the sixteenth century as the present culture stands in contrast with that of the Catholic Reformation. In some significant ways, these universities are closer to that ideal now than they were thirty-five years ago because theology has begun to develop in the seriousness of its teaching and scholarship. Now there are creative new possibilities by which theology can bring into integration the various schools and departments that constitute a university, and principal among them may be its willingness and its Socratic ability to raise issues of common concern. To understand the origin and nature of the Jesuit tradition, however, it might be helpful to explore in much more detail two of the components that gave it character: humanistic studies and theological orientation. This is the burden of the next chapter.

CHAPTER FIVE

Humanism and Jesuit Theology

... según la orden de la summa prouidencia de Dios Nro. Señor, que quiere ser glorificado con lo que él da como Criador, que es lo natural, y con lo que da como autor de la gracia, que es lo sobrenatural.

—Ignatius of Loyola, *Constitutiones*[1]

Introduction

The two nouns that occupy the title of this bifurcated chapter recall in a single phrase preoccupations that have dominated the history of Western culture and have figured decisively in the tradition and character of Jesuit higher education. Though both of these terms are systematically ambiguous—actually more τόποι than terms, variables rather than constants—"humanism" has come to comprise much of a human being's appropriation of the human and "theology" much of a human being's reflection upon the divine. Without much violence, this title could be transmuted into "the place of an educated sensibility for the human within a disciplined reflection upon the divine." The adjective, "Jesuit," specifies this reflection as carried on within the spirituality, education, and intellectual tradition of the Society of Jesus. Thereby hangs not only a tale, but a set of problems.

These two nouns with their attendant adjective also emerge from the previous chapter. It would be better to dwell initially upon the problematic area they circumscribe before attempting to find resolutions to the questions they suggest. For these problems in their turn give rise to others, and these further questions hint towards avenues of approach or further resolutions beyond the compass of this chapter. The first section of this chapter will treat theology and humanism under two headings: the problematic area indicated by the title and the theology that constitutes the Ignatian understanding of the relationship between the divine and the human, that of instrumental causality. The second section will reflect on the realization of this understanding in higher education, taking up the university education in which this conjunction between theology and humanism was embodied.

THEOCENTRIC OR ANTHROPOCENTRIC

Three Aspects of the Problem

These two nouns—"humanism" and "theology"—do not let us off easily. Each of them comes into this discussion freighted with its own lengthy history. "Humanism" was invented originally as a Latin word, "*Humanismus*," by the German educator, F. J. Niethammer in 1808—just as in that same century some fifty years later Jacob Burckhardt was to invent his massively influential "*Renaissance.*" In both terms, the axiom was realized: you create the language and then the language creates you. Both words formulated and bodied forth in a radically important understanding of the history of learning.

Niethammer coined *Humanismus* to designate a Renaissance theory and program of education, one that took the Greek and Latin classical studies as central, in opposition to the upstart but growing demands for a curriculum designed for concerns that were predominantly practical or scientific. Historians in the nineteenth century put this term to good use, expanding it to designate the general culture of the scholars in the Italian Renaissance who had given such an emphasis to classical literature and had embodied it in an academic curriculum.[2] But words have a way of changing our understanding of the reality named and codified, sometimes giving definition and precision to what was in reality far more vague and fluid and often in the process mutating in their own meaning. "Humanism" wandered considerably farther than any confinement within educational projects of the Italian Renaissance. It came to designate, as Paul O. Kristeller has insisted:

> the modern and false conception that Renaissance humanism was a basically new philosophical movement, and under the influence of this notion the old term humanist has also been misunderstood as designating the representative of a new *Weltanschauung*. The old term *humanista*, on the other hand, reflects the more modest, but correct, contemporary view that the humanists were the teachers

and representatives of a certain branch of learning which at that time was expanding and in vogue, but well limited in its subject matter.[3]

This literary program arose out of earlier concerns with grammar and rhetoric, continuing a transformation of the medieval traditions in these disciplines.[4] Its subject matter was literature, especially Latin literature, and its purpose the development of an effective human being in the social order. It focused its educational and cultural energies on the *studia humanitatis*, grammar, rhetoric, history, poetry, and moral philosophy. "And the study of each of these subjects was understood to include the reading and interpretation of its standard ancient writers in Latin and, to a lesser extent, in Greek."[5]

"Humanism" developed even further over the nineteenth and twentieth centuries to denote a number of philosophies or themes or focal concerns which give a decisive place to the cultivation and appreciation of the human as such. Thus, as various analogical concentrations and humane persuasions predominated in different traditions, one came to speak of secular humanism or Christian humanism or Marxist humanism or medieval humanism or the humanism that was appropriated for their pragmatism by F. C. S. Schiller and William James or even the "devout humanism" that Henri Bremond minted and applied to Leonard Lessius and Francis de Sales, while Henri de Lubac entitled his influential work, *The Drama of Atheistic Humanism*. "Humanism," like many other critical terms in Western thought, has become polyvalent, systematically ambiguous.

This career does not leave "humanism" so hopelessly ambiguous as to make all inquiry into its meaning futile. It does, however, dictate that one safeguard the distinction between "humanism" as a cultural and educational program that gave its emphasis to the literature of classical Rome and Greece, and "humanism" as a spirit, a humane sensibility, appreciation, and cultivation of human achievements and enrichment as such. In fact, Renaissance humanism with its *studia humanitatis* can legitimately be seen as one concrete realization of "humanism" in what was to become this more extended meaning, a particular realization of a more general humanistic spirit. When one asks about "humanism and Jesuit theology," this question can be posed about the importance of "humanism" in its broadest sense; but the question can be answered in part by attending to "humanism" as it was used more narrowly by the nineteenth century, i.e., to characterize a particular focus given to cultural studies in the Italian Renaissance.

But there is a further dimension to the problem posed by the nouns in our title, one that extends beyond ambiguous terms. A Jesuit who takes up the relationship between humanism in its broadest sense and theology might do well to recognize that these have already been wedded and their union critically and influentially addressed by Jacques Maritain in his lectures delivered in August 1934 at the University of Santander and subsequently published in 1936 as *Humanisme intégral*.[6]

Maritain certainly numbers among the most sensitive and reflective Catholic philosophers in the twentieth century. One cannot simply pass over in silence that in these influential lectures he maintained that the Jesuit theologian, Luis de Molina, presented to the Western world a "mitigated humanist theology" that possessed great significance in the history of culture.[7] This theology became "the theology of the Christian gentleman of the classical age," seeking to save human freedom at the expense of divine causality, claiming for the creature a share, "a share only, doubtless, but in the end a share, of *first* initiative in the order of good and of salvation." Molinism gave to the creature a primary initiative in the effecting of the good, and so offered a theological representation to the typical "man of the Christian humanism of the anthropocentric epoch."[8] For all of its cultural importance, this modified or mitigated humanist theology possessed the inherent instability of any compromise and eventually resolved its own internal contradictions by giving way to the "absolute humanist theology . . . theology of rationalism" and its doctrine of "freedom without grace."[9]

If Molinism as a "mitigated humanistic theology" was theologically defective in its understanding of the primacy of the divine initiative in human life, its radical anthropological fault as a Christian naturalism lay with its cognate isolation and glorification of the purely natural human being—an abstract "state of pure nature"—in contrast to the full human being marked with the life of grace. This humanistic theology posed grace as an external elevation of nature rather than an organic and healing and permeating transformation.[10] A mechanical and abstract dichotomy between the purely natural human being and the graced human being obtained, allowing for a primacy to be given to human means to accomplish the tasks that human beings found themselves confronting—the creation of their own history. This predominance given to "human means" is the inevitable result and the sure symptom of this faulty, even destructively seductive, "mitigated humanistic theology."

Maritain does not simply or explicitly identify Molinism and Jesuit theology as such. But one could gather the impression that this is implied, that Jesuit theology has an *anima naturaliter molinista*. He locates the character of the entire Society of Jesus and, by implication, of any theology, education, and practice that would bear its stamp, in the spirit of the Counter Reformation, "an absolutist reaction to try to save this spiritual and intellectual unity" that had characterized medieval Christendom. In its emphases, he claims that this historical period was an epoch of predominantly human means. These were chosen

> not exclusively, doubtless, but in a predominant manner—human means, means of State, political means, in order to try to save the unity at once spiritual and political of the social body. . . . To a powerful unleashing of passionate and willful forces, one responds by a supreme tension of the combative energies of the human will drawn up for the defense of the good. This is understandable, even in the order of spiritual life and of sanctity. The Company of Jesus is the type-formation of the spiritual militia in that epoch.[11]

The primacy given to the human in Molina's theology finds its root in the Order of which he was a member. An almost patronizing note sounds in Maritain's comment upon this reliance of the Society of Jesus in its defense of Christianity upon human capabilities and choices—as opposed to the previous emphasis given to the divine initiative:

> No doubt it was necessary that the experience be made of what man is able to accomplish, in the domain itself of the defense of the Christian order, with his human means and his human energies *placed in the foreground of the action*—with his human initiative, applied, in the saints, to the effort to have charity triumph in themselves and in others, and to make more brilliant, to *augment* [emphasis his] the glory of God.[12]

Maritain's reading of the history of Western culture becomes increasingly dramatic as he traces this radically anthropomorphic orientation back to the founder of the Jesuits. He cites René Füllöp-Miller's suggestion that there stands at the beginning and at the decline of the modern age two giant figures of comparable psychic tension, Ignatius of Loyola and Lenin. Whatever the difference in the end that they pursued, and consequently in their methods, there is in both cases "a very significant exaltation of the heroic will."[13] Maritain further comments upon the maxim inaccurately attributed to Ignatius that one should pray as if everything depended upon God, but act as if everything depended upon human effort with the remark: "He who would truly act as if everything depended on man alone would employ, it is clear, if he were logical, human means solely, even to uphold the cause of God."[14] This maxim, of course, is not found in the works of Ignatius—for all of its popular attribution.[15] The fact of the matter is that while this great and gifted

Christian philosopher shows some acquaintance with René Füllöp-Miller's *The Power and the Secret of the Jesuits*, he exhibits almost no knowledge of the actual writings of Ignatius nor of the *Constitutions* nor of the normative documents of the Society of Jesus and of the centuries of scholarship that surrounds them.

Maritain takes for granted that this was what the Jesuits and, by implication, classical Jesuit education was all about: the use of human energies, "the heroic will," and human means "in a predominant manner" to achieve an effect in the order of grace. And he attempts to understand such a strategy through the humanism of Molina's times. Consequent upon such an understanding, the Society of Jesus could not but espouse a theology like that of Molina. It expresses a fundamental acceptance of a primacy of human initiative: an anthropocentric humanism, "man, forgetting that in the order of being and of good it is God who has the first initiative and who vivifies our freedom, has sought to make his own proper movement as creature the *absolutely first movement*, to give to his freedom-as-creature the first initiative of his good."[16]

Whereas "humanism" in its original meaning designated a program of literary education distinguished from theology, Maritain has used it to characterize a theology founded on a faulty understanding of the relationship between human effort and divine initiative. The recognition of the nineteenth century Germanic coinage of a Latin term to cover a fourteenth to fifteenth century Italian program of education and the rattle of musketry from the battlefields *De Auxiliis* may sound curiously distant as the twentieth century draws to its end, but they suggest the problem of the title's adjective.[17]

This raises the meaning of "Jesuit." Jesuit theology is presumably the theology done by Jesuits, but such theologizing has written its own long, varied, and complicated history since that November of 1537 when Pierre Favre and Diego Laínez took up daily lectures at the Sapienza, the University of Rome. Perhaps a word on that history. In the Sapienza, some sixteen years after the excommunication of Martin Luther, Favre was to comment upon Scripture, probably the Epistle to the Romans, and Laínez to hold forth upon the *Lectura super Canone Missae* of the redoubtable nominalist, Gabriel Biel.[18] Obviously, the claims of Romans and the influence of the nominalists were not confined to northern climes. Some twelve years later, in November 1549, Claude Jay, Alfonso Salmerón, and Peter Canisius began their lectures at the depleted University of Ingolstadt, meager German forays into what would write a large page in the history of Jesuit theology. These beginnings were not promising. The papal nuncio, Luigi Lippomano, reported that the three Jesuit theologians were wasting their time at the University of Ingolstadt, having only thirteen or so students in all, ten of whom were "illiterates" and only go to class because they are under constraint to do so! The not very easily discouraged Canisius wrote to Polanco: "Would that there were four or five for whom we could hope that our lectures would be of advantage."[19]

Four years later, in 1553, André des Freux began to comment on Genesis from the newly established chair of Sacred Scripture at the Roman College followed by John Couvillon, commenting upon the First Letter to the Corinthians. Martín de Olabe held the chair of scholastic theology, lecturing on the *Summa theologiae* in the morning and on the *Sentences* in the afternoon. Charlat Quintinus, the Rector, was given the chair of *casus* or moral theology. One cannot pass over without a smile the curious fact that Quintinus used for his textbook the work of the great Dominican commentator Cajetan (Thomas de Vio), engagingly entitled, *A Summary of Sins (Summa peccatorum)*, and that these were delivered on all feast days (*tutti i giorni festivi*)! It is interesting that while originally there was no mention of *casus* or moral theology in the *Constitutions'* description of university theology, when such a chair appeared in the Roman College, 1553, it yielded no pride of time to the more distinguished chairs of scholastic theology and Sacred Scripture, and antedating that of positive theology (1571) by some eighteen years. The chair of Hebrew came also in 1553, but both liturgy and ecclesiastic history had to wait until the middle of the eighteenth century, 1748 and 1742 respectively—some three decades before the papal suppression of the entire Society of Jesus.[20]

With these early lectures in theology and a few in science and philosophy, the Roman College appropriated for itself the heady designation of "university," however modestly that term could be initially predicated. The chair of scholastic theology would soon become two, and would number in its first thirty years such occupants as Diego de Ledesma (1556–62), Manuel de Sá (1556–58, 60–61), Francisco de Toledo (1562–68), Juan de Mariana (1562–65), Francisco Suárez (1580–85) and Gabriel Vázquez (1585–91).[21] It was a remarkable series, one rich in theology and in idiosyncrasy.

One might pause for a moment to gaze ever so briefly at one irascible luminary glittering in that early firmament, the most distinguished among the earliest professors of scholastic theology, Francisco de Toledo. He entered the Society already noted for his theological learning. A disciple of the great Dominican, Dominic Soto, Toledo did not suffer either opposition or fools gladly, and his inability to bear his colleague, Juan de Mariana, made it necessary to adjust the academic schedules of the Roman College. Ricardo Villoslada notes the opinion of Polanco that

Toledo suffered from "an infirmity of head and of humors," and finds him at times "*intollerante e intollerabile*"—by no means the last in the theological tradition of the Society of Jesus who could be so described.

In 1555 a chair of "*Controversiae*" was established with Martín de Olabe as its first occupant and Roberto Bellarmino as its most distinguished (1576–87). In 1560 a third chair of scholastic theology was added to the Roman College, but the University had to wait until 1571 for a chair of positive theology, despite the honor paid to this kind of theology in the *Spiritual Exercises* and in the *Constitutions*.[22] From these pioneer years and often desperate beginnings, the line of Jesuit theologians would wind its way through four hundred years of inquiry and controversies to reach the late twentieth century with such figures as Henri de Lubac, John Courtney Murray, Bernard Lonergan, and Karl Rahner.

This adjective, "Jesuit," then, could present an enormous and insoluble problem, a labyrinth from which no one returns. One cannot explore in this chapter with any thoroughness the massive history of great Jesuit theologians in order to abstract some central humanistic doctrines. If such an ambitious enterprise would not confine itself to rather obvious generalities, it would constitute a daunting task, even for a lifetime of unremitting and concentrated scholarship. An alternative necessarily suggests itself: an exploration of the formative Ignatian documents that lie at the origins of the Society's commitments to humanism and theology, documents that have expressed Jesuit spirituality and so governed Jesuit theology with greater or less success since its inception. Within these normative texts, one can search out the Ignatian understanding or vision of the relationship between the divine and the human, a vision that will serve to form Jesuit theology and inform a Jesuit program of education in the centuries that are to follow.[23]

The Human Defined by the Divine

Jesuit higher education does not come out of a prior philosophy of education. It comes out of a spirituality, out of a pattern or manner of living under the experiences and empowerment of grace, that Ignatius presented as a way to God. If one wishes to ground an inquiry into the Ignatian understanding of the relationship between the human and the divine, and thus uncover the spirituality that serves as the source for his commitment to higher education, one could well begin with the great contemplation with which the *Spiritual Exercises* end—the "Contemplation for Attaining Love." This contemplation brings the *Spiritual Exercises* to their completion by building through four ascending points to some apprehension of God's relations to human beings and all creation.[24] The *Contemplatio* proposes a fundamental understanding of the religious density of all things within and because of the action of God. This is crucially important to register about the Ignatian *Contemplatio ad amorem*. In contrast to Bonaventure's classic *Itinerarium mentis in Deum*, for example, God is not designated from created things; created things are defined by the actions of God. In the progressive understanding of the universe as the contemplation moves through the four points, the primacy in the specification of all things is not the human will, but the divine choice and action.

First, all things are seen as gift—creation and redemption and every particular thing in one's life—and the exercitant is "to ponder with much feeling how much God our Lord has done for me, and how much he has given me of what he has and finally how much the same Lord desires to give Himself to me as much as He can [*y quánto me ha dado de lo que tiene, y consequenter el mismo Señor desea dárseme en quanto puede*]."[25] The initial category for all that is—everything of creation and of salvation, and even God himself—is gifts (*"beneficios"*). "Gift" is, to import the classic vocabulary of metaphysics, a "transcendental," a predicate that is convertible with being, with what is. And the reason that all things are gifts is that God in love has given everything that is, even himself. Creation is God's gift of all that is created; grace is God's gift of God—in a self-communication that will take a central position in the theology of Karl Rahner. Whatever is, is gift.

Second, God dwells within the things that he has created, especially within human beings: " . . . giving me being, life, sensation, and understanding, and making of me a temple, since He created me to the likeness and image of His Divine Majesty [*. . . dándome ser, animando, sensando, y haziéndome entender; asimismo haziendo templo de mý seyendo criado a la similitud y ymagen de su diuina maiestad*]."[26] Everything is not only gift, but sacred—another "transcendental"—because God is immanent within creation, an indwelling presence in all things which God has given and transforming by this indwelling human life into that which is sacred, a dwelling-place of God. This presence defines a human being. *Res sacra homo*, the axiom of the humanists, is founded theologically for Ignatius in this defining indwelling of God. Whatever is, is sacred.

Third, as the *Contemplatio* moves more deeply into the reality of all that is, God is seen not only as immanent within all creation, but at work within it, and at work for human beings: "considering how God works and labors for me within all things created on the face of the earth, that is, behaves as one who labors [*Dios trabaja y labora por mý en todas cosas criadas sobre la haz de la tierra, id est, habet se ad modum laborantis*]."[27] While the first two points of the *Contemplatio ad amorem*, i.e., that God gives and indwells all things, are assertions that one can find throughout mystical literature, the doctrine that God is at work in all things, that he relates to all things as a laborer, that all things are effected and affected by the struggle of God to achieve human salvation, is not so common an emphasis in this same literature. It is, however, a strongly Ignatian perspective. Here the examples given for the location of this struggle are all "of nature," rather than special to grace, ranging from the heavens and the elements to plants, fruits, grains—all things are caught up in the work of God for human beings. Everything is not only gift and sacred, but part of sacred history. All things are, in this sense, "providential"—still another "transcendental"—and God is understood in terms of providence.

God as workman will found two critical characteristics of Ignatian educational theology: that God works in all things, in all events and that one must assign a religious importance—a secondary importance, but real importance—to all natural gifts, talents, and endowments as those gift through and in which God labors.[28] God is present, immanently working within them all, and any theological appreciation of the value of created things and talents must register their place within this divine providence and the resultant sacred history. This is a theme that will run throughout the subsequent writings of Ignatius on education.

Finally, the relationship between God and all things is one of descent: "to see how all the good things and gifts descend from above [*mirar cómo todos los bienes y dones descienden de arriba*"].[29] In sharp contrast with much of mystical literature, Ignatius formulates what is basically a "descent spirituality," i.e., things are seen not so much as moments in a human ascent to God as they are seen as participative realities descending from God; they are *de arriba*: "as from the sun descend the rays of the sun, and as from a fountain descend streams of water." Things not only come from God, they are always of God: "*así como la my medida potencia de la summa y infinita de arriba, y así justicia, bondad, piedad, misericordia*, etc."[30] One can find God in all things because all things descend from God and speak of God.

De arriba becomes one of the critically important terms in Ignatian theology, as one can also find it in the Gospel of John [3:31] and the Epistle of James [1:17]. No one has laid greater stress on this foundational Ignatian vision of all reality than Hugo Rahner: "From then [Manresa] on, his theological thought became a descending movement from God to creatures, in which created things and all earthly beauty, wisdom and righteousness were merely the reflected splendour of what he had already grasped in the immediacy of his mystical contemplation of God himself."[31] In the *Contemplatio ad amorem*, God is not so much known by an intuition or inference founded in the nature of things, as all things are known and designated, and even defined in their depth, by the action of God. To find God, one does not prescind from creation; one enters into it, following out the pattern traced out by the incarnation through the passion, death, and resurrection of Jesus. Whatever is, is God's self-revelation and communication.

This is almost the opposite of Maritain's "anthropocentric humanism." For finally things are understood as gift, sacred, providential, and of God as they are grasped in this descent from God. Ignatius' vision of all that is, his "religious metaphysics" that will furnish the basis for his educational ideal, follows the development of the "Contemplation for Attaining Love." Reality—what is—is gift, sacred, providential and (most profoundly) of divine communication. This explains the paradoxical nature of Ignatian spirituality: all things descend from God as from their source and purpose; every natural thing was to be prized within this descent as indicative of the way that God was present and moving within human life. Even in the most considered mode of making an election—the period of choice in the *Spiritual Exercises*: "The first rule is that the love that moves me and brings me to choose such a thing, descends from above [*descienda de arriba*] from the love of God."[32] In Ignatian spirituality, there is already an absolute priority given to the divine in "the first initiative in the order of good and salvation"—out of which comes everything and by which everything is given its religious density.

The Human United with God: Instrumental Causality

Nothing is finally profane. Precisely because of the divine origin of all things and the quality of the divine presence in all things, every aspect of nature is to be revered and treasured, every science and human development is in its integrity gift, sacred, providential, and of God. Everything, then, becomes a way to God because everything is descending from God. Indeed, it only becomes a way to God when and if it is seen in this primordial descent. For example, the *Spiritual Exercises* opens the three weeks of contemplation on the life, death, and resurrection of Jesus with the contemplation on the Incarnation. This contemplation is the most dialectically drawn of all of the contemplations of the *Spiritual Exercises*. It embodies a "Christology from above," as the Trinity determines upon the Incarnation. It grounds the subsequent contemplations of the individual mysteries of the life of Jesus, even during the passion when "the divinity hides itself."[33]

In Ignatius, consequently, there was no exaltation of human means as a principal agency—not even the "heroic will," to use a phrase from Maritain—by which one would attain the purposes of the Society of Jesus or augment the glory of God. On the contrary, there is an insistent emphasis upon the divine initiative out of which all things must come and with which the Society of Jesus—and its educational commitments—must be in union. The metaphor in which Ignatius understood this union between the active human being and the indwelling, "working" God in the *Constitutions* is that of the instrument in the hand of God, working *ad modum laborantis.* The theology that supports and explains the educational theory is that of instrumental causality—God as workman and God's work in and through all things:

> For the preservation and development not only of the body or exterior of the Society but also of its spirit, and for the attainment of the objective it seeks, which is to aid souls to reach their ultimate and supernatural end, the means which unite the human instrument with God and so dispose it that it may be wielded dexterously by His divine hand are more effective than those which equip it in relation to men. Such means are, for example, goodness and virtue, and especially charity, and a pure intention of the divine service, and familiarity with God our Lord in spiritual exercises of devotion, and sincere zeal for souls for the sake of glory to Him who created and redeemed them and not for any other benefit. Thus it appears that care should be taken in general that all the members of the Society may devote themselves to the solid and perfect virtues and to spiritual pursuits, and attach greater importance to them than to learning and other natural and human gifts. For they are the interior gifts which make those exterior means effective toward the end which is sought.[34]

This theology of the human as the instrument of the divine, as the means through which the divine enters human history, runs throughout Ignatius' writings. From admission to candidacy in the Society, for example, he excluded those who had formally and publicly denied their faith or had ever committed murder because "those who hope to enter the Society in order to be good and faithful sowers in the Lord's field and to preach His divine word will be instruments the more apt for this purpose, the less they are marked by the first and second defects [heresy and homicide]."[35] He saw all apostolic work under this metaphor and urged prayers that God would dispose those with whom and for whom the Jesuits labored "to receive His [God's] grace through the feeble instruments of this least Society."[36] This understanding of instrumentality allowed the primary emphasis to be given to the Jesuit's union with God, but also an importance to be attached to natural gifts and humane development.

An instrument operates under two characteristic determinations: (1) its own nature or structure—a pencil, pen and an ax, a horse or a human being will not do the same things, irrespective of who moves them; and (2) the influence of the agent—as a pen in Shakespeare's hand can write a sonnet, but barely a coherent paragraph in the hand of some high school sophomores. As Aquinas put it in treating the humanity of Christ as the *instrumentum conjunctum* of the divinity, the nature and the development of the instrument is crucial:

> It is proper to an instrument to be moved by the principal agent, yet diversely, according to the property of its nature. For an inanimate instrument, as an axe or a saw, is moved by the craftsman with only a corporeal movement; but an instrument animated by a sensitive soul is moved by the sensitive appetite, as a horse by its rider; and an instrument animated with a rational soul is moved by its will, as by the command his lord the servant is moved to act, the servant being like an animate instrument, as the Philosopher says [*Polit.* i. 2, 4; *Ethic.* viii. 11].[37]

An instrument will be moved, influenced, initiated, and directed according to its own character. What a thing is and the degree to which it is developed determines the kind of activity and function which can be initiated through it: "God moves each thing according to its own measure [*modum*]."[38] Union with God introduces this divine instrument into the determining influence of God, but that influence will be operative according to the kind and development of the instrument in question. Hence the distinctions made by Aquinas between inanimate and animate, sensible or rational, separate or organically conjoined.[39]

Ignatius does not spell out these distinctions, relying upon a general theology of instrumentality and using as his example the inanimate instrument that is wielded by the divine hand. This choice is noteworthy, since his later stress upon obedience will insist upon the volitional and rational union—the free union—between God and those who mediate God's influence to the world. But what this example of the instrument in the hand of God loses in precision in the critical Part Ten of the *Constitutions*, it gains in metaphor and suggestion. It emphasizes contact, the union in touch, the presence, that in some way is found in all mystical experience. It develops further the theology of the relationship between

God and creation carried by the third and fourth point of the *Contemplatio*: God is immanently at work, "even like a workman [*habet se ad modum laborantis*]," and the union becomes that of single action flowing from the laborer directly into the instrument, and through the instrument into the external world of history, space, and time. That "flow" or influence is a descending movement, coming from the agent and through the instrument in a single action: "There is only one action of the instrument and of the principal agent [*instrumenti et principalis agentis est tantum una actio*]."[40]

That this instrumental union was fully conscious and volitional—a deeply affective and free response to God who was the source of each point of the *Contemplatio*—was underlined by the repeated self-offering of the one making this contemplation (*Suscipe*). This prayer followed each one of these points, as one gave oneself over to this influence of God within one's life. But the starkness of the metaphor of the instrument in the hand stresses mystical contact and union, the primacy of the influence of God, and the descending nature of God's presence and influence.

This understanding of the "hand of God," in which all religious instrumentality lay, opens up the entire Part Ten of the *Constitutions*, treating the preservation and development of the Society of Jesus and giving voice to the absolute primacy of the divine initiative:

> The Society was not instituted by human means [*con medios humanos*]; and neither is it through them that it can be preserved and developed, unless by the omnipotent hand [*sino con la mano omnipotente*] of Christ, our God and Lord. Therefore in Him alone must be placed the hope that He will preserve and carry forward what He deigned to begin for His service and praise and for the aid of souls.[41]

But the τόπος of instrumentality further provides Ignatius with a fundamental insight not only into the relationship between human reality and God, between human action and divine influence, but also into the relationship that obtains among human beings and constitutes a basis for humanistic, scientific, and theological learning. In a word, the metaphysics of instrumentality bears upon theology, education, and humanism. For an instrument is not only moved according to its own nature, but has its effect according to this nature and its development:

> When based upon this foundation, the natural means that equip the instrument of God our Lord for [being] with their neighbors [*para con los próximos*] will all help toward the preservation and develop-

ment of this whole body, provided that they are acquired and exercised for the divine service alone; employed, indeed, not that we may put our confidence in them, but that *we may cooperate with the divine grace according to the arrangement of the sovereign providence of God our Lord.* For He desires to be glorified both through the natural means that he gives as Creator, and through the supernatural means that He gives as the Author of grace. Therefore the human or acquired means ought to be sought with diligence, especially well-grounded and solid learning [*doctrina*], and a method of proposing it to the people by means of sermons, lectures, and the art of dealing and conversing with people.[42]

It is crucially important to note that well-grounded and solid learning—education—is that which joins one human being to another, and further that this learning must be coupled with the developed capacity for communication. This latter will support the subsequent Jesuit emphasis upon rhetoric. God wishes to be glorified—to have the divine presence become palpable—in all things: natural and supernatural, human and divine. Everything is to become that in which God is glorified. Things and God, nature and grace, are neither parallel nor in competition for Ignatius. God desires to be glorified in all things, and all are united in a theology of instrumentality.

This emphasis stood in radical contrast to the more pessimistic representatives of Augustinianism during the sixteenth and seventeenth centuries, extolling the glory of God at the expense of the human. One must choose between the glory of the human and the glory of God. John Calvin put this antinomy starkly:

> Man cannot arrogate anything, however minute, to himself, without robbing God of His honor, and through rash confidence subjecting himself to a fall. To keep free of both these rocks, our proper course will be, first, to show that man has no remaining good in himself, and is beset on every side by the most miserable destitution; and then teach him to aspire to the goodness of which he is devoid, and the liberty of which he has been deprived.[43]

Certainly such a statement could be interpreted in a manner congenial to Ignatius: the utter primacy in the order of good and salvation is God's. But it was not often so interpreted. It obtained a grim influence in fixing an antinomy between God and the human and propagating such abstractions as "man in himself." *Soli Deo gloria*, despite its possibility for a graceful interpretation, became the rubric under which this terrible di-

lemma was to be resolved—as if somehow or other God was in intractable rivalry with creation. One had to choose: *aut gloria Dei aut gloria
hominis*. The revolutions of Feuerbach, Marx, and Nietzsche kept that
same ruinous competition, but chose the alternative resolution in the
nineteenth century.

Whatever one advances as the profound and pervasive faults of
Molina's understanding of God's foreknowledge of future and free human choices (*scientia media*), no assertion of Ignatius can be subsumed
under either alternative of this dichotomy. The dichotomy could not be
more foreign to his theology and his educational theory. On the contrary,
the divine descends into the human and into all created things "according to the arrangement of the sovereign providence of God." There is
nothing in nature or in grace that is not from God through God and for
God, and the finality of each is realized through the organic subordina-
tions suggested in the theology of instrumentality. This divine instrumentality provides the basic theological structure for what would later
become the educational program of the Jesuit university. It is the spirituality out of which the Ignatian commitments to higher education will
emerge.

PURPOSE, PROGRAM, AND PRACTICE

Renaissance Transformations in Humanistic Education

To understand the educational program in which Ignatius would realize
his vision of the divine and the human, one must understand something
about the liberal arts of the Middle Ages. The *studia humanitatis* (the
studies of humanity) of the Italian Renaissance—and the Ignatian university, insofar as it was influenced by the Renaissance—proposed to
reform medieval education. Like any reform, a good deal of its definition
lay with what was being corrected or repudiated. What were these medieval liberal arts that needed this Renaissance correction?

When Hugh of St. Victor in the late 1120s wrote his major work on
education, the *Didascalicon*, giving information and directives to students come to Paris to study at the recently founded Abbey of Saint
Victor, he was at pains to distinguish the liberal arts from the mechanic
sciences, insisting that the seven liberal arts "are called liberal either
because they require minds which are liberal, that is, liberated and
practiced (for these sciences pursue subtle inquiries into the causes of
things), or because in antiquity only free and noble men were accus-

tomed to study them."[44] To possess these arts is to be free; to educate in these arts is to educate for freedom.

This liberal education comprised the "circle of the arts," maintained John of Salisbury in 1159, a few decades after Hugh of St. Victor, and it freed the students in two ways: they no longer needed the help of a teacher "to understand the meaning of books and to find the solutions of questions", i.e., they offered the students a new independence in inquiry; they developed an educated sensibility so that freed from the ambitions or cares which dominate the lives of others, they "may devote themselves to wisdom." The liberal arts have achieved the character which they alone can impart when "they liberate us from the care incompatible with wisdom."[45]

One taught these universal arts to students in the Middle Ages because these disciplines would free them. And from this purpose, the name of the "arts" was secured. The student became increasingly free as he learned to read with understanding, making sense out of the greatest books in the history of Western culture, as he learned to analyze and distinguish good arguments from bad, and as he learned to proceed methodologically in literary or scientific creativity. As John of Salisbury wrote: "They are called 'liberal,' either because the ancients took care to have their children [liberos] instructed in them or because their object is to effect the liberation [libertatem] of the human person."[46]

Long before John of Salisbury, Seneca had drawn the connection between liberal studies and free human beings.[47] Drawing upon this tradition as it reached them through the Christian ideal presented in Augustine's De doctrina Christiana and through the unity of the liberal arts initially elaborated by Martianus Capella's De nuptiis Philologiae et Mercurii and standardized by Cassiodorus, the great educators of the early Middle Ages, Isidore, Alcuin, and Rabanus Maurus, formulated a program in the liberal arts that was to characterize Europe for centuries.

What Hugh of St. Victor and John of Salisbury understood by an education in the liberal arts was, then, not so much a command of a particular subject matter as an assimilation of certain universal intellectual skills and sensibilities. The "liberal arts" were not particular subject matters to be mastered. One did not learn "grammar" as one might today learn thermodynamics. It was not a body of knowledge to be understood so much as it was a discipline, a skill, a comprehensive habit that could be brought to bear upon any text irrespective of its subject matter. Grammar was the "art of interpretation"—the art of reading and writing with sense, but also interpreting and criticizing the content of what was written. As such, this skill could be brought to bear upon anything written, i.e., history or poetry or even mathematics. Each of these liberal arts of words (*sermocinales*) was a universal discipline, one not nailed down to a single body of knowledge or a single author. Grammar, thus, was the art of interpretation, as Marius Victorinus had defined it for early Christian culture and Rabanus Maurus had repeated for the Middle Ages.[48] Rhetoric was the art of argumentation—of differentiating good arguments from bad, of formulating arguments from evidence to conclusion—and when mastered, this skill could also be brought to bear upon any subject matter, i.e., the argument of a historical claim, the plot of a drama, the decision that a legislature should make or the direction to be weighed for foreign policy. Logic became an analytic instrument of all discourse and, eventually, a methodological instrument for the advance of scientific inquiry and discourse.

Grammar, dialectic and rhetoric were methods, universal skills that could be introduced to analyze and treat any subject matter embodied in discourse to yield creative new insights and to reveal problems unresolved. Arithmetic, geometry, astronomy, and music were also universal skills which could be applied similarly to things in order to discover the "secrets of all nature." The trivium treated discourse, what was given in language; the quadrivium treated things, what was given in nature.

When the Renaissance criticized this program, it did so bitterly in terms of the universal claims of this education. These medieval "liberal arts" were indeed universal disciplines, not identified with any body of knowledge or subject matter! But as they became more universal, they had also become more abstract, innocent of concrete subject matter and particularity, and so dominated by general rules and complicated schemata that they distracted the student from the life and achievements of men and women. So the medieval *ars dictaminis* inculcated in the students general rules, rather than the preceptive method of imitation, which the humanists favored.[49] Juan Luis Vives was warned by one of his professors at the University of Paris that he would have to make a choice in his studies between dialectics or theology and the grammar that was a component in the arts of humanity. The new humanism made such medieval institutions as the Universities of Paris and of Louvain the object of bitter and scathing criticism.[50]

The Renaissance humanists proposed another program, that of the five *studia humanitatis*: grammar, rhetoric, poetry, history, and moral philosophy, a program that would have as its purpose the formation of the competent Christian leader. Rhetoric they reformed, for example, through an increased focus on the concrete orations of Cicero, an author to be imitated and mastered for his elegant style rather than studied simply for abstract rules to be formalized and applied or for the moral lessons one could garner from his disputations. These classical studies provided the humanists with classical standards to be reached in their imitation of Cicero.[51] History and poetry were added as concrete human achievements; passions and actions were to be studied in their true narrative or celebrated in literature. Moral philosophy was brought into this circle of five because of the revolutions that the humanists were introducing by means of these new arts of humanity. It was not that the humanist thought that knowledge comprised virtue. There were too many learned scholastics to whom they would be unwilling to attribute virtue! Rather there was a way of reading literature that built character, and so literature became a vehicle both of good style and good living. As Vives insisted in a critically important text to which these reflections will return: "The arts of humanity . . . [are] those branches of learning [*disciplinae*], by means of which we separate ourselves from the way of life and customs of animals and are restored to humanity and raised toward God Himself."[52]

Vives is pointing to a more profound shift in education from the Middle Ages to the Renaissance. The "abstract" medieval arts gave way to the concrete humanities, and this focus upon particularity embodied a new orientation towards social action and efficacy and a conjunction between literary education and moral and religious formation.

The humanists of the Italian Renaissance had designated this set of cultural and academic concentrations as the *studia humanitatis* or the *studia humaniora* because the justification of this new literary canon lay with what Vives had stated, i.e., the restoration of humanity to human beings, including, as Vives insisted, both their negative separation from the life of beasts dominated by instinct or by pleasure and pain, and their positive and practical movement towards a godly life, as moral philosophy would indicate it. The students would become like the great or beautiful things that they learned to know, appreciate, and love. They would grow into their own humanity as they assimilated those profound achievements of human culture to which these studies gave access. Hence, a straight line could be drawn between literary studies and moral development. Europe had moved a good way from the medieval liberal arts of words.

The liberal arts of words were transformed into the content-oriented humanities that included literature, history, and philosophy. In this transformation of general education, the liberal arts of words over the centuries became the "more humane letters," and the liberal arts of things became the sciences and various "philosophies of nature." This left a disjunction between the arts and the sciences or between the methods and skills which dealt with texts, documents, and the thoughts of others, and those which dealt with things, while history was introduced to study "true narration of the deeds of human beings."[53] Paul Kristeller maintains that the clearest statement of the literary canon that comprised the *studia humanitatis* is to be found in the one drawn up by Nicholas V as a young man for Cosimo de' Medici. After having listed many books on theology, then the works of Aristotle in logic, physics, metaphysics and moral philosophy, together with works in mathematics and the Greek and Arabic commentators, he wrote: "concerning the *studia humanitatis*, insofar as it looks to grammar, rhetoric, history, and poetry as well as moral [theology] . . ."[54]

These Renaissance humanists did not themselves call their cultural emphasis and consequent academic program "humanism." As mentioned, F.J. Niethammer some four centuries later was to coin this term to designate the Renaissance theory and program of education in the fourteenth and fifteenth centuries, one that took Greek and especially Latin classical studies as central. But those Italian humanists who practiced such a program or actually embraced such a theory during the Renaissance called what they did by the much older term of Varro and Cicero, *humanitas*. This is precisely the word that Ignatius uses for his literary provisions for higher education in the *Constitutions*. The choice of this word gives the clue to the education early Jesuit educators thought essential.

Humanitas itself has an interesting history, and one that bears directly upon the challenge to higher education that is to be explored throughout this book. In the Hellenistic period, the Greek word παιδεία no longer simply meant the processes or techniques by which children were formally educated into their maturity. The term was extended to cover the product of all this education, the humane culture itself, even that which was "pursued beyond the years of schooling and lasting throughout the whole of life, to realize ever more perfectly the human ideal . . . a mind fully developed, the mind of a man who has become truly man."[55] Παιδεία thus comprised both the formal education of children into adulthood and, more importantly, the finality and adult product of this education: the humane human being—one who had come into the promise inherent in his humanity, a mind fully developed.

When the Romans came to translate the word παιδεία, according to the second-century Roman grammarian, Aulus Gellius, they made a pivotal choice, one which would influence humanistic education for two thousand years. One must inspect this critically telling text of Aulus Gellius, for it was frequently invoked as canonical by the Renaissance humanists:

Those who have coined Latin words and those who have used these correctly, did not wish that "*humanitas*" would mean what the common people think it means and what the Greek word "φιλανθρωπία" means, namely an indiscriminate friendly spirit and good will to all human beings. Rather they called "*humanitas*" pretty much what the Greeks called "παιδεία" and which we call "education and training in the good arts." Those who sincerely desire and pursue these arts are the most highly humanized [*maxime humanissimi*] since the care for that knowledge and the training given by it have been bestowed upon human beings—uniquely out of all other animals. And for this reason, it is called "*humanitas*." Almost all the literature indicates that our early writers and especially Marcus Varro and Marcus Tullius [Cicero] have used the word in this way.[56]

This text of Gellius with its separation of "*humanitas*" from "φιλανθρωπία" had an enormous influence upon the Renaissance understanding of the humanities. One became humanized by an education "in the good arts"—what today are called the humanities—and one's "good will towards all human beings" is not specifically part of this education at all. "*Humanitas*" translates παιδεία and it meant "*eruditionem institutionemque in bonas artis*," or as R. S. Crane translates the text of Gellius, "education and training in the good arts. Those who desire and seek after these are *maxime humanissimi* [most highly humanized]."[57] Scholars as late and as great as Henri Marrou have accepted the accuracy of Gellius' translation into Latin, but more recent scholarship has called it into question.[58]

If the ideal of the liberal arts of the Middle Ages was human freedom, the ideal of the Renaissance humanists was humane development.[59] The curriculum for learning in the Renaissance, under the influence of the humanists, came to bear upon "the humanities," or "the more humane letters." In the Ignatian prescriptions, it became in Latin the *litterae humaniores*, or in Spanish, the *letras de humanidad*. And how did the Renaissance humanists propose to develop human beings so that they became humane, *maxime humanissimi*? By the reflective contact worked between the student and the great achievements of human beings, in language and in history, which the student would imitate, incorporate, and assimilate. Such a humanistic education would form the whole person in his moral character and in consequent human achievements that would range from public service to elegant style.

Humanism and Theology: The University of the Society

Not everyone looked upon this Renaissance transformation of education as manna from heaven. The scholastic theologian, Diego Laínez, protested to Ignatius that this educational program for young Jesuits *en cosas de humanidad* would debilitate the intellects of these scholastics, educating them to be so attentive to style and form that they could not engage studies which were more profound, such as scholastic theology. Ignatius directed Polanco, his secretary, to respond, reminding Laínez that

> from times long ago until our own, it has been the common practice to begin with *letras humanas,* with the exception of those periods when barbarism reigned in the place of studies, not just in *letras* but also in human society. With the exception of those years, we gather that this method of beginning with a good foundation in *letras humanas* before going on to other studies, prevailed in Greece and Italy, and I think in other places as well.[60]

The Society of Jesus was committed to placing humanistic studies at the beginning of an extended education: "Such subjects open the mind gradually and prepare it to take subjects of greater consequence."[61] Indeed, so influenced were the early Jesuits by this Renaissance humanism that an extended argument was entertained earlier in this century whether or not their *Ratio studiorum* of 1599 was simply an adaptation of the educational methods of Juan Luis Vives.[62] Humanism, in the broadest senses of that word, has flourished or faltered as its vision has been concretized and realized in an institution of ordered disciplines, whether in the writings of Vives or in the institutions of the Jesuits. But both of these promised an educational program that involved an elevation of the mind to God. Both of them, consequently, raised the question of the relationship between humanistic studies and academic theology.

In the history of thought, these two courses of education, humanistic and theological, have been related in many different ways: they have been opposed as contraries, or one has tended to absorb the other, or one has been found derivative from the other, or some integration has been discovered between them that suggested an organic relation. T.S. Eliot, for example, conducted an extended argument with his former teacher, Irving Babbitt, on whether humanistic education in its fullest sense was possible without a religious component or dimension.[63] The various forms of these ancient battles are as varied as they are prolonged, and their lines need not be of concern here. Two possibilities concerned the scholars of the Renaissance and Catholic reformation: either humanistic studies necessarily entailed religious or theological concerns or theology necessarily entailed humanistic studies.

Representing the first would be the Renaissance Quintilian, Juan Luis Vives, in his work so often compared to the *Institutes,* entitled *On the Transmission of Disciplines, or Christian Education* (1531). In this massive attempt to elaborate a new *"circulus artium,"* one that would stand as a substitute for the medieval pattern and understanding of liberal arts, Christian education was to concern itself with the "arts of humanity": Vives, in the text cited above, had described these, as "those *disciplinae,* branches of learning by means of which we [a] separate ourselves from the way of life and customs of animals and [b] are restored to humanity, and [c] are raised towards God Himself."[64] The humanities were not theology, but they of themselves contribute directly to religious edification and piety as they also further the uses and necessities of temporal life by cultivating the human mind. Humanistic studies, though distinguished both from purely practical pursuits and philosophical speculation, included in Vives both the study of classical literature and—as the Italian *studia humanitatis* had not included—the study of natural science. As such, they fulfilled their theological or religious purpose: "All things, the more exactly they are known, the more do they open the doors of entrance to the knowledge of the Deity, i.e., the supreme Cause, through His works."[65] Though theology was not considered part of humanistic studies—while moral philosophy was—these studies necessarily entailed a theological dimension. If not for theology properly speaking, there was assuredly a necessary place for a disciplined attention to the religious within the humanities.

Ignatius did not necessarily contradict the doctrine of Vives—in fact, many elements in their educational patterns coincide. But his emphasis and consequent structure are different. When Ignatius came to consider the relationship between humanistic development and theology, he treated the question not abstractly in terms of the principles and consequences of natures, but in the practical dispositions that would give structure to a Jesuit university. In the directions for the "universities of the Society," framed so late and influenced by so talented a set of collaborators, the theological justification of the various branches of knowledge and their organic interrelationships have already been noted. Whatever be the intrinsic value of each of these disciplines, all of them existed above all for theology because theology comprised the reflections upon human finality: the knowledge and love of God and eternal salvation. Theology served not only as the principal subject matter to be studied in the university, but as the architectonic or governing discipline in the university. As a subject, it was to include scholastic theology, Sacred Scripture, and positive theology; as an architectonic wisdom, its needs were to dictate the presence of the other faculties and its influence was to draw them into a unity.[66]

In this orientation of all studies to theology, the Jesuit university may have been in some contrast with Vives and other Renaissance humanists who "did not subordinate the development of secular learning to its amalgamation with religious or theological doctrine."[67] Both Ignatius and Vives agree that the arts—however differently they read them—raise human beings towards God himself, the precise finality of theology in the Ignatian scheme.[68] These arts, then, serve both as intermediate goods, possessing value in themselves, and for the further purposes of theology. It is interesting, especially if one considers the subsequent emphasis on rhetoric within the secondary schools of the Society, that the *Constitutions* do not similarly exalt the worth of the more humane letters. In the provisions for the universities of the Society, the humanities are seen as valuable in order to learn theology, and they take their place in the study of theology. It is additionally curious to discover, if one takes up the contrast between philosophy and rhetoric drawn by Cicero and Quintilian, both Vives and the Ignatian *Constitutions* give the priority to philosophy or the "arts or the natural sciences."

This insistence of the *Constitutions* on the integrative function of theology and the estimation given of the *artes o scientias naturales* injected the early Jesuits into the *res-verbum* controversy among the humanists, a controversy reaching back to the arguments between Socrates and the Sophists. Petrarch, beginning the tradition of the Italian humanists, had given the primacy to rhetoric because "it is more satisfying [*satius*] to will the good than to know the truth," and rhetoric is the effective means of moving people to will the good. Petrarch's emphasis upon rhetoric would influence critically the humanistic directions of the subsequent century. Both Lorenzo Valla and Angelo Poliziano made language, especially rhetoric, the center of humanistic education, while Leonardo Bruni and Vittorino in some contrast would maintain that language took its value from its ability to mediate the truth about reality. Pico della Mirandola also asserted the preeminence of *res* over *verbum* and, consequently, of philosophy (arts or natural sciences) over rhetoric. This did not prevail, however, and by the sixteenth century "Italian humanism was primarily a literary pursuit, and philosophy was left to develop on its own."[69] In Ignatius, linguistic and literary studies are distinguished from philosophic, but not opposed, and an organic relationship was worked among them through their relationship with theology, with an obvious edge given to the arts or natural science. This organic subordination says something not only about the resulting humanities, the arts or sciences, but also about the theology for whose learning and employment they were seen as indispensable.

Theology and the Influence of Humanism

If humanistic studies in the university prepared for theology, the spirit of humanism also affected theology. The faculty of theology in the Jesuit university consisted, according to the *Constitutions*—in contrast to actual early practice—of three components: Scripture, scholastic theology, and positive theology. This last took its time to win actual admission into the Roman College, but the provision for its inclusion came with the others in the *Constitutions* and reflected the growing emphasis upon the study of the patristic tradition which the humanists urged.[70] Such humanists as Leonardo Bruni and Desiderius Erasmus had attacked both the method and the style that marked scholastic theology: "barbarous, excessively and uselessly subtle," producing only abstract and sterile knowledge, unconnected with the life of the gospel. But the "humanists assail a thing only for the sake of replacing it. In place of the *disputatio* and the dialectical method, they want to see the texts and the exegetical method cultivated, the Bible text first of all and next the ancient authors."[71]

To meet this attack and to respond to the needs out of which it sprang, a theology known as "positive" emerged. Perhaps the term was first coined by John Major in 1507 in his commentary on Book Four of the *Liber sententiarum*, attacking those "who profusely and at length insert into theology useless questions from the arts and assail frivolous opinions with a prodigality of words . . . Wherefore I decided as far as possible to pursue theological matters almost totally in this fourth part, now *positively*, now *Scholastically*."[72] Ignatius locates this same distinction in the eleventh of his famous rules, "*Para el sentido verdadero que en la Yglesia militante debemos tener.*" One should be ready and prompt:

> to praise positive and scholastic teaching and learning [*doctrina*]. For just as it is more characteristic of the positive doctors, such as St. Jerome, St. Augustine, St. Gregory, and the rest to stir up our affections toward loving and serving God our Lord in all things, so it is more characteristic of the scholastic teachers, such as St. Thomas, St. Bonaventure, the Master of the Sentences, and so on to define and explain for our times the matters necessary for salvation, and also to refute and expose all the errors and fallacies. For the scholastic teachers, being more modern [*modernos*], can avail themselves of an authentic understanding of Sacred Scripture and the holy positive

doctors. Further still they, being enlightened and clarified by divine influence, make profitable use of the councils, canons, and decrees of our Holy Mother Church.[73]

Melchior Cano—one of the great dyspeptic theologians of the sixteenth century—attempted to integrate such positive theology (without ever naming it) into theology by making it that part of theology whereby it "establishes its principles or works on its foundations or datum." The fuller sense of positive theology as a basic kind of theology parallel to scholastic, having its own approach to texts and its own finality, carried the day. In 1591 Gregory of Valentia, for example, accepted theology as divided into scholastic and positive, while only two years previously Louis Carbonia maintained that "Christian theology is usually divided into Scholastic and positive."[74] By incorporating this division into the structure of the theology faculty, the Ignatian university registered a notable influence of the humanistic movement.[75]

Yves Congar explains and distinguishes extensively between the use of positive theology as it was elaborated by Ignatius and as it was programmed by Cano. Congar's reduction of the former to "a literary conception, according to which positive theology represents a certain *manner* in working out theology" seems inadequate. In Ignatius, positive theology has its own affective finality with its immediate realization in life and even its own "great books" or authors who are to be studied. Scholastic theology, in contrast, seems to recall the questions and disputations whose finality includes definition and explanation "for our times," inquiry and the correction of errors. On the other hand, Ignatius does indicate that the scholastic doctors—being *moderni*—have been able to incorporate into their theology the positive theology of more ancient times as well as the subsequent decisions about dogma and discipline in the church.[76]

What was also critical for the future of Jesuit theology was the provision that the scholastic theology should be "*la doctrina scholástica de Sto. Thomás.*"[77] During the Middle Ages, the textbook for lectures on scholastic theology was that of Peter Lombard, the *Liber sententiarum*. This gave to the most diverse kinds of theology—that of Thomas Aquinas, Bonaventure, Duns Scotus, William of Occam, Durandus, etc.—a common set of texts, a common language, and a common series of problems which allowed for a continuity of tradition and language together with a pluralism of theologies. With the rejection of this massively influential textbook, Catholic theology has never been able to retrieve this commonality of texts, tradition, and language "within which the conflicting theologies . . . could contact and speak intelligibly with one another."[78]

Aquinas had not written his *Summa theologiae* to substitute for this great book of common texts, but to aid the Dominican students at the *studium provinciale*, to prepare for preaching and confessional work those friars who would not attend the university.[79] During the sixteenth century, a revolution took place—in lesser but important ways fragmenting the culture of Europe as did that religious division which would splinter Christianity during the same decades. Major Dominican thinkers began to comment not upon the *Liber sententiarum*, but upon the *Summae theologiae*. Most influentially, the great Francisco de Vitoria introduced this novelty into Salamanca in 1527. Ignatius would have the Jesuits follow suit, teaching the scholastic doctrine of Saint Thomas.[80] He also allowed, as previously noted, for lectures on the *Liber sententiarum* or upon "some other compendium or book of scholastic theology that would seem better adapted to these times of ours," but Saint Thomas and his masterpiece carried the day.[81]

How faithfully the Jesuits of the sixteenth century followed this prescription can be gauged from the examinations prescribed in the *Ratio studiorum* of 1586. Five "public acts" or public examinations were to test the student in the course of his progress to the final degree. For the first public act, somewhat more than fifteen theses were selected from the first part of the *Summa theologiae* and defended by the examinee—with the examiners and candidate going at it for two hours and a half in the form of scholastic argumentation; for the second, a similar number of theses from the first part of the second part of the *Summa*; for the third, another fifteen or so from the second part of the second part of the *Summa*; for the fourth, the student took up a similar number from the third part of the *Summa*; for the last—the "atto generale," the candidate faced fifty theses "*de universa theologia*" in an examination that lasted for five hours.[82] One must contrast this early Jesuit emphasis on the *Summa theologiae* in the Roman College both with that of the great universities of Louvain and Paris where the Master of the Sentences still held sway and with the Spanish universities of Alcalá and Salamanca, where the chair of Thomistic studies was matched with those championing the thought of Scotus and of the nominalists. While for the first four of its early years, there was also at the Roman College a chair for the study of the *Liber sententiarum*, Villoslada maintains that this was a concession to external pressures and notes that in any case that from 1557 on "there are no other chairs of scholastic theology than those for the study of Saint Thomas and there was no other text than the *Summa* of the Angelic Doctor."[83] Ignatius' own prescriptions had been considerably more liberal.

The *studia humanitatis* told on the profession of theology in many ways, perhaps most evidently in the introduction of positive theology, albeit overshadowed by the massive presence of the *Summa theologiae*, and in the insistence that learning must be coupled with skills in communication and lead to affect. But one can perceive something of its spirit in the commitment of the teachers to students and of the relationship between various fields of learning and theology. This can be seen in the actual teaching practices of those who occupied the major chairs of theology and Scripture of the Roman College. Often they would have spent previous years in teaching the humanities and the arts or natural sciences, moving year by year with their students, before assuming their positions in theology and biblical exegesis. Professors of philosophy would often teach all three years of these subjects before making their entrance into theological instruction. A remarkable insistence upon a prior experience in teaching humanistic and philosophical courses formed the Jesuit professor for his teaching of theology. This progressive movement through the humanities and the arts or sciences towards theology, then, not only measured out very concrete stages through which the students of these Jesuits would advance to the study of theology, but often also measured the various stages their instructor might pass through with them as he moved to assume a position of theology at the Roman College. The career of André des Freux has already been cited.[84] Achilles Gagliardi could furnish another example of what was a host of such teachers. The fall of 1562 found him teaching ethics; two years later he was lecturing in physics; in 1565 he was teaching metaphysics; in 1566, he assumed the third chair in scholastic theology, but only for a year; ten years later, 1576, he held the second chair in scholastic theology and served as prefect of studies. And in addition to all of this, Gagliardi is numbered among the more distinguished of the Jesuit ascetical writers in the early years of the Society of Jesus.[85]

In Summary . . .

The development of a theology intrinsically related to a humanism that was both preparation and influence constituted a natural product of a spirituality that found God at work in all things. The wellspring for the Ignatian commitment to higher education is a spirituality that lives off of that religious conviction. The paradigmatic experience of this is of those who have been led through the *Spiritual Exercises* to give themselves over to this pervasive and immanent action of God in the world, giving themselves over to mediate instrumentally that divine presence and providence into the lives of other men and women. The theology of instrumentality provided for a union both between the human person and God and between the single person and other human beings. This was a single principle for theological and humanistic unity. Goodness and virtue, especially charity, purity of heart, familiarity with God in prayer, and a zeal for souls for the sake of the glory of God—these were the means which united one with God.[86] A developed humanity, solid and well-founded learning, a knowledge of how to be a part of the lives of others were among the principal human means that united this same one with his or her fellow men and women. Through this union, the influence of God could descend *de arriba* into the world. In this way, grace was to enter and transform all human learning, bringing this learning to a completion far beyond its own powers. Humanity could be united with divinity through this mediational instrumentality as a single action passes from the providential God through this human instrumentality into the whole of human life.[87]

As humane development was caught up in divine influence, so humanistic developments—both the *studia humanitatis* and all arts or natural sciences—became a preparation for learning and an inherent necessity for doing theology. Each of these faculties contributed immediate skills, but also habits of mind that entered into theological wisdom—to be communicated through linguistic skills and to be furthered through the knowledge of nature. The human was an essential component of divine instrumentality in the world; so the human was to be a reflection of the divine glory within the world—enabling one both to apprehend something of its nature and presence, and to communicate this through "sermons, lectures, and the art of dealing and conversing with men and women."[88]

Human beings united with God, humane intellectual disciplines and achievements united within the reflection upon God: everything was to be united without being identified. And the more palpable became this unity, the more it emerged in human experience, consciousness and affectivity, the greater in the ways of men and women became the glory of God. "For God desires to be glorified both through the natural means that He gives as Creator, and through the supernatural means that He gives as the Author of grace."[89]

PART THREE

Contemporary Signs of Contradiction

CHAPTER SIX

The Search for a New Humanism: The University and the Concern for Justice

... a search for a new humanism ... which will enable human beings to find themselves again.

—Paul VI, *Populorum Progressio*[1]

The Issue

For a Jesuit university, the persistent call for evaluation of its meaning as an institution of higher learning has been heightened also by two significant recent developments: one within the church and the other within the Society of Jesus. Both bear upon the humanistic and theological commitments that constitute the character of such a university.

Within the church, renewed realization is emerging that the suffering of the vast majority of humankind stands in judgment upon its life, upon the vitality of its proclamation of the gospel, and upon the authenticity with which this gospel is embodied in the practice of those who are educated within it and who confess it as the truth of their lives. The issue for the church is not just that a civilization or an economic system that destroys or exploits other human beings is a constant provocation for resentment, bloody reprisals, war, and the vicious cycles of repression. Everyone can understand that if human beings are not given a chance for a human life, they will become murderous—the revolutions of those who have been so dehumanized have always been terrible. The Christian point, however, is that the lot of the oppressed and of the poor in the world is in itself, prescinding from any consequential argumentation, a sinful destruction of human life and a denial of the human destiny that God has willed for those whom he has made and whom he cherishes.

The millions who face genocide and slaughter in Middle Africa, the crowded and hopeless urban proletariat dying on the streets of Calcutta, the refugees from East Timor, the Sudan, and Bosnia—yes, but also the migrant workers who follow the crops in California and see their children uneducated for any future that can be different, the black youth who now endures massive unemployment in Detroit, the large percentage of Hispanic youth who cannot find work in San Diego or those who prey on one another in East Los Angeles, the poor who live off of food stamps, and the millions of old people hidden away in cheap rooms in our cities, waiting to die. *The Economist* for October 1997 reported that thirty-six million Americans live in poverty and the number of the very poor in 1996 actually rose by a million.[2] Was it for this, asks the church, that "God so wondrously established human nature and even more wonderfully established it anew?"[3] In the Easter of 1967, Paul VI opened one of the greatest documents of his pontificate with the following words:

> The development of peoples has the Church's close attention, particularly the development of those peoples who are striving to escape from hunger, misery, endemic diseases and ignorance; of those who are looking for a wider share in the benefits of civilization and a more active improvement of their human qualities; of those who are aiming purposefully at their complete fulfillment. Following on the Second Vatican Ecumenical Council, *a renewed consciousness of the demands of the Gospel* makes it her duty to put herself at the service of all, to help them grasp their serious problem in all its dimensions, and to convince them that solidarity in action at this turning point in human history is a matter of urgency.[4]

The period after Vatican II was an epoch of "renewed consciousness." The Synod of Bishops of 1971 asserted that "action on behalf of justice and participation in the transformation of the world fully appear to us as a constitutive dimension of the preaching of the Gospel."[5] However affected by the subsequent dispute between those advocating "constitutive" and those advocating "integral," the episcopal message urged that the ministry of the gospel and the word of the church must include a concentrated engagement with human misery, that the structures of society must respond to human needs, that a gospel or a Catholic educational institution without this care for the pain and despair of men and women is false in claiming to be Catholic.

Within this context, on 2 December 1974, representatives from all over the world met for a rather rare occurrence in the history of the Society of Jesus, a congregation called not to elect a General but to deal with problems that could not be resolved by the extensive powers of the General. As no previous Congregation of the Jesuits, this lengthy, lengthy meeting confronted the great ocean of misery in which so many human beings are submerged. Voices from all over the Order demanded that a serious confrontation take place between the conscience of the Society and the wretched condition of the majority of human beings—letters came with the terrible self-reproach of Lear upon the heath:

> Poor naked wretches, wheresoe'er you are,
> That bide the pelting of this pitiless storm,
> How shall your houseless heads and unfed sides,
> Your loop'd and window'd raggedness, defend you
> From seasons such as these? O, I have ta'en
> Too little care of this![6]

Much of the effort of the Society of Jesus—its college and university commitments, its literary and scientific journals, even its retreat houses and metropolitan churches—was too much associated with the financially comfortable, even in some countries with the ruling and exploiting classes. It had not always been so. It was not even now the case with the vast majority of its commitments. But wherever it existed and to the degree that it existed, it demanded review, acknowledgment, and reform.

And so the Congregation spoke in the name of all Jesuits:

> The Society of Jesus, gathered together in its Thirty-Second General Congregation, considering the end for which it was founded, namely, the greater glory of God and the service of men and women, acknowledging with repentance its own failures in keeping faith and upholding justice, and asking itself before Christ crucified what it has done for him, what it is doing for him, and what it is going to do for him, chooses participation in this struggle—the crucial struggle of our time: the struggle for faith and that struggle for justice which it includes—as the focus that identifies in our time what Jesuits are and do.[7]

The vocabulary of faith had always been present; but the heavy word "justice" was given a new predominance, one—with all of its unsettling ambiguity, challenge, and historical heritage—geared to signal a deeper and more pervasive commitment to the wretched of the world.

This decision radically marked each of the major decrees this Congregation formulated. It reconfigured the Jesuit formation of its own members, the dynamics of its community and religious life, its identification of its own members, and above all the ministries to which the Jesuits give themselves.[8] The Congregation demanded that every Jesuit enterprise be evaluated and finally judged by these two criteria: its service to the faith and its promotion of justice—every Jesuit engagement, even the university[9]:

> Greater emphasis should be placed on the conscientization according to the Gospel of those who have the power to bring about social change, and a special place to the poor and oppressed. We should pursue and intensify the work of formation in every sphere of education, while subjecting it at the same time to continual scrutiny. We must help to prepare both young people and adults to live and labor for others and with others to build a more just world.[10]

So seriously does the Congregation intend this, so urgent is this focus of Jesuit efforts, that the Order is to withdraw from those institutions when its commitment to them would be indifferent to the revelation of God in Christ or impervious to the cries for justice and humanity all over the world.

> A decision in this direction will inevitably bring us to ask ourselves with whom are we identified and what our apostolic preferences are. For us, the promotion of justice is not one apostolic area among others, the "social apostolate"; rather, it should be the concern of our whole life and a dimension of all our apostolic endeavors. Similarly, solidarity with men and women who live a life of hardship and who are victims of oppression cannot be the choice of a few Jesuits only. It should be a characteristic of the life of all of us individuals and a characteristic of our communities and institutions as well. Alterations are called for in our manner and style of living so that the poverty to which we are vowed may identify us with the poor Christ, who identified Himself with the deprived. The same questions need to be asked in a review of our institutions and apostolic works, and for the same reasons.[11]

This radical reorientation of the work of Jesuits, a reorientation so that these works address more directly and explicitly the conditions of human misery in the world, was received in different ways—not unlike the parable of the sower. Some Jesuits hardly heard it, content to keep business as it was and better it along the same lines; others heard it, received it with enthusiasm, but under tough negative criticism and the wear of time, it died; still others conscientiously attempted to embody it, but the pressures from other obligations and unmet responsibilities simply crowded it out. But in the many places where it did take hold and as it increasingly has taken hold, it has changed, deepened, and revitalized in its Christianity the work engaged.

This fundamental decision radically altered in its turn the public perception of the Jesuits. In May of 1990, for example, the distinguished English Catholic, Lord Peter Rawlinson, published a work, *The Jesuit Factor*, in which he deplored the influence of the previous General of the Society upon the work and direction of the Society of Jesus. It was under Pedro Arrupe, wrote Lord Rawlinson, that the Jesuits moved into a "sympathy or association with Marxism." This divided the Society into two camps, he maintained, the traditionalist versus the progressive, the social activists versus the spiritual purists, the Eastern Europeans versus the Latin Americans. His accusation became something of a *cause célèbre*, evoking from the May issues of the London *Tablet* a rather damaging review of his work and a defensive response from its author.[12]

Lord Rawlinson possesses no monopoly in this assessment of the Society of Jesus. One could have found a similar minatory moment in the editorial pages of the *Wall Street Journal*. Still further, in 1982 Manfred Barthel finished his not unsympathetic history of the Jesuits with the admonition that "they must not try to set earth above heaven, or Marx above Jesus."[13] Perhaps most accusatory was the spectacularly imaginative piece by Malachi Martin, explaining that the influence of such as Pedro Arrupe, Karl Rahner, and the American Arthur McGovern had betrayed the direction and the religious traditions of the Society of Jesus.[14] The popularity of Martin's fiction is an index of the almost hopeless general ignorance of the subjects he entertains.

Within the culture of higher education, the attack against this orientation expanded into questioning far more considered: a serious focus upon justice perverts not only the purpose of the Jesuits but the nature of their universities precisely as the forum defended in chapter 7. The university is a place where one raises questions and conducts inquiry with a necessary pluralism of voices. It is not a place for indoctrination, social or political or economic. Over this century, some universities of South America were reportedly crippled by making them centers of political activism and social revolt. Some recently created universities in France were at their beginnings almost destroyed when in 1968 Maoist students brought them to a halt and physically threatened and even assaulted such distinguished thinkers as Paul Ricoeur. There were institutions of higher learning in Europe, one heard, where it was very difficult for a political moderate to find a position. For a good portion of this century, the world recoiled as freedom of inquiry was suppressed in the Communist world by iron political controls and constant indoctrination.

This objection has much validity, and it warrants careful weighing. The university always suffers when the doctrinaire curtail its freedom, when its conclusions are already in and the function of its faculty becomes persuasion. If student agitations obstruct free speech or if a political system or politically correct opinions makes honest discussion impossible, then the university suffers mortally. Its life and its discourse die. Propaganda is not the function of the university. In many ways, it is the intractable enemy of the university.

Fear of such an inhibition made the reception of the decrees of the Congregation that much more problematic. Sometimes the decrees were criticized out of existence, the enthusiasms of the Fathers Congregate deplored before the demands of "the real world," the differences insisted upon between the needs, even ideology, of South America and the First World, and the dangers of such an orientation—if taken radically—to the integrity of the educational mission. On the other hand, Jesuit colleges and universities have increasingly taken up something of the challenge. Service has become an growing part of their vocabulary. Fordham, for one example out of many, sends over seven hundred students a year into community service programs among the very poor and marginalized. For years, Georgetown has sent students to work among the desperately poor in Peru and Latin America. Throughout the country the Jesuit Volunteer Corps, both national and international, has grown, fed by graduates of Jesuit universities, and has flourished. Similar stories can be narrated about every Jesuit university in the United States.

Still further, many of these universities have incorporated a steady involvement in the world of human misery into the education offered to all of their students though programs such as the PULSE Program at Boston College and the East Side Project at the University of Santa Clara. It would be false to say that much has not been done; it would be true to say that these institutions of higher learning are just beginning to realize the academic possibilities of this challenge. For it is not enough—although it is marvelous—to have service projects on the side and academic programs open to the idealism and commitments of the young. But a disciplined concern for the suffering in the United States and the exploited throughout the world is still to become, by and large, part of the basic education itself.

The central question remains: how can this be done without betraying the very nature of the university? For the past few years, higher education has confronted capture by the politically correct. As far back as October 1990, the distinguished scholar Richard Bernstein warned about the rising domination of the universities in the United States by a "cluster of politically correct ideas," a "liberal fascism." In the subsequent year, Eugene Genovese voiced the same concerns in the *New Republic*.[15] So the question which one can level at the General Congregation of the Society of Jesus, and at the church and the needs of the world which lie behind it, is this: Can you orient the university whose very life is open question and inquiry, can you orient this institution so that it deals with human misery, with the wants of the vast majority of human beings, and not destroy it, not betray its very nature as a university, not refigure it as a propaganda mill for a new political or social orthodoxy?

This question ranges much further than simply within those institutions that bespeak a Jesuit tradition or even those which carry a Catholic character in their organization of questions and curricula. The contemporary university is a very complicated mixture of schools and of faculties, of general education, higher education, and professional education, with the accent falling now on one of these and now on another. Such an institution is "consecrated to—and even constituted by—the unhindered movement of inquiry."[16] Can it, then, without internal and fatal contradiction, respond significantly, even intensely, to the need for social justice within this cruel century of unparalleled slaughters, massive totalitarianisms, continuous economic exploitation, and seemingly endless sorrow? What is at stake is more than the Jesuit or even the Catholic university, though the question has been occasioned by events within the Society of Jesus and within the church. What is at stake is the relationship between the university itself and the exploited throughout the world, between the students, the faculty, the administration and the hopelessly poor. Should there be some bond between them? What is the responsibility of the university as such before the pain of the world?

The Humanistic Education

This chapter will argue for a position whose lines may be stated as follows: that the university, as such, can and should foster in its faculties and in its students a profound and educated concern for a just social order; that this engagement or care for "the development of those peoples who are striving to escape from hunger, misery, endemic diseases, and ignorance" emanates from the very nature of the university itself; that this educated attention to the human condition, to fellow human beings, and this corresponding care to develop among all members of the academic community a disciplined sensitivity to human misery and exploitation, is not to champion a single political doctrine or to approve as orthodox a particular system of economics; that the university fosters this kind of habitual concern as it fosters "the arts of humanity," a humane sensibility and an educated awareness, to be achieved anew within the demands of these times as a product of an education whose ideal continues to be that of the Western *humanitas* and whose fundamental proposition is *res sacra homo*.

In one form or another, *humanitas* continues to indicate a cultural value around which the university clusters, however divergent the units by which it is constituted.[17] One may, and indeed must, distinguish professional education, higher education, and general education according to the specific aim that gives each of these its unity and internal consistency. The values of one will not be absent from the purposes of another, but the central values of each will give a unique constellation and a proportional importance to the presence of the others.

Professional education, almost by title, intends to shape human beings to a career or to a task by which they may earn their living as well as make a contribution to the common good of society. It inculcates knowledge and insists upon the mastery of skills so that engineering or medicine or business will be well done. Higher education proposes a training in specialized research. It promotes in a human being those capacities and habits of reflection by which discovery may be advanced and the scientific or technical extension of knowledge promoted, with the obvious contribution this makes to the commonweal. General education, liberal or humanistic education, is oriented directly neither to the promotion of a career nor to the advancement of a collective body of knowledge. It proposes the humane development of the students as such, whether that humane development be framed in terms of a freedom which emerges from the liberal arts, both literary and scientific, or in terms of a humanism that comes from a disciplined and profound acquaintance with the works which bespeak human excellence.

It is not that the courses of one kind of formal education will be absent from the curriculum of another. Literature and history, science and ethics, mathematics and composition have their place in professional and higher and general education. But the governing aim, the reason given for its location and the extension accorded its pursuit, will differ in each. General education is foundational for either higher or professional education. The general development of a human being will promote certain skills whose further enlargement or specialization will be directed towards a profession or towards the advancement of knowledge. It has become fashionable to oppose the general knowledge given by the humanities college with the particularized expertise of higher education or the concrete mastery demanded by a profession. Actually, all three forms of education are coordinate, and their interdependence has been indicated by the halting efforts of undergraduate professional schools to introduce a basic curriculum in the humanities or, conversely, by the profound effect which higher or professional education can exercise upon the undergraduate program.[18] What they share in common, when their aims are unconfused and their sequencing coherent, is a common commitment to human development, whether that development is into general excellence or into a sensitive engagement in a human profession or into a life given over to the advancement of knowledge. The university, as such, insists upon a profound commitment to the human, and the commitments that it makes to the disciplines and the professions already imply convictions about the human. As the university advances the humanistic in general, professional, and graduate education, so is it founded upon a sense and conviction about the human.

The university has always been a place, for example, where persons ask questions, all questions, any questions judged humanly significant. The universities began with the disputed questions of the Middle Ages and continue into this century with free inquiry and instruction. To erect such an institution is already to be involved in common assumptions about the nature and development of a human being: that to be human is to be able to question seriously and to derive answers and to grow in an atmosphere of progressive description and analysis; that there is a profound value in the progressive assimilation of skills and the mastery of subjects, that one grows as a human being in this way; that the human race benefits when inquiry and discussion are freed from alien pressures, integral with their evidence, and unimpeded in their progress. In these three statements alone, among the hundred which any university community would insist upon, there is already a humanism, a general view of what it means to be a human being, a lived and accepted experience which can be articulated and examined in such disciplines as psychology, literature, philosophy, history, sociology, education, and theology and whose content, whether examined or unexamined, will always lie at the foundation of such professional schools as those of business, law, and medicine.

From its inception, the university has proposed to educate human beings because it believed that they could be developed, and the church began and fostered these institutions because this was to collaborate with the "power" of God, a divine presence which was effective when human beings progressed to become what they essentially are. Any justification of the promotion of justice as a commitment of the contemporary university must be grounded on the basic conviction that the university exists for the humane growth of its students. It is to foster the cultivation of mind through the refinement and enlargement of awareness, sympathies, disciplines, and judgments, and its finality is attained in that soundness and harmony of skills, affectivity, and knowledge that indicates personal culture. This does not exhaust the purposes of the university, but it is included as central within them. If the university is to foster a passion for justice, it is because this has its place in the sensibility and understanding, the discriminating concerns and disciplined inquiries that mark *humanitas*.

As mentioned, the Jesuits' entrance into education takes up during the revolution worked by the *studia humanitatis*, and the *Constitutions* of Ignatius indicate the transitional period in which they were written (1540–56). The liberal arts for the Jesuit university became *letras de humanidad*. These comprised the grammar and the rhetoric from the Middle Ages—albeit changed in their character and new location—and the poetry and history of the Renaissance, to be followed by the natural sciences and the study of philosophy.[19]

But just as the medieval liberal arts were criticized for becoming too universal, too abstract, so the Renaissance humanities wrote their own history of the liabilities inherent in their program. Their emphasis was upon particular subjects to be mastered, rather than on universal disciplines to be brought to bear upon any subject matter. Their liability was exactly the opposite of that of the Middle Ages: endless subdivision into greater and greater particularity. Consider one example. Poetry was to be studied, as such, no longer simply as one of the subjects upon which medieval grammar would be brought to bear. Poetry was divided into Greek and Latin. Greek poetry became further divided over the centuries that followed between early Homeric and later lyric and tragic, and, still later, pastoral. Latin underwent similar divisions as classic poetry was distinguished from that of the Middle Ages and from that of the sixteenth century. Classical literature was to be distinguished from vernacular. Vernacular literature divided further into English, Spanish, Italian, French, etc., with each of these further divided into such stages as one finds in the English curriculum: Anglo-Saxon, Middle English, Renaissance and Shakespeare, Milton, neoclassical, romantic, etc. The Renaissance transformation of the humanities has issued in the fragmentation that characterizes so much of contemporary higher education. The university suffers now from centuries of this endless subdivision into further and further particularities, with the fields so individualized and specialized that it can be difficult for scholars in one field to communicate seriously about their subjects with those from another. This deficiency has been repeatedly noted in this century, and out of its recognition have come the various programs at Columbia, Chicago, and St. John's to reform general education.

But the beginnings and original genius behind this concentration was a noble one: the humanistic program was to humanize the student through content, through bringing students into contact with the great accomplishments of human beings. The student would become more profoundly human by learning to appreciate critically the poetry of Homer, the history of Tacitus, the political rhetoric of Cicero, the music of Palestrina, and the physics of Aristotle. Each was an extraordinary human achievement, and the student was humanized by assimilating it. Students developed a disciplined sensitivity and acquired a concrete knowledge that changed them profoundly: they became like what they loved.[20]

It is almost universally agreed that a radical reform is again needed in the liberal or humanistic education of our time, whether that education be seen as the content of general education—an education valuable in its own right—or a necessary element within or before professional or higher education. This agreement allows for a further advance in programmatic education which has humane development rather than simple vocational training as its governing purpose.

The contemporary world presents its own inhibitions to human freedom and development. Students are to be humanized in a world of massive manipulation, of technological sophistication, of increasing isolation and narrowness produced by progressive specializations, of globalization and developing responsibilities within an international community. This is a century in which human beings are increasingly called to take responsibility: not simply to care for their own lives, but—by democratic, political, and social instruments—to influence and better the economic, political structures of society. Increasingly, the people of the world sense that what is, does not have to be, that either radical resistance or steady, planned, careful effort or the unplanned spontaneity of human interchange can alter the structures of society, can build a world that is "a more humane [humanior] society." Education must make such a sense of social responsibility and its resultant public directions possible. The university cannot simply return to the solutions of the Middle Ages or of the Renaissance, however much it can learn from their genius and incorporate their achievements. It is faced with problems whose special character demands its own response and whose continued presence demands continual rethinking of the humanistic aim of the university.

Deficiencies in the Contemporary Settlement

The first of these problems has already been noted and can be left to a subsequent chapter: the fragmentation consequent upon the progression of the liberal arts as subject matters or fields. The concentration upon these particular fields has left the pursuit and practices of each increasingly isolated. It has fostered the divorce between "science" and "the humanities," as if it were inevitable that Western intelligence would live in two different worlds. The increasing recognition of separation and isolation of academic fields has led this century to the search for methodological disciplines or skills, "universal arts," such as language, history, and method, that are common to all of these fields and whose mastery would allow for communication and mutual influence among them. Much of this labor effected the reformation in general education at the University of Chicago during the middle of the century, under the influence of one of the major figures in American philosophy of education, Richard P. McKeon: "Interdisciplinary education and research cannot be achieved simply by juxtaposing, adding, or uniting disciplines conceived as fields. . . . We need new disciplines to identify and transmit the arts by which men act and integrate their purposes and knowledge."[21] But fragmentation is not the only problem and not the one to be addressed here.

The second deficiency of contemporary humanistic education has only gradually and recently emerged as a concern of educators in the twentieth century: the isolation of the student or the institution from the ordinary life of the desperate, the poor, and the exploited, an isolation that inculcates indifference, narcissism, and unconscious cruelty. Some crude sense of this alienation lay behind the shrill demands for "relevance" from the students of the past decades and occasions the sense of uneasiness about student apathy, repeatedly voiced by concerned faculty over more recent years. It lies behind the charges from the Third World that American universities do not educate their students to any understanding of their impact upon the world, that they do not develop in them a sense of an international human solidarity. This charge found another voice in the Maoist contention that such institutions estrange the students as a privileged caste from their fellow human beings and continue a system built upon indifference and exploitation.

These criticisms, certainly more radical and more telling, emerge from outside the university—equaling in their intensity the charges Rabelais and Erasmus leveled at the education of the Middle Ages. This contemporary criticism lodges a savage indictment against institutions whose purpose is the production of the *maxime humanissimi*. It might be phrased in a series of questions:

"What are the students you produce, even if your programs of intellectual assimilation of the great human achievements in knowledge and in deeds is successful—which they seldom are? Even if your students do depart with such a sensitive development that they can appreciate the craftsmanship and content contained in the poetry of Goethe, Dante, and Eliot, or in the sweeping histories of Thucydides and Gibbon, or in the beautifully and carefully crafted argumentation of George Kennan, John Henry Newman, and George Steiner, what have they really become? They have been touched by some of the greatest achievements in human culture. As they learned to appreciate and love them—they changed. They developed. They became more human—as every person becomes what she has learned to know and to love, as it becomes bone of her bone and flesh of her flesh, a world she inhabits, an educated sensibility that marks her understanding and taste. Yes, all of that can be true. I grant all of this. But has your student become humane?

"Have you not heard from Dorothy Thompson what she found in the homes of the SS administrators in Dachau—of the 'men who, in a modern bureaucratic manner, according to card catalogues, dossiers and files, gave the orders which resulted in tortures, carefully calculated famine, and corpses piled like cordwood, when the crematories were too full?' She found the lyric poetry of Goethe and the musical scores of Schubert. Did not this sensitivity to great music and deathless poetry compound the horror of what these 'cultivated' men were doing with their power and with the lives of others, isolating them with refinements that drugged them to the inhuman depravity of which they had become instruments?[22] Do you not remember how sharply, how ironically Pushkin drew his contrast: the cultivated Russian nobility with their educated appreciation of life in drama and in ballet while for hours their coachmen waited for them freezing in the snows of St. Petersburg?[23] Have you never read Fyodor Dostoyevsky's *Notes from the Underground* and contrasted his treatment of the gentlemen with that of Newman's *Idea of a University*? His country had been ravaged by the Napoleonic invasions, and the serfs of Russia had earlier been surrendered wholesale into slavery by such cultivated and enlightened monarchs as Catherine the Great. Starvation had decimated Ireland and the Civil War in the United States had taken over six hundred thousand lives. With great bitterness Dostoyevsky wrote: 'Have you noticed that the most refined blood-letters were almost without exception the most civilized gentlemen? . . . Because of civilization man has become if not more bloodthirsty, then surely bloodthirsty in a worse, more repulsive way than before.'[24] Eric Maria Remarque has Paul Bäumer watch the shattered bodies brought into the German hospitals during the end of the

First World War and cry in despair about the betrayal of the educators: 'How senseless is everything that can ever be written, done, or thought, when such things are possible. It must be all lies and of no account when the culture of a thousand years could not prevent this stream of blood being poured out.'[25] This is not a voice simply from the past. Within the last decade, George Steiner has posed it once again to our culture: 'We cannot touch on the experiencing of art in our personal and communal lives without touching, simultaneously, on moral issues of the most compelling and perplexing order. . . . Does the cry in the tragic play muffle, even blot out, the cry in the street? (I confess to finding this an obsessive, almost maddening question.)'[26]

"Or to be more specific: over the nineteenth and twentieth centuries, Jesuit colleges in the United States have had any number of boarders from Latin American countries—talented, educated men. Did they return to their countries—where the suffering of the poor and the exploited often calls to heaven for vengeance—resolved to change this as they had been educated to experience the misery around them and to move towards its resolution? Or did they become more part of the problem? Have any studies even been done on this question?

Reformulation of Liberal Arts and Humanities

If the university is to meet this searching criticism, which is far more telling than these few paragraphs can suggest, it must encompass among its educational objectives not only liberating skills to be mastered as in the Middle Ages or human achievements to be known, appreciated, and assimilated as in the Renaissance. The university must also instill a profound attention to and disciplined appreciation of the world of pain and misery in which so many live. Expansion and innovation in the humanities today must advance an educated sensibility to what it means for human beings to live in suffering, with no political or social hope for themselves or for their children. Humanistic education must inculcate a perceptive care for human beings in the lot that is so often theirs, not as skilled or as idealized only, but in the lived human life when it is wretched and impoverished. Such an education comprises sensibility and knowledge, developed skills in appreciation, and carefully disciplined habits of intervention.

As students once gave themselves to the Latin grammar of Donatus and learned to love the Sixth Book of the *Aeneid*, so they must become more human also by growing in sensitivity and care for the individual person in suffering, the tragic mystery that is inherent both in every human being and in the world community. Humanistic education must develop an educated awareness that includes a profound sense of human solidarity and a spontaneous sympathy for human pain. As students were once freed, liberated through a command of dialectics and a discerning taste for Shakespeare, now their academic maturity must comprehend as well the suffering of humankind, the desperate problems with which other people struggle. As one would never say that an indifference to beautiful poetry, to sound history, to a well-reasoned argument, and to the advances of science are consonant with a liberal education, so insensitivity to human pain and sorrow, isolation from the international experiences of exploitation and misery, and indifference to the great questions of economic justice and human rights must mark a human being a savage in the twenty-first century, whatever his or her humanistic conquests in terms of literary skills and refined taste.

To bring the students to such a developed sensitivity that human pain and social injustice speak to their lives—and speak so effectively that they draw the students to further specialized studies and consequent actions—is neither indoctrination nor partisan pleading. It is a humanistic education whose product is a sensibility, a set of skills, and a knowledge that is profoundly humane. It is part of what Paul VI called the "search for a new humanism that will enable human beings to find themselves again."[27]

Such a "search" on the part of the academic institution looks to a reformulation of the liberal ideal proper to these times and essential to an integral humanism whether in general, professional, or higher education. This concern that human beings live lives of human decency and open possibilities is both an advancement and the contemporary embodiment of what has been so long a slogan within the humanities, a slogan now rearticulated against a consumer society and massive power structures: *Res sacra homo*—a human being is a sacred thing. A responsiveness to human sorrow and exploitation and a consequent passion for social justice are simply part of what it means to be a developed human being. A serious concern about justice is an essential dimension of a contemporary humanism.

For the settlement about *humanitas* given in the second century by Aulus Gellius—his dismissal of the opinion of the common people and his preferred reading of Cicero and Varro—demands serious critique and revision. It permitted or fostered a concept of humanistic education ridden by profound inadequacies. *Humanitas* cannot simply translate παιδεία; it must also, as the people understood it and as de facto both Varro and Cicero also understood it, translate φιλανθρωπία. This is also the Christian humanistic heritage. When Jerome, for example, came to translate that exquisite phrase with which the Epistle to Titus speaks of the Incarnation—ὅτε δὲ ἡ χρηστότης καὶ ἡ φιλανθρωπία ἐπεφάνη τοῦ σωτῆρος ἡμῶν θεοῦ (when the goodness and loving kindness towards human beings of God our savior appeared), he translated φιλανθρωπία as *humanitas*.[28] Clearly, contemporary understandings of *humanitas* also must cover this comprehensive care for the human. This is not an arbitrary command of God; it is an inherent necessity if a person is to become a human being.

A critique of the narrowness of what has been classically considered the humanities or the more humane letters is not simply a product of these times nor one that issues under the challenge of Karl Marx and Marxist humanism—*pace* Lord Rawlinson. One can find it also among some of the finest minds of the Italian Renaissance. Giovanni Gioviano Pontano, for example, in his *De sermone*, explicitly distinguished *humanitas* from *comitas*, and in his explanation of the humane he adumbrates an understanding of a humanistic education that embodies much of what is being suggested here. To be touched deeply by the pain of others is characteristic of *humanitas*:

> *Humanity* differs from *comity* in several ways. For whoever is moved by other persons' injuries, inconveniences, captivity, grief, poverty, banishment and other ills, him we call "humane," yet not in any sense "companionable."[29]

This advances considerably beyond the educational ideal of Aulus Gellius. It indicates a cultural, educated sensibility such that one is moved (*moveatur*) by the injuries and hardships and grief and poverty of other human beings, and suggests in contrast that one who is not so touched is humanistically underdeveloped. What Pontano advanced as theory, he exhibited in his description of the person and life of the philosopher Giovanni Pardo:

> He was humane [*humanum*] toward every kind of human life and action . . . the accidents of friends and citizens weighed heavily upon him; he consoled the suffering, helping them as much as he was able, visiting them, assisting them, giving his direct help; he stood by anyone at any time as a gracious and affable companion.[30]

Such an understanding of *humanitas* definitely does move the educational ideal of the Renaissance beyond that of Greek παιδεία—a Hellenic or Hellenistic education whose background included a slave society and the exploitation of great masses of people. Pontano moves the humanistic ideal into a social φιλανθρωπία, that gives cultural precedents to the call of the Jesuit General Congregation to all involved in education:

> There are millions of men and women in our world, specific people with names and faces, who are suffering from poverty and hunger, from the unjust distribution of wealth and resources and from the consequences of racial, social, and political discrimination. Not only the quality of life, but human life itself is under constant threat. It is becoming more and more clear that despite the opportunities offered by an ever more serviceable technology, we are simply not willing to pay the price of a more just and a more *humane* society [*humanior societas*].[31]

Academic Strategies

It is in its curriculum that such humanistic ideals meet the call made upon the university by the poverty, suffering, oppression, and exploitation of millions, a call for the development of humane students and for "a more humane society."

What does this mean in the concrete? It means that the university with this more complete humanistic ideal must determine again or anew what are the skills and what is the knowledge that is most worth having. The humanistic development of the student will continue to be recognized as valuable in itself and as an indispensable foundation for further specialization and professionalism. But the humanities themselves must advance in their self-understanding to cultivate the kind of human being who can respond to this contemporary world of suffering. The humanities must, of course, continue to develop skills in interpretation and argument, in reading and composition—as in the Middle Ages—together with a discriminating appreciation of those disclosures of the human that we find in great literature and history, in science and in mathematics, as in the Renaissance. But a humanistic education must do more. Liberal or humanistic education must advance to a third stage in the maturation of its academic programs and their goals. It must also aim at evoking within the students a profound sensitivity to human misery as well as to human achievements. The consciousness of the students must be drawn to the millions of homeless that walk the streets of one of the wealthiest nations in the world, to the aged poor hidden away in convalescent hospitals waiting to die, often drugged into insensibility, to the searing hopelessness—the poverty and the joblessness—in the ghettoes of our major cities that expresses itself in addiction and murder. The students must learn to understand, to care, to feel for such people—if these students are ever to become humane, enlightened, developed human beings.

In the *Poetics*, Aristotle asks what is that at which artists aim, what they wish to embody in their work—whether the matter with which they work is color or music or language or stone. He answers that artists imitate the deeds—the actions and passions, thoughts and emotions—the dimensions of human beings.[32] Artists embody in different media, some aspect or dimension of the human—something that speaks about the human and appeals to the human, but in a new way. Literature and history, the creation of fictions and the narration of fact, disclose the human. They develop a sensitivity, a set of habitual insights into what it is to be human. Just as they evoke from the students a growth in skills and tastes, so they extend their disclosure to elicit an appreciative understanding of human misery. With no eisegesis or social propaganda, literature and history express the human condition in its abundance, and this contains a massive component of suffering as well as revelations of heroism, goodness, achievement and beauty. As the students attend—as their attention is focused!—to what is disclosed, they advance into a more humane sensibility.

But a humane sensibility must become an educated sensibility. It is not enough to feel deeply; one must also know. Deep care without concomitant skills and knowledge leads only into enthusiasms. From this appreciation must come an educated awareness of what these students can do with their lives and with their education to better the human condition. The university must awaken both a sensibility to the suffering of human beings—both nationally and internationally—and an educated commitment to address this suffering if the university is to educate the students into a humanism adequate for our times. Within this context, the social sciences can take on a significantly humanistic dimension. If the university proposes to develop in students both social sensibility and a sound understanding of the great social problematic of our times, it must insist upon courses in economics, political science, and sociology precisely as those are geared to continue the humanistic development of the student. This obviously does not mean that one solution or one orthodox set of solutions, one kind of politics or social analysis or correct economics is to be inculcated—that would merit all of the reservations which Richard Bernstein and Eugene Genovese have expressed. It does mean that the students should be both introduced into some appreciation of the human condition of the vast majority of human beings and equipped with some of the disciplinary tools that will enable them to analyze these problems and move to their resolution with an informed intellect as well as an awakened sensibility. Jesuit educators must urge such educational reforms or developments if they are to be true to the religious genius of their contemporary vocation. Both the university and the Society of Jesus must envisage an education that comprises both this developed human sensibility and specialized social knowledge.

There are classic educational strategies by which such a development could take place within a humanistic curriculum. There is a triadic pattern that courses in literature can follow, progressing from studies in appreciation to those in literary criticism to those in aesthetics. So a similar developmental pattern could obtain here: from courses that awaken social sensibility to those critical disciplines where this awareness is educated in economics, sociology, and political science, to those courses by which this development is brought into theological and ethical reflection. Perhaps just as grammar and rhetoric or arithmetic and geometry became the liberal arts of the Middle Ages, universal disciplines applied to almost any subject matter, so now political science and sociology, economics and anthropology could be transformed into such similarly general disciplines brought to bear upon all the forms of human life. In this transformation, the social sciences would be taught as "arts" essential both for developing humane sensibilities and for providing tools by which the human condition can be thoughtfully addressed.

Perhaps an example: when Priscian wished to teach in extreme detail the nature of Latin case, number, and gender, he composed his influential grammatical work, *Partitiones duodecim versuum Aeneides*, an extensive analysis of the first twelve lines of the *Aeneid*. He thus put literature at the service of grammar, one of whose parts was the *enarratio poetarum*.[33] But it is quite another thing to read precisely the same masterpiece of Virgil for what it says of war and family, of human striving and failure—to bring the students gradually to recognize and feel, with John Henry Newman, Virgil's "single words and phrases, his pathetic half lines, giving utterance, as the voice of Nature herself, to that pain and weariness yet hope of better things, which is the experience of her children in every time." James Joyce had Stephen Dedalus catch the pain of life, first in his own family and then in the generation after generation of children, from these words of Newman: "He heard the choir of voices in the kitchen echoed and multiplied through an endless reverberation of the choirs of endless generations of children: and heard in all the echoes an echo also of the recurring note of weariness and pain. All seemed weary of life even before entering upon it. And he remembered that Newman had heard this note also in the broken lines of Virgil 'giving utterance, like the voice of Nature herself, to that pain and weariness yet hope of better things which has been the experience of her children in every time.'"[34] In this convergence of life, nature, and literature, one can absorb something of the pathos of human existence and in that lesson learn an abiding compassion and discover one's own humanity:

> For I have learned
> To look on nature, not as in the hour
> Of thoughtless youth, but hearing oftentimes
> The still, sad music of humanity.[35]

This educated sensibility could open up to a curriculum whose courses would be brought to bear upon social issues, one which would fulfill the goals of Robert M. Hutchins for a college student: "He may even derive from his liberal education some conception of the difference between a bad world and a good one and some notion of the ways in which one might be turned into the other."[36] The transformation of the social sciences into the social "arts" might be one way to educate the students to understand the desperate situation of the Irish at the turn of the century, their history of famine, exploitation and oppression, the lack of an industrial base, the contempt they suffered from their English masters, the narrowness of their ecclesial leadership, the grinding poverty in the countryside. They could come to understand the social, political, and economic structures that effect the painful world of *A Portrait of the Artist as a Young Man* and what could be done to realize this "hope of better things." And these "arts," in their turn, could introduce the students to the fundamental issues to be considered in social ethics and moral theology, foundational courses that would give grounding to the awareness and analysis that had preceded them. Such a curriculum would thus follow the triadic structure of appreciation, criticism, and philosophy.

This triadic strategy, this humanistic program could be formulated in the rhythmic unity of development which Alfred North Whitehead has outlined as romance, precision, and generalization. Most education, he maintained, either formal or informal, moves through these three successive levels of involvement and understanding.

First, there is a cultivation of sensitivity and interest, of wonder and the heady excitement which attends wonder, of experience and the growing appreciation which experience evokes. From this "romance" with the subject matter, another desire grows: to explore it more in detail, to master its internal structures and particular facts, to analyze what has been the object of immediate experience and appreciation.

Finally, from this stage of precision, one moves to that of generalization, such a grasp of the fundamental ideas and of the basic premises that one can apply them to many more fields and to subjects other than those whose original excitement and subsequent analysis have brought the student to this point. Romance, precision, and generalization are a single cycle of human evolution; they are the dialectical moments inherent in any and all human development; they are cycles within cycles within cycles. "All mental development is composed of such cycles, and of cycles of such cycles."[37]

Both of these formulations of "strategies" point basically to the same stages of development. In all education, there is an initial and crucial awakening of interest when one learns to read or attends to nature. One is caught up in novels or in histories or in biology or in astronomy. An introductory course could have no finer product than this awakened enthusiasm, this "romance." But it is not enough for the student to develop this first appreciation for literature or for physics; appreciation must develop into literary criticism or into an understanding of the methodology of the science. The second stage of educational growth, then, inquires why this novel is well written or how one does sound physics or history. The advancing criticism or the work of science becomes methodologically careful and precise. Finally, just as appreciation develops into criticism, so criticism gives way to foundational studies, to those more generalized philosophical inquiries into the principles of mathematics, the metaphysical basis of the sciences, and the aesthetics of the art object, which enable the students to see the connection of one field of knowledge with all the others.

These three stages present a line of organic development that any early enthusiasm assumes in an educational pattern: unless inhibited, the early engagements with the arts and sciences move into wisdom, into the generalization of causal influences or foundational studies in what has been the initial subject of wonder and analysis. Literary studies have a consecrated terminology to designate this progression: appreciation, literary criticism, and aesthetics, but it is a pattern common to all the arts and sciences if they are allowed to develop under their own intrinsic dynamism.

One might hope for the same pattern of development in a humanistic education whose focus would include a concern "to distinguish between a bad world and a good one, and some notion of the ways in which one might be turned into the other."[38] Such a program would aim in its initial stage at developing awareness and a sensibility for the pathos and sorrow in human life—as well as for its great achievements and joys. The classic subject fields of the humanities all conspire to make such a sensitivity possible, and they could be augmented by the introductory social sciences which can expand the area of facts and introduce middle-class students to experiences that lie beyond their immediate world.

Second, this developed sensitivity for the lot of the poor, oppressed, and exploited can lead naturally to those life sciences and social sciences that are both descriptive of the human environment and critically analytic of the economic, social, historical, and ideological structures that have brought them about or by which they can be changed. Appreciation for the human situation leads inevitably to questions about the influences that have made such a life actual for so many and about the strategies by which they can be addressed.

Third, just as appreciation gives way to criticism, criticism gives way to those more general studies that involve the foundations of human life, its value and its direction, studies such as those in social ethics, jurisprudence, political philosophy, and moral theology, by which an evaluation of the situation once experienced and analyzed can be obtained and the vocations for action discerned. One of these stages cannot substitute for another. To paraphrase Kant, social ethics with little knowledge of economics or political science is empty, but economics or political science not evaluated by social ethics is blind.[39] The humanistic development within the students of a passion for justice must pass through all three stages of its internal evolution: a sensibility to the human condition moving into the social and life sciences by which this condition is described and analyzed and finally into the ethical and theological wisdoms by which it is finally weighed and acted upon.

It should come as no great surprise if a humanistic, religious education evokes from its students a new social compassion and concern. Rainer Maria Rilke had suggested that this should be the result of an encounter with great art. Before the "Archaic Torso of Apollo" he recognized that:

> here there is no place
> that does not see you. You must change your life.[40]

And George Steiner comments that

> The archaic torso in Rilke's famous poem says to us: "change your life". So do any poem, novel, play, painting, musical composition worth meeting. The voice of intelligible form, of the needs of direct address from which such form springs, asks: "What do you feel, what do you think of the possibilities of life, of the alternative shapes of being which are implicit in your experience of me, in our encoun-

ter?" The indiscretion of serious art and literature and music is total. It queries the last privacies of our existence.[41]

As a corollary of this conclusion: not only should the university be so concerned about the forms of human justice, but there is a unique place which only the university can occupy in this more general care for justice. The university offers, as no other institution can offer, the reflective atmosphere and the broad range of studies that can awaken and refine humane sensibilities. It possesses an organization of scientific courses by which the issues in social justice can be carefully considered. Finally, a Catholic university demands or should demand from its students those foundational studies, theological and philosophic ethics, by which sensibility and knowledge are grounded in their presuppositions and brought into an integration with Christian life and the commitments of holiness.

It is here that the serious teaching of Christianity meets the humane concerns of the university. What Christ preaches and embodies is the Kingdom of God—that God might permeate and direct the understanding and the affectivity of human beings. From the time of the great Hebrew prophets, the Kingdom of God entails a just social order, while the influence of sin lives in the negation of this rule of God. The university moves against injustice as it does against the inhumane. The church moves against injustice as it does against sin and the denial of God. Both pose serious issues for the intellectual life of a Catholic, Jesuit university. In the conjunction of both is found that purpose which has been noted twice as definitional of the "arts of humanity" and with which the great Spanish humanist Juan Luis Vives shaped the Renaissance's reform of Christian liberal education: the humanities are "those branches of learning [*disciplinae*] by means of which we separate ourselves from the way of life and customs of animals and are restored to our humanity and raised towards God Himself."[42] That is not a bad statement for the humane concerns and skills, for the sensitivities, the critical powers, and the theological orientation—in short, for the goals, the meaning and the value of what is to be done in a Catholic university.

This, then, is the basic argument of these pages: that the university, precisely as such, should foster a development in social compassion and a sense of justice both in the sensitivities and skills which it imparts to its students and in the order of the curriculum by which this humane development is attained; that this orientation is consequent upon its very commitment to disciplined humanistic education, whether in the undergraduate or the graduate schools or in the schools of professional education; that this orientation has taken on a new urgency in our century and is native to the single continuous purpose of the university, in light of which it has periodically reformed its basic education radically, whether in the Middle Ages or in the Renaissance; that the Catholic character of this institution gives to this orientation a special exigency and gravity.

CHAPTER SEVEN

The Catholic University as Pluralistic Forum

Academic Freedom is a modern term for an ancient idea. . . . Its continual history is concurrent with the history of universities since the twelfth century.

—Richard Hofstadter[1]

The Issue and Its Situation

There is still another issue that the Catholic, Jesuit university must engage, an issue inevitably evoked by its Catholic identity and its university liberties, an issue that has excited more confrontation possibly than any of those bruited about on its campus over the past thirty years. This problematic situation can be understood and phrased in so many variations, but all bear upon joining freedom of inquiry, conversation, publication, and profession with responsibility to a tradition, a revelation, a community, a trust. How can they be coupled? How realistic is it to deny that freedom of inquiry and constancy of commitment are de facto somewhat antinomic within any university? Is there any university that permits research unbridled by ethics or whose fundamental values are socially questionable in practice? Can one provide for any continuity and human morality if everything is open to question, but can one provide for pervasive, honest inquiry if the university is grounded upon the dogmatic or moral commitments of a community? Can one profess and still question, or does not some, possibly hidden, profession actually lie at the basis of serious questioning? All of these formulations swirl around the polarities of religious identity and intellectual inquiry, but the religious scene has no monopoly on them. It merely raises to a more

129

pronounced degree the polyvalent paradox of commitment and inquiry, a paradox that confronts every reflective human being as well as all institutions of higher learning and research. This paradox poses a pervasive and inescapable problem, but that itself may not be a bad thing.

It was John Dewey who argued that reflection, human thought, originates only in confrontation. Organic life tends spontaneously toward pleasure fulfillments, and the difficult job of thought is engaged only when that path is blocked.[2] This "block" can be seen as the *aporia* of Aristotle, the obstacle that impedes free movement and before which one must consciously pause and inquire. For Dewey, as for Aristotle, hindrance is also possible incitement. For "the obstacle" through reflection becomes "the problem," and it is only "the problem" which initiates human inquiry. A problem is the conscious experience of ignorance and from the beginnings of disciplined reflection, human beings "began to philosophize in order to escape from ignorance."[3] The process of resolution, of question and answer, is itself uniquely human. Inquiry and contemplation mark human life; they are the movement and fulfillment proper to a human being and constitute the path to wisdom. Our humanity emerges in the measure of our deliberative confrontation with a problematic situation.

If this is so, Catholic educators have not been unblessed by the continuing tensions both within the Catholic university and between the Catholic university and its interested publics. These institutions have been caught up over the past forty years in issues of identity and of mission, of public or ecclesial expectations, and of academic integrity as profound as anything in their history. These constitute a crisis whose constituents are variously placed as consistency with a past heritage versus the demands of the present or the directions of the future; the American understanding of the university versus the teaching and governing mission of the church; fidelity to orthodoxy versus openness to inquiry; the Catholic specificity of the university versus its incarnational presence in American culture.

What is the teaching church now to expect from such an institution? The question has been a pressing one over these thirty years. As early as 1969, Robert J. Dwyer, the late archbishop of Portland, in an action almost unprecedented within the American church at the time, condemned the Catholic University of America in the public press for its failure to meet, in his words, "an obligation incumbent upon a university which describes itself as Catholic to conform to the common teaching of the Church." To have allowed professors of theology to engage in public criticism of Pope Paul VI's Encyclical, *Humanae vitae*, the archbishop wrote, was for the Catholic University to range itself "with any number of secular institutions of higher learning . . . which acknowledge no spiritual allegiance and feel bound by no obligation to revealed truth." In sanctioning this public dissent, the archbishop charged, the University's Academic Senate "failed miserably and totally to reckon with . . . its Catholic commitment."[4] Unique as it was then, this sort of attack on Catholic institutions of higher learning has been repeated any number of times, has become even somewhat ordinary over these intervening years. Archbishop Dwyer initiated a public criticism premised upon a common enough expectation of a Catholic university.

Addressing the presidents of Jesuit universities in November 1985, in a much gentler manner, Archbishop John P. Foley, the then president of the Pontifical Council for Social Communications, referred to what he considered the scandal inherent in the presence on Jesuit university faculties of those who do not reflect authentic Catholic teaching. When he has complained to the news media about inviting such persons to represent the universities on their programs, he has met with the response: "How can we be faulted for selecting for our program those who appear to have the Church's seal of approval because they hold positions on the faculties of Catholic universities?" The archbishop comments: "I know the demands of academic freedom—and I also know its purpose: to pursue truth fearlessly and without pressure. May I suggest, however, that a truth already possessed may sometimes be compromised in the face of other fears and other pressures by the officials of Catholic universities: the pressures of government regulation, the allure of public funds, the fear of faculty reaction, the unwillingness to endure apparently bad publicity."[5] The archbishop could appear to be saying that the administrators of Catholic universities periodically compromise the Catholic character of these institutions because of their desire for money and the fear of trouble. This is by no means an isolated opinion, and his willingness to discuss it openly does credit both to the much respected archbishop and to the presidents who listened. But the remarks of both major prelates would raise the question for some Americans whether there can be such a thing as a Catholic university at all. George Bernard Shaw's dictum is well known: a Catholic university is a contradiction in terms.

In sharp contrast, a previous president of Fordham drew severe fire for his statement that "Fordham will pay any price, break any mold, in order to achieve her function as a university."[6] This was attacked as a betrayal of Catholic education, a secularization. Implicit in this attack lay the unspoken premise that tension necessarily exists between the academic orientation of a university and the teaching mission of the church, that the establishment which results from these diverse forces is at best a balance between them. Over these past years, most Catholic universities have not been strangers to disputes that have arisen out of the attempts at such a "balance": to charges of betrayal or obdurance, to diagnoses of decadence or narrowness, to the rhetoric of progress or that of decline, to serious philosophic controversy, and to covert political cabals. Running like a theme through these variants is the question: What are we about? What is our purpose? What is a Catholic university?

These are decisive moments characteristic of all organic and conscious life: discriminations between development and disintegration, between growth and decline. Catholic academic institutions are attempting to continue their existence into the future, while justifying both the commitments of its tradition and those changes that contemporary cultures demand. The controversy itself is not alien to the intrinsic commerce of the university, and it could well contribute substantially to its life, unifying into a common conversation divergent philosophies and viewpoints within its community by drawing them all into a single centralizing question. This question, then, can become a source of academic unity, of common university discussion, as it already has become the occasion of diversity. What unites intellectual divergences into a community is not necessarily a single doctrine, but a common problem.

Concretely, these interchanges have themselves generated a theoretic content far richer than the prudential decisions made about a particular direction to be chosen by a particular institution. The charges and countercharges have constituted a matrix in which a somewhat new understanding of Catholic higher education has been emerging, one whose impetus lies not with any particular section of the university so much as with the university community as a whole. One can only welcome such contributions to this discussion over these decades as those of David J. O'Brien, John Tracy Ellis, Philip Gleason, Peter Steinfels, Theodore M. Hesburgh, C.S.C., Paul Reinert, S.J., and many others.

When Canon Salzbacher assembled his observations in 1842 on the American Catholic Church, he drew the attention of Europe to such "institutions of higher learning as colleges, academies and universities." He noted that the bishops of the United States had placed these institutions high among their priorities: "It has long been the ambition of the bishops to erect such higher institutions of learning and to supervise them in order that these young men, who otherwise would attend the public state schools, might not go astray."[7] The Viennese prelate was quite accurate; such "institutions of higher learning" were very much a growing phenomenon, and "might not go astray" put their purpose very well—in fact, it let the cat out of the academic bag!—for they were conceived essentially as what one may term a "custodial institution."

Such an institution transmitted a teaching, the common teaching of the *magisterium*. This body of doctrine afforded a criterion by which faculty was selected, curriculum chosen, and morals enforced. Counter-positions within the university were permitted more as token, as a stimulus to study and refutation, rather than as serious presence and a significant challenge to influence. Such universities were "Catholic" because their elements were Catholic: their teachers were clerical, often religious under vows, with Catholic laymen added as clerics or religious proved insufficient; their students were Catholic, frequently coming from families deeply concerned that the faith of their children be safeguarded from secular universities; their textbooks and libraries were often ecclesiastically censored. These universities were custodial, safeguarding the faith and morals of their students. At their worst, they conducted or condoned indoctrination through the exclusion of alien influences; at their best, they transmitted the books and cultures of generations much richer than themselves.[8] These universities were "custodial" not only in content, but emphatically in purpose. Religious orders or national hierarchies sponsored such institutions as a service to the American Catholic Church, and the bishops often recognized this importance. Archbishop John Ireland of Saint Paul spoke for many: "In love, in reverence, in hope I salute thee, Catholic University of America! Thy birth—happy omen!—is coeval with the opening of the new century. The destinies of the Church in America are in thy keeping."[9]

Such a picture is by no means parody—nor is it by any means peculiarly Catholic. It is as much American as Catholic, part of the heritage of the sectarian considerations in which American universities were founded, rather than descendants of the great medieval universities. Thomas Jefferson, certainly one of the most enlightened educators and statesmen of his time, wrote a resolution into the statutes of the University of Virginia, which he had founded, that outlawed disagreement with Locke's *Essay on Civil Government* and Sidney's *Discourses on Government* in their understanding of liberty, the rights of human beings, nature, and society.[10] "Custodial" would describe those philosophy departments, for example, that, having found light and nourishment in a particular philosophic tradition, turn that tradition into a "sect" by marginalizing the history of philosophy, dismissing Continental philosophy, and excluding metaphysics as nonsense. In the custodial institution, there is always a tension between dogmatic commitments (however disguised) and the native orientation of the university to open, free discussion, unhampered research and argument, and the positive representation of all forms of human knowledge and serious opinion.

Internal Contradiction

But the failure in such a settlement is evident. A university is essentially an open place. It is ideally a forum for discussion, mutual collaboration and debate, where any position may be considered and evaluated and any significant tradition welcomed. The medieval universities took their rise and their greatness from the freedom of debate; the pervasive method of instruction as these institutions developed became the disputed question. The strength of the university lies with the vigor of the discussion and debate within the community—of teachers with students, and, perhaps even more important, of teachers with teachers. Ideally, the research university is a community of scholars talking and working with one another, and the students are educated by being drawn into these discussions and projects. Thus, whatever external pressures—ecclesiastical or civil—which would limit the questions or hamper the dialogue, strike at the very nature of the university itself.[11]

There was, then, in the custodial conceptualizations of the Catholic university in the United States, a fatal conjunction of mutually contradictory ingredients, whose internal contradiction time would reveal. The university by its nature is to represent in its faculty and in its curriculum the "universe of knowledge"—whatever passes muster as serious inquiry within the academic community has its place necessarily within the university, and students, policies, and the institution itself are the poorer for its absence; yet in this custodial understanding, such lacunae were held to characterize the very essence of the university's Catholicity. It was Newman who insisted as the major premise upon which his *Idea of a University* is argued, that "as to the range of University teaching, certainly the very name of University is inconsistent with restrictions of any kind."[12] Second, the university is consecrated to—and even constituted by—the unhindered movement of inquiry, of question, of examination, of discussion without bias, without prejudice, without any antecedent determination that inquiry must issue in this conclusion, that this question can only be answered in this manner.

This does not mean that the university is a place where convictions are absent. Just the contrary. Convictions are strongly present. They lie at the foundation and structure of the university and justify its existence. There are values that the university simply by being a university embodies and is to nourish. Even to ask a question is to imply a radical set of humane commitments. Further, it is important that faculty and students not only question, but profess. If the professor refuses to profess, he or she courts or idealizes a moral nihilism, one that would subject a university to its own destruction in the conflict between loud fascist voices and an academic community that itself stands for nothing. It is not simply an accident that the German universities were among the first institutions to capitulate to the pressures of Nazi ideology and political power. Convictions are fundamental to academic inquiry and discussion; indeed, they make such a life possible.

But even these convictions are open to analysis and discussion. Theology itself as a university discipline is classically religious faith moving methodologically to its own analysis and understanding, and education at the great medieval universities submitted any proposition to the dialectical question. Yet the "custodial university" is by definition an institution whose most important conclusions are radically unquestionable either in their meaning or in their truth, where searching and public inquiry can easily be taken as moral disloyalty, and whose energies are bent only upon defense of these conclusions, their presentation or their inculcation.

Aristotle distinguished sharply between scientific inquiry and rhetorical method: inquiry begins with the question and moves toward its resolution; rhetoric begins with the conclusion and moves towards its justification. The significant error in the early understanding of the Catholic university in the United States, perhaps, lay with the crippling restriction of its components and in the forensic determination of its purposes. Such a university has been termed a "custodial institution" and the Second Vatican Council is as good an event as any to signal the beginning of its end.

A new concept of the Catholic university has been emerging over the last decades, however, out of the death of this previous understanding. Put dialectically, the initial conception of the Catholic university corrupted, moved into a period of alienation and self-doubt because the simplicity of its early formulation included factors that history would demonstrate and has demonstrated to be mutually exclusive. Catholic universities, as argued in the third chapter, have been passing through the tensions inseparable from dialectical growth—the second moment of which is that of objectification and of the disintegration of an earlier unity. But this should not be taken as the end of the road, as if the Catholic university is simply in decline. On the contrary, this may well be a critically important moment within growth. If so, further progress will consist in a denial of the alienation of church and university through a more profound understanding of each.

It is impossible to speak here of all Catholic institutions of higher learning; there is too much differentiation among them. But in many cases, Catholic universities seem to be moving, evolving into a further stage in which their profound service to the church is synthesized with their renewed commitment to pluralism and to inquiry. Further, in this newly articulated unity, inquiry and Christian faith are already being commonly understood as mutually supportive and enriching, rather than as limiting constituents. For while Catholic educators are moving away from the university as bastion and redoubt, they are coming to grasp better its nature and unparalleled value as forum.

To say that the university is essentially a forum is to assert it is formalized, structured, constituted, made to be what it is, by an order of discussion. Both words are operative: "order" and "discussion." To begin with the second term first . . .

Discussion

"Discussion" indicates a collaboration in inquiry, either by the mutually supportive labor of human beings concentrated upon a single problem, exchange, or project, or by their mutually critical debate in the testing and verification of variant positions and resolutions. Discussion is the formalizing activity of the university, and the refusal to discuss is the destruction of its life. Each time a professor will not discuss with students, or students with one another, or professor with professor—something of the university dies. The major effort of the academic administration should be to provide the instrumentalities with which the members of this academic community can talk seriously and systematically to one another. This is the energy center of the university. The students are not there simply to be informed of the faculty's conclusions, either recent or historic, but to be drawn into their discussions, their controversies, and their mutual projects. The only limitation upon discussion should be the intrinsic features of inquiry itself: time, place, energy, subject matter, and interest—not prior dogmatic commitments or alumni pressure. More specifically, to attempt to protect Christian morals or Catholic theology by a restriction of contradictory discourse or by the elimination of all but token queries is not to teach theology at all. It is to destroy the university which should contextualize its life and minister to its vitality.

This is not to say, however, that Catholic thought is to be overwhelmed by sheer numbers or drowned out by eclectic heterogeneity. That would be an equally unacceptable destruction of its discussion and of its character. It is imperative that there be a strong Catholic voice in Jesuit universities, one that represents the richness and the reflection of the Catholic intellectual tradition and the knowledge that embodies this tradition. If the university is to be Catholic, one must repeatedly insist upon the strong presence of Catholic intellectuals and of the Catholic intellectual tradition within the university. If this is absent, there is no possibility for a Catholic university in the usual sense of that word. In such a situation, the questions and knowledge considered critical by a Catholic culture will never be engaged with the depth and the steadiness that give the university its Catholic character. The hiring of the university must be conducted in terms of its mission, otherwise that mission will cease to exist.

This obviously does not mean in any way, however, that the faculty is to be restricted to Catholics. The principle remains: whatever passes as serious knowledge must also be present on the campus, insofar as this is possible. If the Catholic tradition is not in continual and serious contact with the pluralism that reflects the universe of knowledge, it will possess neither a university nor a significant theology. If the Catholic is the only voice, one does not have a university, but has at very best, perhaps, what some would recognize as a seminary. University pluralism means that whatever the intellectual traditions represented, faculty of the greatest diversity must be able to contribute to the mission of the university, be willing to enter into the discussions that constitute its life and so contribute to the purposes that specify it. Catholic intellectuals must confront within these universities the pluralism, resources, and the real challenges that exist within the universe of knowledge. This exchange makes for the life of the university.

This brings the argument of these pages to suggest an alternative to the position of Archbishop Foley. The theological discussion that constitutes a university as Catholic must be free. In no way does a simple appointment to the faculty constitute what the archbishop called "the Church's seal of approval" of a particular member of the faculty. Nor should it be seen as such. What it does or should indicate is that such a person can represent part of the universe of serious discourse that a university embodies and with which Catholic theology must be in living and honest contact if it is to be true to itself and become a vital part of American culture. What the archbishop calls "truth already possessed" can be more deeply understood, developed, purified from its cultural accretions and misconstruals, and steadied in its assertions of the message of Christ, only if its reflections occur in an atmosphere in which its questions and its evidence are taken seriously and challenged by the questions of others with academic care and freedom and in which it achieves a reflective presence within the disciplines and research that form the universe of human knowledge.

No other institution except the Catholic university can offer this service to the church, can provide a place in which the sweeping experience of Christian faith can be analyzed comprehensively in both its opposition and in its support, and in which theological formulations and systems can be developed, discussed, challenged, and criticized. This kind of institution in its essential function will be destroyed if the freedom of these interchanges is inhibited under the impression that orthodoxy can only be protected by restraining honest, considered disagreement. Academic freedom, with all of its attendant challenges and abrasive moments, is essential not only if a university is to be a university, but essential also if its theology is to be sound. It was Cardinal Newman again who wrote: "That is no intellectual triumph of any truth of Religion, which has not been preceded by a full statement of what can be said against it. . . . Great minds need elbow-room, not indeed in the domain of faith, but of thought. And so indeed do lesser minds, and all minds."[13]

One must note that to argue in this way for complete freedom of discussion is not to advocate some form of totally unrestrained conduct. Open discussion does not provide a license for any kind of action. To make free discussion possible in a Catholic university, both civility and the ethics of the Christian heritage are necessary. Without civility, there is no rational interchange; without Christian ethics, there is no vital Christian community in which that interchange is taking place. To sustain its own life, academic freedom cannot countenance the promotion of violence nor instigations to racial, gender, or religious discrimination which would intractably divide the university nor the destruction of a fundamental Christian decency that gives to this community its social identity. A forum itself is made possible by law. For its own life as an open forum, the university depends upon decencies of exchange and the civil behavior of moral human beings. Both of these should be strengthened within a Catholic university. Discussion must be free if there is to be any university at all, but American universities in past decades have witnessed moments in which the deliberate, brutal, unrestrained advocacy of fury destroyed that freedom of discussion. This the university cannot tolerate if it is to continue to exist.

The difference between a Catholic university and one from another tradition cannot and must not be that in the latter, serious and responsible discussion ranges freely while in the former it is inhibited and circumscribed. That would simply mean that one is a university and the other a custodial institution of some stamp or other. The special character to the education given in a particular university—among many other factors—lies much more with the questions to which priority is given, the knowledge that is considered most worth having, the divergent understanding of the habits that mark an educated person, and the spirit that pervades the academic life of interchange that is a university.

Further, it must be stated: academic freedom in no way inhibits the serious responsibility of the *magisterium* to teach what is of Catholic faith and to characterize as such what is its negation, what is opposed to it—whether this takes place within a university or outside of it. The bishops have their obligations; the university has its obligations. Granted the complexity of each issue, the freedom of the university professor to speak does not of itself touch the freedom and the inescapable responsibility of the bishops to make their own judgments about the orthodoxy of what is said. The bishops may always evaluate the coordination between statements made within a Catholic university and the teaching of the church, as they may evaluate such statements anywhere. Insofar as the university becomes what it is, a *locus* of serious and open discussion, where meanings are clarified in careful exchange and counterpositions advanced and considered, the Catholic university can actually contribute to the depth and the accuracy with which the teaching church understands positions that strike one initially as strange or extravagant or even as heterodox.

While academic freedom, as such, is in no way contradictory to the freedom of the *magisterium,* the presence of a diversity and disagreement within the university is not only essential to its nature as a university but to the soundness and vitality of Catholic theology. There is no need to choose between the presence of an open, responsible discussion representing the world of serious knowledge or reflection and the vital presence of a Catholic orthodoxy with its fidelity to the gospel and to the παράδοσ's through which this gospel has come into the twentieth century. That both are present and present in vital interchange is the serious responsibility of those who are called to govern such institutions.

Order

This brings up the first operative term, "order," in the phrase "order of discussion." If the forum is to be a forum—more than a chaos, more than an anarchy of voices in which the loudest finally prevails because of a sophistic command of techniques, the selection of popular topics or even a willingness to pander, however covertly, to the prejudices of the less discerning—there must be order, a prior and posterior of subject matter, to allow those discussions, inquiries, and even research that give to each its warranted importance. The university will determine its character by the hierarchy it establishes among subject matters to be mastered and questions to be explored. In initially making this determination, either consciously or not, each university will reflect its source within a culture and the purpose it is to serve. A university will take its initial order of instruction and research from the questions of its parent culture. It lives off its surrounding and generating civilization in this way. But the university's discussion may radically alter the culture's predominant conclusions about these questions, conclusions which have formed the underlying ethos of the culture and out of which issued these initial questions themselves. Then a new order of discussion arises from the changes worked through education.

A technological community will evoke a university whose order is quite different from that emerging from the church, as one can see sponsored in the nineteenth century both the new Free University of Brussels and the ancient Catholic University of Louvain. Neither the church nor the scientific community with an eye to its own interests proposes an institution that impedes inquiry, but the priorities of each are different. These priorities disclose themselves in their selection of the questions that will dominate the institutions, the ones judged cardinal, questions that evoke research or drive curricula or focus academic habits or inspire structures. Thus the doctrinal commitments of the church tell upon the universities it fosters. These come into the university as the subject matters or fields and as issues the church holds most important. A Catholic university will have an academic structure and a spirit profoundly reflecting the concerns and the commitments of the church, and it will evince its character through its disciplined awareness of the great mystery of God, revealed in Christ and in the Spirit; human life as the choice of God and all of the forms of its development in knowledge and love, practice and grace, sciences, literature, and art; human communities and the purposiveness of society; the claims of social justice and the Christian imperatives for a life of service; the seriousness of life and the responsibilities of human beings; and so forth.

If the initial citation from John Dewey is correct—that reflection originates only in problematic confrontation—then the church stands in serious need of the Catholic university; its authorship of these institutions is not an accident of history, but a realization within its own history of the dialectical implications of its mission. Within these or like institutions, the greater efforts of Catholic theology have taken their origin or their rise: the Cappadocians drew from the philosophical and rhetorical instruction of the School of Athens; the "Schoolmen" flourished within the universities of the Middle Ages; one recalls the work of Rahner in Innsbruck, Munich, or Münster and Schillebeeckx at Nijimegen. The university—not the secondary school or the seminary or even the individual theologate—is the proper locus for theology, just as an altar is the proper locus for sacrifice.

The church must have theology. If the church is to have theology, it must have universities or, at least, a university presence; and if these institutions are to be universities, their discussion must not be ecclesially limited. This is not to maintain that the Catholic university is needed because the church must educate all Catholics or most Catholics, much less that hereby it is forming leaders for tomorrow. Whatever the truth of such statements, they do not capture the point. The church needs Catholic universities, realizing each of these terms in its fullness, so that the church can think theologically. This theology will be as vital as its contact with the other knowledges engaged at the university and it will realize itself in so many different ways, ranging from the formal research, instruction, and writings of its faculty and graduate students to the disciplined ability of its undergraduates to appreciate and recognize sound religious reflection and to distinguish this from the enthusiastic or the bogus.

The Identity of the Catholic University

Can one gather from what has been said some delineations of the Catholic university, assertions that disclose something of its unique character? Not in the custodial sense of Catholic through exclusive selections among faculty, students, books, and curriculum or in its defensive posture. To respond to this question demands that some of the statements of previous chapters be repeated, if only to offer a response that is unified. If the previous arguments are correct, this university is Catholic in four ways: through (1) the community out of which it comes and by which it is sustained; (2) the purpose that it is to serve; (3) the spirit and structure that informs it; and (4) the serious presence of Catholic tradition and reflection as one of its most significant components.

The Catholic university comes out of the faith of the Catholic community, which, in the teaching of the Second Vatican Council, "strives to relate all human culture eventually to the news of salvation."[14] Notice this is "all human culture," all modes of discourse and thought, no matter how varied and contradictory in expression or in actual content.

Second, the university is Catholic in its deliberate determination to render to the church and the broader world this unique service: to be an intellectual forum, a center of higher studies, where in authentic academic freedom the variant lines of Catholic tradition and thought can intersect with all human learning and contemporary reflection, moving toward a unity of world and Word, that all things be assimilated into the Christ. This mutual implication of human culture and religious faith takes place within the intellectual and moral habits of the students and the instruction and research of the faculty.[15] No other institution within human culture can render this critically important contribution to the Christian community, and without it the commitments of faith disintegrate into sectarian polemics or indoctrination whose only strength lies in their isolation from contradicting contact.

Third, such a university is Catholic because of the spirit and activity that energizes it. Academic exchange in thought and collaborative inquiry formally constitute the specifying activity of any university. The only spirit that can further specify any community as Christian is charity, that love of friendship for God and for other human beings that bespeaks the influence and teaching of Christ. To the degree that the university's characteristic interchange is permeated by a love both for the truth to be explored and for the human beings who are to come to know it and that this in its turn mirrors the love and influence of Christ as it comes through the church—a love found in the concern that human beings share so great a good as that of sacred and profane knowledge, of reason and of revelation and that by their influence, especially teaching, they make this same development possible to others—is that university Catholic in its spirit. It is confirming to note that when Ignatius proposed to begin universities, he began his educational program with this articulation of its motive: "*eadem caritatis ratio.*" The universities were to be begun from "the same motive of charity" as had drawn the Society of Jesus to secondary education as well.[16]

The structure of such a university will be set by the priority of questions it entertains and by the knowledge that is agreed is the most worth having. Both these issues and this knowledge dictate the presence and influence of theology and philosophy as architectonic wisdoms within the curricula and research commitments of the university. This will be explored in the next two chapters.

Fourth, strong and influential, but not exclusive, among its elements must be the serious presence of Catholic intellectuals, those who understand the church in her tradition and in her teaching and for whom faith has been found illumination. Those who embody this Catholic intellectuality are indispensably present. They constitute the source through which the many different philosophies and theologies whose inspiration is the manifestation of God in Christ and through the church reach out to contact another world whose inspiration is other, but whose commitment to dialogue is no less real. Without the presence of a diversity of intellectual traditions, there is no university. Without the significant presence of Catholic scholars and professors, the Catholic identity of these institutions will inevitably fail—its last presence being lived in the official catalog and dreary pronouncements of the university after the faculty has long since ceased to espouse this vision. This dictates to the Catholic university that it have in place the policy of hiring for mission and that it take concrete means to assure that Catholic intellectuals number strongly among its faculty.

This presence of Catholic intellectuals is necessary, but not sufficient. Essential is the presence of faculty of other traditions, both religious and humanistic. They should find in the Catholic university a support for the religious and humane values they represent, support that they would not find elsewhere. *Gaudium et spes* states that whatever is human enters with peculiar efficacy into the concerns of the church, which adds its own religious sense of urgency to those values that engage all human desire and longing.[17] For this reason, members of the faculty who represent a tradition other than Catholic should never find themselves alien within this world. The diversity of traditions and philosophies they represent is essential for the university, necessarily extant that the university be a university, that universal human culture be present. Their high human and religious values, the humane achievements and concerns divergent traditions cherish are treasured also by the Catholic culture of this university. The value of Catholic intellectualism should manifest itself in recognizing in other traditions and cultures the humane and religious values that are there, while those who represent these values should find themselves supported even more strongly as this culture conjoins to an educated sensibility and moral development an additional religious inspiration. It can be legitimately hoped, even expected, that all faculty will find the values they love strongly affirmed in a Catholic university.

What faculty share, then, both among themselves and with the students are the values and concerns of the university as a whole—if not all of them, enough of them so that each person finds his or her humanistic and religious values confirmed in the common affirmations of the university and themselves drawn into the community that results from their common possession. What is asked of all faculty is a commitment to the mission of the university. As William Neenan, S.J., former academic vice president of Boston College, put it: "Since the faculty, through the hiring process, their curricular decisions, and the research and scholarship options they choose, will ultimately determine whether Boston College remains recognizably Catholic and Jesuit into the next century, it is imperative to develop a faculty consensus concerning the values that are consistent with the Jesuit educational tradition."[18]

One can legitimately argue that such a Christian commitment, far from militating against the genius of a university, strengthens and merges with it. A Catholic university should be more truly a university precisely because it is Catholic. Its parent culture, the church, evokes, encourages, and sustains those questions of ultimacy, which have for at least three thousand years framed the wisdom of any intellectual community. At the Catholic university, they are to be given a primacy in consideration and in argument, rather than ignored as a matter of state policy or smothered under technical curricular obligations of tertiary educational value.

Further, the faith of the community should ideally provide a more sound foundation for academic freedom than the calculations of politicians or the corporate integrity of trustees. For it is precisely the obligation of faith that all positions must be considered, that all things ultimately be taken up into Christ. It was Newman who maintained that "among fairly prudent and circumspect men, there are far fewer instances of false certitude than at first sight might be supposed. Men are often doubtful about propositions which are really true; they are not commonly certain of such as are simply false. What they judge to be a certainty is in matter of fact for the most part a truth."[19] To discover this truth in the richness and diversity of human traditions becomes an imperative for the Catholic university. That this has not been the case is historically evident, but it points to the seriously defensive understanding of revelation and the custodial nature of these institutions in the past.

Finally, the spirit of a Christian community can make for that respect and trust, that civility and honesty of interchange which allows the university to become, in Robert Maynard Hutchins' words, "the incandescent center of independent thought."

The distinguished philosopher and psychotherapist, William J. Richardson, S.J., argued twenty-five years ago that the purpose of a Catholic university today is "to represent the Church in Academia, i.e., to serve as that corporate person through which the Church becomes present to the community of academic institutions and they to it."[20] The position argued here is complementary to his: that the church must sponsor institutions of critical controversy and discussion so that it may have a reflection sound in its own tested structures and in dialogue with the issues which arise within other fields as well as within the universe of human knowledge. This reflection can be embodied either in the research of its faculty or in the habits of theological reflection to which the undergraduates are introduced.

An Objection and a Conclusion

Let these remarks conclude with a final, more specified question: how do these imperatives and these characteristics of a university apply to an institution whose major emphasis is undergraduate education—as is the case with many Jesuit and Catholic universities? These are usually not institutions heavily engaged in research, which are intensely specialized in their departments and demand of their faculty above all continual original contributions to specialized fields. Their concern is rather with general or liberal education, a concern that the undergraduates be broadly educated, even though few of them will initiate original scholarship and research. Is not the purpose of this institution instruction rather than inquiry, the inculcation of skills and intellectual habits, the transmission of a heritage of learning and of a body of knowledge already established, rather than an orientation to the genuinely problematic, which the students are not technically trained to handle competently?

Much recommends this objection as serious and significant, but it does not comprehend the actual needs of the students. There is much to admire in the Catholic university but two serious defects can inhibit its growth: the faculty does not adequately collaborate in disciplined discussion with one another on any except the personal or the casual or the occasional moment, while the academic administration does not engineer policies and procedures that encourage or even demand this interaction; and second, many students—perhaps partly as a result of the absence of this faculty interchange—evince very little interest in academic questions. Many of them impress one as wanting a grade, technical and marketable skills, a diploma, and out—and as painlessly as possible. The life of the intellect—the intellect as life—often has very little resonance in the conduct of their lives or in their implicit value structures. Many factors might explain this phenomenon, i.e., students with few searching questions. But whatever its causes, any subsequent education will be only technical training until an interest in the problematic is evoked and situated as the critically important intellectual movement of a human being. The task of liberal education in our institutions, then, has as its first moment the evocation of interest in the life of the intellect, the awakening of real questions, the incitement to the issues and culture of the mind. This will be developed more fully in the next chapter.

If this is true, then some restructuring of the liberal arts college would seem necessary, especially of the introductory courses. Against the background of the history of the liberal arts and of the humanities that has been reviewed, the question can be asked: in our culture, in our universities, what is that which will first free the students to be intelligent, reflective, and compassionate human beings, that is, liberalize and humanize them?

An answer will not be found by simply repeating either the training in skills of the Middle Ages or the content-centered humanities of the Renaissance, though obviously it would be mad to think Catholic education could not draw profitably and heavily upon both. The liberal arts core curriculum cannot be ordered only to skills or to the appreciative grasp of subject-fields. It must be ordered initially to an apperception of meaning, to the importance of thought; in a phrase, to the problematic within life. What is needed in the introductory courses in the liberal arts is a serious attention to the discovery of problems. Such would be courses that center not simply around abilities to be won or fields to be mastered, but around problems to be experienced, appreciated, described, discussed, debated, and resolved. The liberal education of the students should consist initially in evoking in them a sense of problems.

In the Middle Ages and Renaissance, devices were taken from the *De inventione* of Cicero to set up a liberal arts curriculum. One might suggest that the contemporary university might do something of the same: elaborate problem-courses in terms of topics, τόποι, the places wherein arguments and issues are found—problems of love, of community, of the poetic, of the political and economic order, of life and of death, of beauty, of Christ, and of God, etc. Students could be introduced to the standard fields of English, sociology, history, and theology by an initial and serious concentration upon the problem.

Students will begin to be liberated from advertisement, television sentimentality and propaganda, from money, power, and publicity, from superficiality and banality only when they are overwhelmed with the questions within which they live—whether these questions leave them in wonder or in doubt or in anguish. Only then will they care to find the ways in which human beings and Christian culture have engaged these questions. To give to the undergraduate curriculum an increased emphasis upon the problematic would be to accomplish two things: to promote university education, even on the undergraduate level, as an order of inquiry and discussion; and to provide that free forum in which the students can increasingly apprehend the richness and possibilities of their humanity and their religious engagement can grow into a deeper understanding of its promise.

The university as a pluralistic forum is a picture of what the Catholic university over the past decades has been gradually, painfully becoming. One can understand the struggles, self-doubts, debates, and discussions that have preoccupied Catholic universities in these decades only as one can understand any process, i.e., in terms of its direction. The Catholic universities are changing, growing into institutions which are more truly universities, and precisely in this way, more truly Catholic. Rather than failing to realize their Catholic commitment, as the late archbishop of Portland charged at the beginning of these years of charges and counter-charges, the Catholic universities in many cases are beginning to measure up to it. What are emerging are those universities which are Catholic in their faith and catholic in their pluralism.

PART FOUR

Towards the Love of Wisdom

CHAPTER EIGHT

Philosophic Grammar and the Other Disciplines

To be a philosopher is not merely to have subtle thoughts, nor even to found a school, but so to love wisdom as to live according to its dictates.
. . .

—Henry David Thoreau, *Walden*[1]

The Problem

Over the centuries two disciplines within the tradition of Catholic higher education came to function as architectonic wisdoms: philosophy and theology. They served as the far-reaching learning that gave to other learning integration and coordination. Classically, philosophy could draw the various disciplines into a coherent unity. One could consider in metaphysics their disparate subject matters as complementary aspects of reality or their engagement as an ethical or political imperative for integral human development or their constructions as exhibiting a unity and diversity one with another that are found in things well-made. Catholic theology, in contrast, did not so much analyze the disciplines. It rather assumed their results. These furnished the questions that inevitably bear upon the self-revelation of God and upon the faith in which that is received. They also furnished the conceptual structures through which, in Bonaventure's felicitous phrase, "the credible is made intelligible."[2] The first of these kinds of wisdom occupies this present chapter; the second, its subsequent companion. And the question here about philosophy lies precisely with the contemporary possibilities of its architectonic role.

Instruction in philosophy has long occupied an essential place within Catholic universities and was accorded an integrating function within the general education offered. In the decades preceding the Second Vatican Council, philosophy was attended with much greater academic seriousness in these institutions than was theology. It exercised, consequently, greater influence than did the required but often debased courses in "religion." Ask average graduates from the schools of that period which courses were found most engaging during their collegiate years and most memorable afterwards; more often than not the answer will return: philosophy. Its depth and influence were due in large measure to the retrieval of Thomism, to seminal thinkers who represented its genius well, such as Jacques Maritain and Étienne Gilson, and to institutions where it flourished such as the Medieval Institute of Toronto, the University of Louvain, and St. Louis University. At its best, instruction in Thomism instilled a common language and charted a progressive movement through serious issues in concatenated courses. It offered a careful, sober methodology by which philosophic inquiries and conversations could be conducted. It inculcated a respect for problems of ultimacy and for the vast range of the human intellect. It carried a living tradition of wisdom that retrieved ancient philosophy, uniquely drew upon the thought of the Middle Ages, and engaged issues of modern and contemporary philosophy. One was introduced into philosophic reflection under the dispensation of that time by being introduced into Thomism.

Much has changed since those bracing days. Most striking is the collapse of the organic coherence in philosophical education Thomism once provided. Its hegemony and the incremental philosophical development fostered by its steady pursuit exist now for the most part only as a memory. In its place one finds an eclectic richness, perhaps even a chaotic pluralism. A student can typically pass from one course offered by an analytic philosopher to a second by a Heideggerian to a third by a Marxist—with surveys of the history of philosophy that resemble for all the world careening through the Metropolitan Museum of Art on rollerblades: a blur of color, a patch here and there of concepts and patterns, languages hardly apperceived and remembered, and a growing sense that what is presented so earnestly now waits only for a moment to be replaced by another. If narrowness and dogmatism were the faults to which Thomism was liable, a weary confusion or skepticism threatens—if it does not invariably characterize—much in the contemporary settlement. From the impressive variety of courses and texts offered, the student picks those statements and insights that strike home—very much as one might underline parts of a book that arouse a sympathetic response. And the justification of the selection is made through vague appeals to "experience."

Still the problem today is not whether philosophy should be present in the curriculum—this still remains unchallenged—but rather whether in the accepted pluralism and diversity it can function as it once did, as a discipline that could bring much of the academic life of the university together. More specifically, with the collapse of the previous academic covenant in Catholic universities, can the student be brought to reflections that are both foundational and integrating?

When Thomism was in its zenith, its breadth opened up possibilities for the interrelationship between philosophy and the other disciplines. Its thinkers wrote major works in the philosophy of science, the philosophy of art, the philosophy of work, the philosophy of nature, and the philosophy of history. Its own intellectual integrity could allow it to relate to each of the sciences and the arts. But in relating them to itself, Thomism related them to one another. The unity of philosophy allowed for a unity of the curriculum and in the discourse about the curriculum. Obviously, in some places this was more successful than others—in many places, it did not exist at all. But this academic coherence was at least something that Thomism made possible. It must be noted emphatically that to praise the accomplishments of any period is not to wish that it return, but to recognize that it possessed achievements from which the contemporary age can learn. To retrieve what is of value in the past is not an essay in restoration.

Now the question must be raised whether the contemporary pluralism in philosophy within the Catholic university has not rendered such a unifying function impossible. Is it not necessary simply to abandon any fancy talk about an architectonic and straightforwardly to treat philosophy like any other field within the humanities or sciences? We give instruction in mathematics, physics, history, English literature; can we not also teach philosophy? Is it not a discipline a body of knowledge like any other, alongside of every other? Is it not taught by instructors in so many ways the mirrors of their colleagues and equally isolated from others in other disciplines? To afford it a special and integrating function seems pretentious—as voices such as Richard Rorty assert.[3]

One can push this problem about the integrating function of philosophic education a bit further. Three additional difficulties significantly augment this issue and raise the much more fundamental question whether philosophy can be taught at all. Paradoxically, these three objections may well serve as coordinates within which one may chart a response, if not an answer, to the question about the integrative function of philosophy.

Three Additional Dimensions of the Problem

The question of philosophic education belongs to an academic institution, not only because it touches some form of instruction—however ambiguous this activity—but because "wisdom" itself is associated with the history and purposes of education: with the Academy, the Lyceum, the Stoa, the Garden, the University, and the College. Yet any human being engaged in the academic profession of philosophy must recognize paradoxically that he or she belongs to a company uniquely censured within its history—from the Platonic condemnation of the sophists who exacted tuition and claimed to teach wisdom through the medieval reserve about *philosophus* to Schopenhauer's savage question: "How could philosophy, degraded to become a means of earning one's bread, generally fail to degenerate into sophistry?"[4] In this century, Martin Heidegger has acknowledged: "The misinterpretations with which philosophy is perpetually beset are promoted most of all by people of our kind, that is, by professors of philosophy."[5] Ludwig Wittgenstein attempted to dissuade his pupil, Norman Malcolm, late of Cornell University, from a career as a philosophy professor, because he judged that a normal human being could not be a university instructor and an honest and serious thinker. One might easily see why. The teacher had to pretend to an omnipotence he did not possess, one which could not afford to stay with questions for years because of the demands of the weekly lectures and the quarter-syllabus. The teacher was expected both by students and administration to rhetorize serious, painstaking philosophic inquiry, to dazzle students and gain the reputation and tenure of an "interesting teacher." To Malcolm, Wittgenstein wrote: "The temptation for you to cheat yourself will be *overwhelming* (though I don't mean more for you than for anyone else in your position). *Only by a miracle* will you be able to do decent work in teaching philosophy. Please remember these words, even if you forget everything I've ever said to you."[6] The antinomy here lies between the search for the wisdom that one loves and the public or paid profession of it. The history of philosophy indicates the depth of the estrangement.

The difficulty with instruction in philosophy lies not only in the antithesis drawn between teaching and wisdom, but also within the sources and character of wisdom. "Wisdom" runs like a theme through Western thought and educational institutions, but in various locations its meanings differ profoundly. It can denote "knowing all things, though not in detail" or the Socratic reflexive realization that one knows nothing while others think they do.[7] "Wisdom" has embraced either conclusions reached or the methods by which they are reached or the principles from which these methods proceed and by which these conclusions are justified. "Wisdom" can be either a habit of thought or a manner of choice or a conditioned sensitivity to values or a life which issues from reflection, decision, and perception. It can be a particular human achievement

or a comprehensive divine gift which subsumes them all. However variant in its definitions and location, "wisdom" always touches upon something ultimate, something absolute enough to have other things related
to it or evaluated by it.

Whatever its pluralism of meaning and realization, is it not the
case—even increasingly the case—that in Anglo-Saxon countries serious
students have turned from philosophy courses and begun to look elsewhere in the academic curriculum for the fundamentals or ultimates in
life? As in Socrates' Athens, wisdom is derivative for these students from
other disciplines and pursuits: the conclusions of poets, dramatists, scientists, and artists—even of enthusiasts and seers of the New Age—are
taken for wisdom, even though they may be unable to ground or explain
their own propositions. Logistic methods of mathematics in their exactitude or operational methods of science in their productivity are taken
for wisdom and used paradigmatically to judge the seriousness of other
methods and other forms of discourse. Transcendent principles of religion or immanent principles of revolution or human principles of sensitive interrelations are taken for wisdom, as if what is most profound may
be beyond reason but not beyond emotion, action, or experience. But
wisdom as a unique, a philosophic concern and focus—one with its own
principles, methodologies and resolutions—is neither very much the
subject of courses in "philosophy" nor the object of programmed instruction evoking anything like a comprehensive, all-governing "love."

In any consideration of instruction, the ambiguous position of the
professor and the derivative nature of wisdom compound the difficulties
with an additional term of this question: the college students. Here the
issue becomes: how can college students be brought "to love wisdom"?
Can so radical a commitment of life, so pronounced a character of moral
life, be taught to these students, actually form the product or even the
content of three unit courses? Is there any other subject matter within
the contemporary liberal arts curriculum that speaks of love as its finality with wisdom as its object? Do you not trivialize philosophy, in this
fundamental sense of the word, when you take it into the undergraduate
college classroom? If "experience" for William James was a double-bar-
reled word, denoting both the activity and the content, what can be said
about this term that seems triple-barreled—denoting the content of a
discipline, the activity of radical reflection by which this content is considered, and the all-encompassing, affective habit of heart and mind by
which such activity is sought and engaged? You are asking this of the
college student?

Philosophers have habitually considered youth too callow or too
enthusiastic to care about much besides pleasures, wars, ambitions, and

loves. Contemporary educationalists have judged them either too inexperienced or too financially preoccupied to give themselves to an education that was neither specialized in its departments nor geared to a career. Under this persuasion, the undergraduate college in so many universities has lost its unique and demanding teleology. Professional schools and graduate departments have reached down into the college to train students even earlier for the specialists they are to become or for the careers they are to enter. How much of liberal arts education has become entertaining, precious or soft—sometimes a veneer of unrelated courses in the humanities from which the student emerges virtually unscathed by what went on in the classroom. There seem to be undergraduate curricula—how many?—content to train the student in this way, because this is what he wants or what he needs or where "he is at" or where he is going.

The assumption of the possibility of philosophic instruction, then, conceals under the obvious problem of fragmentation a threefold diremption: between the academic profession of philosophy and the undeviating search for wisdom, between curricular formation and the love of wisdom, between the cultural orientations of young students and any commitment to wisdom. The split involves, in complicated antinomies, the teacher, philosophy, the student, and wisdom. Yet, to repeat, the tracing of issues involved in these antinomies may actually shed light on the problem of philosophical education within a culture of fragmentation.

Patterns in American Education

The history of philosophic instruction within American higher education has done little to resolve these alienations or to heal these lesions. Such instruction has passed over a markedly varied course as the orientation of its teaching reflects the manifold influences and involvements predominant in each period. To paint with shamefully broad brush strokes, three moments can be isolated, moments that reflect three distinct structures within American higher education and that sponsored three divergent approaches to philosophic instruction: the religious colleges of the seventeenth and eighteenth centuries, the rising, Germanified universities of the nineteenth and early twentieth centuries, and the technologized multiversities of our own times. Corresponding to these patterns of education, one finds three different understandings of philosophy: forensic, historical, and technical.

Philosophy as taught in the early religious colleges of the American colonies and of the newly formed nation conceived its subject matter as the content of statements, a heritage of wisdom, an array of conclusions; "theses" they were called in the older Latin textbooks, in the English manuals, and in the Harvard *Broadsides*. With appropriate variations, this same understanding could be traced back to the Protestant and the Catholic universities of the European continent. These theses articulated the conclusions regnant in Renaissance and sectarian versions of Christian theology or in the rising political doctrines expressing or countering the persuasions contextualizing the rise of the nation-state. The function of instruction was the assimilation and defense of their truth. Philosophy was conceived, even if at times unknowingly, within the classical, rhetorical tradition. A truth is laid down for defense (a "thesis"), places ("topics" in rhetoric) are searched for its proof, debate is indicative of its mastery, and persuasion is the finality of its engagement. When this enterprise was well conducted, it contained rigor in its definition of terms, clarity in its distinctions, and cogency in its argumentation. In one of the variations of this educational tradition, the debater could be expected to repeat the counterargument of his opponent in the precisely ordered relationship of the terms, to distinguish the term or the proposition which was at issue, and to indicate how this modification bore upon the conclusion. The procedure could be precise and elegant. As it appeared to its critics, however, it was over-simple in its propositions, unnuanced in its elaborations, and unconvincing in its "proofs."

When this form of philosophical education began to disintegrate, its ignorance of history, its failure to consider the fundamental and central works of its own tradition, and its isolation from the current discussion among original philosophers often left it seriously unfair in its consideration of adversaries, significantly uninteresting in its presentation of a problematic, and without the stimulus, honesty, and challenge of even responsible debate. It became the education programmed by the manualists. Under the influence of the pontifical institutes and Roman universities, some remnants of this "thesis-method" lasted in the scholastic education of the Jesuit almost a century after it had passed from American higher education in general. Indeed, this was true of content as well. When Étienne Gilson examined the metaphysical *quaestiones* current at Harvard College before 1670, he commented to Samuel Eliot Morison that their "general inspiration is distinctly Scholastic, and most of them would still today be upheld by a Neo-Thomist."[8]

The second method of instruction in philosophy, one might venture, was adopted from Germany to remedy the obvious limitations of the first. While philosophy had been forensic rhetoric, now its guide was history. This second approach conceived wisdom as that which philosophers taught, and the study of philosophy became the study of philosophers and their contextualizing influences. "Histories of philosophy" replaced or marginated the systematic textbooks or manuals. These histories were not the medieval commentaries upon a single philosophic inquiry, a careful following of a philosopher as his inquiries progressed more and more deeply to reach their resolutions. They were rather a more or less readable compilation of conclusions contextualized by antecedent philosophers, systematized into an assimilable unity, and evaluated in importance by the influence these conclusions or methods were to attain with successors. Or courses became the archeological study of single classical works: when contradictions or variance was discovered or read in these texts, it could be resolved by applications of such devices as "earlier" and "late." Philosophic instruction—no matter how much this accusation was denied and no matter how much the great figures in American philosophy escape it—often became subsumed into some form of the history of philosophy. This history incorporated the nineteenth century's enthusiasm for progress in which each successive continental philosopher found in the past the preparation for his own definitive achievements. Philosophy as history was given its unity not by subject matter and argument, but by chronology or influence or system.

When the enterprise was well done, it displayed care in its textual analysis and assignations, an acquaintance with major works of genius, concern about systematically ambiguous terms and propositions, and vision in its elaboration of historical patterns. It could be engrossing and stimulating. As it appeared to its subsequent critics, however, it was superficial when it attempted to cover vast periods of philosophy in survey fashion, unphilosophic in its failure to deal carefully with argument and principle, and deadening both in its tendency to locate questions only within the past and in its pedantic muster of detail. While the first approach in its manual elaborations failed to come to grips with original philosophers, the second failed either to grasp or occasion philosophically rigorous argument and proof. The first approach presented the student with a series of conclusions to be defended. The second offered a series of facts and philosophers to be assimilated. Both lent themselves to collegiate courses in which the major problems or figures within philosophy could be resolved either in a summary fashion or in agonizingly contrived dissection of a text into divergent times and influences. Both of them initiated the study of philosophy as the study of propositions already enunciated, either historically or defensively conceived.

Both approaches to education in philosophy left their impact on twentieth century Anglo-American philosophic inquiry, feeding into it either an enormously varied series of propositions whose protection was philosophy or an overwhelming heterogeneity of historical opinions whose progression was philosophy. The dominant philosophies in this century became linguistic in their focus; and some of them, highly technical, attempted precision in meaning through semantics and accuracy in implication through logical syntax. Rudolf Carnap asserted in 1934: "Philosophy is to be replaced by the logic of science—that is to say by the logical analysis of the concepts and sentences of science, for the logic of science is nothing other than the logical syntax of the language of science."[9] Whether the concerns of philosophical analysis devolved upon syntax or upon semantics, the object of philosophy was consistently linguistic.

With the "linguistic turn," philosophy became "analytical philosophy." No matter how far ranging the diversity among its adherents, it distinguished itself by two beliefs: "first, that a philosophical account of thought can be attained through a philosophical account of language, and, secondly, that a comprehensive account can only be so attained."[10] So also philosophical concentration was not upon divergent subject matters as aspects of the real nor upon methodologies and systems emergent from comprehensive concepts, but upon language, whether the language was specialized to the sciences or "ordinary language." Dubious of metaphysical speculations and of classic German epistemological criticisms, philosophy could resolve propositions of the past into nonsense. As the history of philosophy was apprehended as a tissue of errors, many made this discovery the preoccupation of philosophy. As Professor Vere Chappell put it: "It follows that the way to achieve success in philosophy—and this again means understanding and the solving of problems—is to determine how our language is in fact used, and thence show where and how philosophers have gone astray."[11]

In its finest usages, linguistic philosophies have encouraged a careful honesty in terms and propositions, precision in methodology, and a modesty in assertions. In the eyes of its critics, however, it has often become trivial in its interests and controversies, arrogantly over-simple in its dismissal of vagueness and ambiguity, ignorant in its unnuanced reading of the philosophic tradition, and outdistanced in logic and semantics by the coordinate disciplines of mathematics and linguistics.

Much in contemporary American philosophical usage cannot adequately introduce the student into the philosophic task because—to put it most simply—the etymology of the question fails to tell in its resolution: how to bring the student to love wisdom—not to defend it, not to possess it even, but to love it. What philosophic instruction aims to elicit as the defining characteristic of the philosophic habit of mind is this attitude of reverence, longing, and dedication—the deepest affection for the truth that will energize and guide a person's entire life.

It is this love that is the goal of initial instruction in philosophy. The question of any initial philosophical education is how to awaken such a love. Neither debate positions nor historical and textual facts nor linguistic precisions and refinements seem happy resolutions of the issue. Love is awakened and sustained neither by cleverness nor by erudition nor by precision. It is awakened by a revelation of the good, sometimes in the form of the beautiful. One is drawn into love and its commitments by the disclosure of an immense good that had been hidden. Love is elicited by this revelation of worth, of value, of what is humanly the object of desire and joy.

If philosophy is to be initiated and "taught," it must above all be through disclosure and vision, a disclosure that the philosophic enterprise engages the object of the deepest and most human love. Whatever human beings long for most radically and however they ennoble themselves through this longing, whatever they move towards with desires that issue from the deepest part of their person, the reflexive grasp of these is legitimately called "wisdom." Wisdom—either as thought, choice, or life itself—comprises these ultimates that human beings love, and by which their lives are structured, and by the discernment of which their counterfeits are recognized. One is taught to love wisdom through the revelation of its human good. Merleau-Ponty has put this very simply: "To philosophize is to seek, and this is to imply that there are things to see and to say."[12]

One can value this search only because of some prior glimpse of its object. The invitation to philosophize is an invitation to "radical reflection" (again Merleau-Ponty's expression), and this entails asceticism, moral seriousness, and a resolute honesty. Reflection becomes "radical" only if it is willing to dig to the roots of whatever is under consideration. Philosophy, so conceived, becomes not simply one course out of many, but a way of life—a very demanding way of life. Students can become willing to embark upon such a life if and only if they can apprehend something worth this commitment. Students will accept the invitation to radical reflection only if they find deep within themselves a love for the radical. Even academic instruction in philosophy can effect this revelation of the depth and the expansion in which a person already lives—albeit unaware—or of the possibilities of a world in which they could live or of the internal alienation worked within human life because its reflective promise is never to be realized.

Introduction through Disclosure

Philosophic instruction as the disclosure or revelation of what is at depth in all human enterprises—with all of their commitments and desires—would move forward quite differently from an approach that conceives of philosophy under the analogues of rhetoric or history or linguistic precision. It would begin with the student's experience and interests, with what Aristotle calls the πρόχειρα, i.e., those things that are before one's hand, the proximate and the immediate.[13] These are certainly not the possibility of movement or Thales on water or propositional calculus! The task of initial instruction would be to inquire into the student's commitments, to probe them for their assumptions in concepts, principles, and methods, to ask what is implied in them or why they are of worth. Socrates began with generals and asked about the nature of courage, an ultimate value foundational to their lives; he would ask a good man about justice, or a teacher about wisdom and instruction. The *data* with which one begins depend very much upon a student's immediate interests or situation. The initiation into the philosophic enterprise is the *question* leveled at that data—the question with which one probes towards the ultimates involved in any human interest. And the *method* is to move—in a thousand different possible ways—from these *data* that are proximate and that have meaning and worth to those concealed but fundamental *principles* upon which they depend and through which they are understood and loved.

Now any educational institution confronts enormous problems with an understanding of initial philosophic instruction as the disclosure of what assumptions and issues underlie the commitments of the students. Whatever be their external conformities, students differ among themselves at that depth to which philosophic inquiry must appeal. Each lives within a unique history and experience, peculiar aspirations, idiosyncratic attitudes and choices. How can such diversity provide any common ground for philosophic questions, how can it do anything but divide a classroom of some twenty-five? Does this not make rhetorical apologetics or historical studies or technical instruction a necessary and practical, albeit a less ideal, program?

It need not. The personal choices of the students have already involved them within communities of learning present in collegiate education. The students have opted for those studies that placed them within the major divisions of undergraduate education. They are involved in humanistic studies, social sciences, physical and biological sciences, or the professional schools. One can begin here—with the studies seriously entertained and the knowledge prized in any of these studies—and probe to the philosophical level by question and inquiry about these commitments. Moreover, as they move through one of these divisions in questioning towards the fundamental commitments or assumptions latent within them, the students will find themselves involved in certain constants which run through the same considerations for all of their peers. One may begin with the student's immediate academic interests; one does not end here. The ultimates which underlie or structure any particular human enterprise in knowledge or love will be found to pervade every human enterprise in knowledge and love; inquiry into one field will inevitably involve inquiry into another. This program sounds very abstract. A concrete example might provide water in the desert.

If the students were studying physics, one might well begin with either quantum mechanics or relativity theories. If with quantum mechanics, the class might well analyze Niels Bohr's major essay that recounts his discussions with Einstein over thirty years. The essay is interesting because it immediately introduces the question of ultimates in physical theory. Both Einstein and Bohr agree upon the findings of the sub-atomic physics of their period, but they are in radical disagreement about its implication. As Bohr stated the question of the discussion: "Whether the renunciation of a causal mode of description of atomic processes involved in the endeavors to cope with the situation should be regarded as a temporary departure from ideals to be ultimately revived or whether we are faced with an irrevocable step towards obtaining the proper harmony between analysis and synthesis of physical phenomena."[14] The problem of cause, interpreted here as antecedent determination, comes out of physical research itself. The assumptions about the inescapable presence of prior causal necessity in all physical data—a basically metaphysical assumption—will dictate the diverse interpretations given to the facts of quantum mechanics.

But the problem of cause reaches far beyond physics; it can be found equally in social and humanistic studies. Thucydides poses the entire analysis of the Peloponnesian War upon the distinction between the alleged reasons for the conflict between Athens and Sparta and the actual underlying cause, a distinction in causality between the phenomena and the real: the growth of power within the one and the inevitable fear that this occasioned in the other. What is causal in history is power, and thus the grasp of the power-factors within political movements will allow those who follow his inquiry to predict future events when such power blocs amass again in conflict.[15] In Dean Acheson's *Present at the Creation*, one can find a similar explanation of political and economic movements, explicating the American entrance into World War I with the growing power of Germany and the fear and distrust this awakened in the United States. To understand power is to understand historic causes. In sharp contrast, the students could read Brüning's analysis of the fall of the Weimar Republic, a catastrophe brought about by a series of accidental and unpredictable choices.[16] In Thucydides and Acheson, the grasp of power as causal factors enables one in some way to predict and to control the political future; in Brüning, neither is possible.

Further, the purpose of Coleridge's *Biographia Literaria* is to search out the principle or cause of greatness in poetic construction, the works of talent being located in the fancy of the artist while those of genius can be traced back to the comprehensive esemplastic imagination that fuses the diversities of words, image, movement into a wholeness and unity.[17] The cause of great art is not power, but imagination. Frank Lloyd Wright defines organic architecture in terms of a diversity of causes. Indeed, Wright's description reads almost like that of a schoolman: A building should be a living organism, proceeding by way of natural inspiration, from the nature of the materials and the nature of its purpose in order to gratify the nature of the human person.[18] Within theology, commitments on causality occur and occur critically. Rudolf Bultmann, for example, accepts as the fundamental principle for the differentiation of myth from history, a doctrine of irrefragable causality: the course of nature and history cannot be interrupted by the intervention of supernatural powers; cause and effect are phenomenal and form an unbreakable nexus. Anything that would represent the transcendent as if it were within history, as if it were a cause of the normal, ordinary order of events is myth.[19]

Notice that the students began with sub-atomic physics, have localized a term of critical importance to its understanding, and have found this term critically present in issues of history, political science, literary criticism, architecture, biblical exegesis, etc. Two things emerge: that some doctrine of causality is present in any of these human enterprises and that understandings differ on what causality is. The issue is then joined: What is the meaning of causality? What is its evidence? How does it function? Why is it present?

And so the inquiry of the students moves to a more radical stage of philosophic reflection. To start with the πρόχειρα, with anything at hand, and to question it in depth is to move analytically to the philosophic commitments and presuppositions which underpin and justify these obvious data. Further, there is no single doctrine about "cause" that runs through these disciplines; "cause" operates like a variable, given different values in different settings. The unity that it gives to the greatest diversity in different works from different disciplines is not doctrinal or systematic, but thematic. While "cause" can issue out of any human enterprise, it is limited to none. Conversely, while proper to none of these individually, it relates them all in common thematic assumptions and language. Every human project makes critically important decisions about the nature of causality. Philosophic inquiry probes for these assumptions, shows their influence and variety, and then judges their adequacy.

What must be further noted is that the doctrine about causality implicit in one field will have a telling, even if unexamined, influence on another. Atomic doctrines of causality can jump over into Pointillist painting. Evolutionary conceptions of biological causality can move into understandings of dogmatic development, historical progress, and educational or moral instruction.

The terms and assumptions that underlie any field of knowledge and relate it to another are a focus of philosophic inquiry. Any science or art subsumes or implies such presuppositions, either in individual words or in statements. Philosophic reflection is to disclose and to judge them, not simply to clarify their meaning, but to judge the adequacy of their understanding and employment. Philosophic questioning selects such presuppositions and examines them within metaphysical inquiry as aspects of the real, within ethics and politics as they bear upon human conduct and development, and within poetics as their employment engages some form of human making. The alternative to such an examination, to philosophic inquiry, is not that human beings will have no philosophic assumptions, but that they will be culturally determined and immaturely accepted. Philip Frank, the great Harvard physicist, has put the matter very well, à la Whitehead:

> Quite a few great thinkers who belonged to very divergent schools of thought have been unanimous on one point: if a scientist believes that he has no philosophy and keeps tightly to his special field he will really become an adherent of some "chance philosophy," as A. N. Whitehead puts it. This great contemporary metaphysician with a solid scientific background assures us that for a scientist deliberately to neglect philosophy "is to assume the correctness of the chance philosophic prejudices imbibed from a nurse or a schoolmaster or current modes of expression."[20]

Philosophic interest can be awakened in the undergraduate and in the liberal studies of the college, then, as assumptions or commitments that are philosophical are perceived to ground inescapably any human enterprise and to unify them all thematically. Such disclosures can free the students from the narrowness of their own context by a reflexive grasp of its particular structure and an expanded understanding of alternative possibilities. Questions about causality are allowed to emerge in a pluralistic context: "cause" is expected to mean many things. Thus it is that every philosophic tradition moves back to a grasp of principles, whether through such inquiries as a metaphysics of first causes or a critique of the possibilities of knowledge or a foundational study of science and mathematics to determine radical meanings and referents. Philosophic inquiry discovers by such analysis both a thematic unity between every discipline and philosophical reflection and a pluralism that cannot be subsumed either by a single system or reduced to an arbitrary relativism that understands all judgments through perspectival discriminations.

Programmatically, philosophic instruction should not begin with the conclusions of a particular culture to be defended nor with the systems of many philosophers to be assimilated nor with linguistic usages to be analyzed as if they were final rather than disclositive. It should take its data from the students, from fields and disciplines other than those classically called philosophic. It should lay against these data questions which will take the students into a deeper examination of their underlying presuppositions in foundational concepts, principles, methods, ideals, etc. The processes by which one moves through these initial data to the ultimates that give them intelligibility are many. One can begin with the appreciation of a film, for example, move to a consideration of critical principles implicit in this appreciation, and come finally to a consideration of the principles of art and beauty that inform both the appreciation and the criticism. In other words, one can move from the educated development of taste ("what do I like?")—to the formulation or recognition of principles of criticism ("why is it good or bad?")—to aesthetics and metaphysics taken for granted ("what kind of thing is it and what kind of coherence should it have?").

Notice, one is not continually introducing into this process new data. The inquiry is working, questioning what is already present and assumed. The philosophic goes beyond appreciation and criticism precisely by entering into them, by inquiry into the meaning and validity of concepts and methods which either appreciation or criticism take for granted. Indeed, philosophic inquiry begins when one questions what is taken for granted—not to deny it (which would be as dogmatic as its gratuitous assumption) but to call it into radical reflection.

Granted that this is a valid philosophic procedure, is it a possible educational program? Only within a liberal arts college or curricular program possessing two characteristics: (1) the members of the faculty take their mutual collaboration seriously enough to be willing regularly to discuss with and to learn from one another, and (2) the administration encourages the interchange within the undergraduate college as its academic unity, a unity whose formal structure is this intellectual exchange and among whose liberating skills are the abilities to move from field to field with an understanding and a recognition of basic assumptions, if not a technical grasp of each discipline. In such a college, the initial "courses in philosophy" would not be either doctrinal or historical or perspectival. They would not simply be set alongside the other courses in English literature or second-year calculus. They would be transition courses, "bridge courses" in which major works in a particular field were examined for their underlying assumptions—be those assumptions of principles, methods, concepts or ontologies. Philosophic instruction would not begin with philosophy!

Each major division of the college could offer such courses: the physical scientist could begin with the works of Galileo, Newton, Maxwell, Einstein and Heisenberg. Basic terms would operate through the discussion of each of these works, but as variables, i.e., their meaning and their applications would vary: motion, space/place, necessity, probability and chance, time, force, cause, etc. Methods would be seen to differ as one shifted from the mathematical models of Galileo, brought to bear upon physical phenomena to yield fruitful results, to the strictly logistic composition of forces and movements in Newtonian mechanics, as one eventually constructed the *Systema mundi* from the initial corollaries of the parallelogram of forces. This serious, careful reading would give the students neither a single doctrine on "causality" and "motion," nor an entire history of the question, nor a set of perspectives to be aligned. It would open up the term itself for inquiry, and the projects of great thinkers would suggest some of the radical variations possible in its pluralistic resolution. The social sciences could offer similar courses in the concepts and methods common to critical projects in their own field: institution, freedom, human being, history, power, and law—for a selective example. Art and literature could present philosophic inquiry with works of appreciation and criticism which presuppose such concepts as imitation, creativity, beauty, art object. The Committee for the Analysis of Ideas and the Study of Methods at the University of Chicago offered very successfully precisely such a program.[21]

Even the separations among the major divisions of the university will yield before this kind of examination. Fundamental terms and presuppositions will be seen to be common to the humanities, the social, biological, and physical sciences. Time, for example, and its relationship to place, is as critical a question in the structure of the *Magic Mountain* and in the theology of Augustine as it is in the physics of Einstein. The infinite figures in the universe of Newton, in the mathematics of Galileo, but also in the *Opus Oxioniense* of Duns Scotus and in the critical theories of Ruskin. It is important to note that this is not to investigate physics or history or criticism for answers to the philosophic question about the ultimates that are already assumed and give structure and intelligibility to this field. A field does not evaluate its own fundamental commitments. Much less is it to question these disciplines for theological propositions. Physicists are not asked to decide about ethics, and dramatists are not queried about God. One is interested in what is necessary in order to do physics or drama, what is to be assumed by way of meanings and methods. The point of this kind of philosophic instruction is to probe any disciplined human enterprise and to show the radical assumptions and commitments that lie at the heart of this enterprise and then to perceive how these themes weave their way through all human projects.

Such "transition courses" would be "liberal" in the medieval sense of grammar: an ability to read and to interpret so carefully that the elemental constituents are forthcoming. It would be philosophic grammar in that its inquiry is towards these fundamental, pervasive concepts and towards the foundational thinking necessary to disclose and appreciate them. One can adapt here something of the understanding of grammar offered by Martianus Capella. *De nuptiis Philologiae et Mercurii* presented grammar as comprising not only correct reading, but "the added duty of understanding and criticizing knowledgeably." Then Capella comments: "These two aspects seem to me to be shared [by the grammarians] with the philosophers and the critics."[22] Once such fundamental conceptions and assumptions are isolated, once a human project is found to be irrevocably shaped by suppositions in concepts and principles, one can move from philosophic grammar to the history of philosophy or even to philosophic inquiry itself: to courses whose explicit focus is the nature of motion, the character of art, the reality of institutions, the possibilities of freedom.

"Philosophic grammar" could enrich subsequent philosophical instruction both with a pluralism that forestalls a single determination of meaning and with its disclosure that philosophy carries an inescapable relevance to every human project and, hence, to the life of the students. Just as interest or need has led them to art or biology, so art and biology ineluctably involve them in philosophic commitments and questions. While many undergraduates may not be capable initially of sustained and serious work within philosophic investigation, these same students are paradoxically capable of philosophy itself—of seeing the need for wisdom in their lives and longing for it, of experiencing this love as it is embodied alternatively in desire and in joy. Once this fire takes hold in the student, a more formal training in philosophy itself is not only possible, but imperative.

It is here that the issues uncovered in all of the disciplines by a philosophical grammar meet the issues posed by Catholic theology. The sciences and the arts embody assumptions whose investigation is properly the object of that radical reflection that is philosophy. Similarly, the needs of theology continually pose issues for philosophy. When Aquinas, for example, justifies the ascription of *persona* to the members of the Trinity, he does so only after an explicit weighing of the meaning of "person," of its differentiation from other pivotal terms such as the first and second substance of Aristotle, and of the ontological density of the personal that dictates its necessary predication of the divine.[23] Theology, if it is to deepen, places such subjects and issues before philosophical reflection upon the objects of universal human experience and uses the terms so precisely specified and adapted for its inquiry into the reality of God, the nature of the Eucharist, the ontological constitution of the church, etc. So much of contemporary Catholic theology cannot be done without a background in the history of Western wisdom, while for its own part theology has encouraged the development of that very philosophy—not by giving it conclusions but by presenting it with problems.

Philosophy can and must be distinguished from theology, but the distinction does not mean indifference, separation, and isolation—let alone hostility. There are many reasons for this. Questions can be common among these two architectonic disciplines, though treated in very different manners, i.e., under a different aspect and with different evidence. A vital Catholic theology must encourage and even incorporate inquiries that are classically considered philosophical, still allowing philosophy its own autonomy and integrity. Such philosophy can constitute a moment within theology. This interrelationship between philosophy and theology has left its mark on both disciplines. It is out of this history that the much debated designation of "Christian philosophy" arose. Philosophy so touched by the situation and the questions of Catholic theology has classically been called "Christian philosophy."[24]

Ideally, all of the great philosophical traditions and methodologies should be represented within any academic community of higher learning, and the university is simply poorer for their absence. But a Catholic university bears particular responsibility towards Christian philosophy, i.e., for a philosophy in vital contact with the possibilities and influence of a Christian theology, its intellectual traditions and experience, a philosophy to be realized in the curriculum, the faculty, and the students. Christian philosophy is not simply Christian thought or reflection. It is philosophic inquiry conducted with all of the rigor and autonomy requisite for that inquiry, but within a problematic situation and complex of issues set by theology among other influences. This is not the place to spell out the character and content of such a Christian philosophy, but only to draw attention to its necessity if the Catholic university is to realize the richness of its heritage and if its curriculum is to be coherent. Indeed, for such a university, it should be inescapable.

When it was suggested that the *data* offered by a liberal arts curriculum or by the other divisions and professional schools of the university should be the initial subject of philosophic questioning, a number of *fields* were designated in which assumptions, concepts, and methods could be isolated: literature, physics, history, etc. This was done because since the Renaissance, the common conception of humanistic studies is that of various fields, various subject matters, the command over which supplies a new humanization of the students. But as mentioned earlier, there is an older conception of humane education, one dating from the Middle Ages, that conceives the liberal arts as universal *disciplines,* as *skills* which can be applied to any subject matter or any field. Philosophic education within the liberal arts could function here as it functions with the more obviously recognized fields: isolate their assumptions and question them. Such a course in the Committee for the Analysis of Ideas and the Study of Methods at the University of Chicago, for example, explored the meaning of rhetoric as it moves from a pseudo-art in the *Gorgias,* to one of the universal arts in Aristotle, to the universal method of all philosophy in Cicero's influential textbook, *De inventione,* to furnish the scientific method for the *Novum organum* of Francis Bacon. Such an investigation of rhetoric—or any other of the methodological disciplines—would again reveal a pluralism of possibilities and the subsequent matter for an innovation and an organization of sciences and arts for this time—a task of proper philosophic inquiry.

Earlier, this chapter presented a threefold ambiguity within which philosophic instruction moved: the dichotomy between teacher and wisdom, between philosophy and wisdom, and between the student and wisdom. The evoking of philosophic questions out of the various areas of knowledge to which the students have already committed themselves might contribute towards the resolution of these antinomies. For, *pace* Wittgenstein, the teachers need not pretend to a competence in wisdom, but to a love embodied in desire that draws them continually to ask questions and to isolate the assumptions which underlie every human project. Further, philosophy does not surrender its subject matter, its methods, and its conclusions to the other forms of human knowledge, but indicates that each of these branches of knowledge presupposes those things that form the subject matter and issues of philosophy. In the end, the inability or disinterest among the students in the face of questions of ultimacy could yield before a program that moves through the students' own interests and life-long commitments to those great realities, as yet unexamined, by which these interests are evoked and by which these commitments are judged, purified, or justified.

The question whether the contemporary fragmentation of philosophy allows it an integrating role within the university—which constituted the initial problem of this essay—could be addressed by a program in which philosophy contacts the various disciplines in two generic ways. The coherence among the disciplines and between the disciplines and philosophy could be realized through the discovery of the common themes that form the presuppositions of the disciplines and through the examination of the meanings and validity of these themes as the object of properly philosophic inquiry.

Philosophic grammar brings the other disciplines together philosophically to forge not a systematic unity among them, but a thematic unity in their basic concepts, terms, methods, etc. Philosophic grammar yields a pluralism of meanings of major philosophic terms. Philosophic inquiries differentiate these into subject matters to be investigated. Divergent methods are framed by which these investigations are to be pursued and varying principles advanced by which these questions are resolved. The irreducible pluralism of issues, concepts, methods, projects, and interests found in all human disciplines explains the pluralism in philosophies and dictates that this pluralism is inevitable—part of the rich possibilities that go with the human. The unity between philosophy and the other disciplines is established from the beginning. These disciplines are the initial subject matter for philosophic grammar and they yield the objects that will constitute the questions for further inquiry.

The pluralism of philosophies does not suggest that all are equally right or useful; some are twisted and injurious. But it does suggest that there are philosophies both rich in the possibilities they offer to reflection and complementary in their relationship to one another. Pluralism is not the same as contradiction. This pluralism of philosophies suggests that the roads to wisdom are many and not self-contradictory and that wisdom's confirmation of itself in so many varied ways gives the lie to a relativism and a skepticism that would reduce this wisdom to ideology and arbitrary perspective.

Philosophy in Catholic universities has changed significantly. There is no longer the rule of a single philosophy that is uniquely "true" and in battle with the sorry errors that constitute so many works reviewed in the history of philosophy and that are present in other universities. The hegemony of Thomism to the exclusion of the systematic presence of other philosophical schools is past, and both the universities and Thomistic philosophy are the richer for its passing. But it would be tragic if the gains obtained from the retrieval of Thomistic philosophy and theology were lost in a new dogmatism. The historians and philosophers of the last centuries have opened for contemporary Catholic thought some of the riches of its heritage and, in particular, of medieval wisdom. Catholic thought would be much the poorer if it did not draw upon that wisdom for its own reflection, development, and philosophic instruction.

One last point for discussion: if the pluralism is not to become chaos, a department or faculty must choose a philosophic tradition or traditions in order to give continuity and coherence to its instruction. There must be some linguistic community and a methodological set of skills that the students learn if they are to progress through philosophic questions. There is not enough time to do everything. The department must foster some continuity and coherence from course to course if the student is to develop.

The department must, then, ask itself if in their common collaboration it would be possible to establish some philosophical communities within which it wishes to teach—something that would give them a common tradition, language, set of methods, and possibilities of student development, etc. Not that each professor would limit himself or herself to this community. A selection of a common linguistic and methodological community would not exclude the additional presence of other schools and, in particular, the philosophic inquiries, criticisms, and persuasions of the individual instructor. If, for example, the department chose two traditions, Lonerganian and analytic, then it would stipulate that one of these would be represented in any core course. But together with them, the instructor would be able to introduce (1) philosophers thought to be important on the issues to be treated and (2) the philosophic tradition the instructor represents or espouses. Both of these have a place together with the philosophic traditions chosen by the department to give its instruction continuity. Thus basic systematic courses would have both that philosophic continuity which allows for incremental development and that diversity which represents the pluralistic prodigality in the history and the contemporary practice of philosophy.

Is such a settlement—or some modification of it—possible?

CHAPTER NINE

Wisdom, Religion, and the Liberal Arts: Towards the Construction of Theology

What would happen if we had to pay our debts towards theology and the metaphysics of presence?

—George Steiner, *Real Presences*[1]

It is astonishing to register what is taking place in the study of theology within the United States. As never before, tens of thousands of undergraduate students in Catholic universities are devoting significant academic attention to the study of theology. As never before, thousands of lay women and laymen are doing graduate studies in theology and assuming their places in the theological leadership of the church. Both of these developments are unprecedented, and the promise they offer for the future richness of theology is enormous.

Both of these developments, however, demand more urgently that Catholic universities look carefully at the construction of theology. These students will significantly shape the theological reflection and professional theology done in this nation. The character of their contribution will depend in great part upon the theology to which they were introduced as undergraduates or which they were expected to assimilate as graduate students. If their theological education lacks an understanding of authentic theological inquiry, of solid evidence and sound argument, the results will tell very harmfully in the future. It could corrupt into fad or prejudice or ideology the self-understanding of the Christian mysteries that is theology. If the theology taught at Catholic universities is sound, disciplined, and enlightened, these characteristics will mark the work and influence of these quondam students.

The achievements of the rich theological tradition of Christianity can suggest ways in which such a development of theology can be fostered. For the accomplishment of genius is both resource and inspiration for any educational enterprise: resource, because achievement is an endless quarry from which the present can select and with which it will build; inspiration, because human greatness stands as the embodiment of value, as an abiding influence which draws and inspires later generations to their own achievements.

For the problem raised here, accomplishment does indicate what can be done, but it is important to remember that one never simply repeats the past. To attempt to repeat would be to play false even to that historical moment which was not itself the repetition of its predecessor. The past is not the present, nor can it be made to function for the urgencies and problems that are now. They are simply different kinds of time. But the foundational persuasion of any humanistic education is that the past does continue to exist and to instruct within the present.

It is in this context that one might consider the influence of the liberal arts upon the formation of theology, drawing from the time when both the liberal arts and theology had attained a remarkable development, the Middle Ages. Educators might garner from that period suggestions that would contribute both to the theological education of students within the Catholic university and to the advancement of theology itself as serious inquiry. Both of these bear upon the construction of theology, either as a set of academic habits or as the components that advance theological investigations.

In a remarkable essay, the late Richard P. McKeon once sketched something of the achievement of those who numbered among the greatest of this distinguished medieval assemblage, Bonaventure and Aquinas. He joined them in 1974 on the seven hundredth anniversary of their deaths not to demonstrate that one was right and the other wrong, but to indicate the extraordinary comprehension of both: the integration within their theologies of the divergent enterprises of science, history, and philosophy, the uniqueness, energies, and methodological strengths of each, and the complementarity of both. Professor McKeon called his outline an "inquiry" rather than an "exposition"; he presented it as an investigation which he invited others to join in order to discover the bearing of the works of these theologians upon the problematic of our times—not to study Saint Thomas or Saint Bonaventure, so much as to study under them.[2]

This chapter proposes to take up McKeon's invitation and to continue these reflections upon Catholic, Jesuit education. Specifically, it investigates what resources these two medieval masters and the epoch they represented so well provide for contemporary theology. How can one learn from them to strengthen theology as a discipline of higher education? The persuasion of these pages is that this can be done in at least three ways:

1. The restoration of theology within these universities as an architectonic knowledge, as a wisdom different from, yet in serious connection with, the other arts and sciences whose study occupies the university community.
2. The establishment within theological inquiry and education of universal theological arts, i.e., arts in the medieval sense of disciplines and methods, skills which permeate and are employed in all theological reflection: systematic, constructive, moral, ascetical, liturgical, comparative, and legal. Among these arts, already present and busy, are four: hermeneutics or semantics, methodology, philosophy, and history. Each of them particularizes for theology those liberal arts or *studia humanitatis* which have entered into liberal or humanistic education in general. Each of them is present and active whenever theology is well done.
3. The derivation of theological study out of the specifically religious inquiries of men and women, whether these emerge from the reach of other disciplines beyond themselves or more immediately from human questioning and longing. Academic theology must attend more seriously and more carefully to the occasions of its existence and vitality in the religious implications of any human inquiry or engagement and to the experience and desires of men and women.

Part One: Theology as Architectonic

It is a commonplace that thirteenth century theology was in vital contact with the sciences and arts of its time. Bonaventure and Aquinas maintained and insisted upon this contact, but did so in radically different ways, and in their differences one can perceive some small sample of the pluralism in Catholic theology.

Bonaventure "reduced"—led back—all of the sciences to theology and theology to the mystical union of God. This was not simply because for Bonaventure any knowledge which stopped short of God's revelation in Christ and which attempted completeness and autonomy was finally false. One cannot come to the knowledge of any finite thing unless through the Word of God through which and for which it was made.[3] Christ defines each thing in the universe. Thus theology must enter dialectically into each human inquiry and demonstrate that these kinds of knowledge were particularizations of the light which enlightens every human being and which drives human beings to discover various meanings—from artifacts to natural forms to intellectual truths to truths that save "because the multiform wisdom of God, which is lucidly taught in Sacred Scripture, is hidden in every knowledge and in every nature. . . . And it is also clear how full is this way of illumination and how in everything which is sensed or known, God Himself lies hidden within [*interius lateat ipse Deus*]."[4]

Sacred Scripture is the key to all knowledge because each thing in its deepest truth resembles the Word of God in which it was uttered, and so each thing can suggest both the ways in which human beings should live and the mystical union between God and the soul.[5] The organic unity of the sciences with theology in Bonaventure lies both in the illumination out of which they come and in Christ who is the *radix intelligentiae omnium*.[6] As Christ, the Incarnate Word of God, is the reality in which all things are created, so to know them in any depth is to know them in him. He is the medium of all sciences.[7] It would be difficult to exaggerate the centrality of Christ in Bonaventure.[8] He is the ultimate intelligibility or meaning of each thing—and so the inquiry of any science only reaches a definitive or stable grasp of its subject matter when it is found in its relationship to Christ, the integral subject of theology.[9]

Thomas Aquinas, in sharp contrast, distinguishes irreducibly among the sciences in terms of their proper subject matter, but his theology unites them without annihilating these distinctions. There was that theology which was metaphysics, whose essential function as first philosophy was the analytic examination and establishment of the initial presuppositions of all the other sciences: their initial assertions, axiomatic sets, foundational prerequisites, and primitive concepts.[10] There was that other theology that "pertained to" or, perhaps better translated, "belonged to" *sacra doctrina*. Its relationship with philosophy or the sciences was threefold:

In *sacra doctrina* we are able to employ philosophy in three ways. First, to demonstrate those things which are the preambles of faith, which it is necessary to know in faith, as those things which can be established by natural reasons about God, as for example that God is, that He is one, and other things of this type or whatever is established about either God or the human being in philosophy,

which faith presupposes. Secondly, to clarify [*notificandum*]—
through some resemblances—those things which are of faith, as
Augustine in his work *On the Trinity* employs resemblances taken
from philosophic teachings to clarify [*manifestandum*] the Trinity.
Thirdly, to resist those who speak against the faith, either by showing
those [objections] to be false or by showing that they are not necessary.[11]

What Aquinas is elaborating in the formation of this kind of theology
is an intimate unity between *sacra doctrina* and philosophic reflection. It
is done without a reduction of one to the other, a unity that would
constitute this second kind of theology, a theology that would belong to
sacra doctrina without simply identifying with it. In three or four different
ways, *sacra doctrina* catches up philosophic inquiry with itself. Philosophic reflection or science stands as the human propaedeutic to the
disclosures contained in sacred teaching; *sacra doctrina* conjoins the
philosophic to its own inquiries "to make more manifest" the intelligibility and truth of what is being taught as revealed; and finally *sacra doctrina*
judges the products of other inquiries as coordinate with or repugnant to
its own assertions, turning to philosophic investigation for the examination of these alternative positions.[12] *Sacra doctrina* in its use of philosophy generates "the theology that pertains to/belongs to *sacra doctrina*."
For Aquinas, theology integrates the work of the other sciences like a
medieval cathedral, not by merging or identifying with these sciences nor
by changing them simply into theology, but by giving them coordination
or coherence, a context in the radical orientation of the human person
toward truth, since it belongs to wisdom to give order and judgment.[13]

The point is not that either Bonaventure or Aquinas is uniquely
correct—the ambiguous vocabulary and divergent patterns of inquiry
suggest pluralism rather than simple contradiction. Both of them make
theology a different kind of inquiry from what we usually consider it to
be: an architectonic knowledge in serious and systematic sympathy with
the sciences and arts of their times. The *Summa theologiae* or the *Reductio artium ad theologiam* evince this contact, and still further possibilities
of ways in which such a conjunction could form are indicated within the
writings of their colleagues and successors.

This is not so much the case in contemporary theology—and not
because "knowledge has expanded beyond the possibility of a single
person to comprehend what is known." One suspects that this has been
the case for thousands of years. Rather, since the Renaissance, theology
has become more a "science," as opposed to a "wisdom": that is, a
specialized knowledge alongside of others, one knowledge among

many—sometimes forensic, sometimes constructive, often out of touch with scientific investigations or, at worst, finding itself either supplanted or more threatened than enriched by the new science. The physics and mathematics of the thirteenth century posed vital questions to theology as it touched upon the transcendence or simplicity of God, the nature of infinity, the character of the hypostatic union, etc. It would be difficult to trace a similar dialogue in the nineteenth century, as the location for Christian theology had often become the isolated seminary or the professional and self-sustaining divinity school, with textbooks as well as the practice of theology becoming more polemical and parochial, and theology simply feeding off theology, theology responding to other theologies.[14] Even today, despite the enormous changes within divinity studies, it remains true that, by and large, systematic theologians are relatively unimportant within American intellectual culture—that they neither enlighten nor contextualize vitally what the national culture is about—and that the "architectonic" has passed to sociology, education, and psychology, to novelists such as Thomas Mann or James Joyce, or to dialectical philosophies, hermeneutics, and whatever is left of attempts at the "unified sciences."

As a consequence, theology has not achieved a position of academic interchange and respect within American intellectual culture. Michael J. Lacey of the Woodrow Wilson International Center for Scholars has described the present situation as follows: "In my experience Catholic theology, indeed theology of any kind, has very little standing at all in this vast scholarly enterprise [of the American academic community]. For the most part theology is simply absent from the ongoing discussions and arguments that drive the disciplines at their topmost level. I doubt that five percent of the nearly 1300 scholars who have worked at the Wilson Center since it opened could identify by name any Catholic theologian of the twentieth century, and I am quite certain that fewer even than this have actually read theology."[15]

If this is true, then the retrieval of a vital contact and interchange between theology and the other disciplines and the rearticulation of the architectonic role of theology becomes a primary task for contemporary theological methodology. The urgency of this task increases as attempts are forthcoming to frame a theory adequate for Catholic higher education. How can theology engage the other disciplines, the arts and sciences, the various works of human beings? These essays have attempted to address this question very partially in the first thesis of chapter 2 arguing that these human projects constitute something of the problematic situation in which theology is to be done. But in no sense does that comment claim to be adequate or comprehensive.[16]

In attempting to frame a more adequate response, one will not repeat the solutions or even the metaphors ("queen of the sciences") of the times of Bonaventure and Aquinas because today's questions and intellectual culture are different. Contemporary theologians will move to a resolution structured by variant theological methodologies and occasioned by the unique cast of their problems. Much of the vitality and the energy of theology today should issue from the questions and concepts, the experiences and reflections that at first blush have nothing to do with theology, that emerge in the "secular" inquiries of human beings as they search into vastly different aspects of the human. Theology will obtain a depth of contact with the human even more effectively when it is mediated through the arts and sciences, mediated by study, discipline, and refinement.

Part Two: The Liberal Arts in Theology

All this, however, is not enough if theology is to exist as a serious academic knowledge. It must not only be related to the other sciences as source for its questions, but it must possess a reflective solidity about its own procedure which would insure the validity and soundness of its assertions. Another reason that so much constructive theology fails to tell upon contemporary culture may lie with the internal weakness of the discipline itself. Would it be unfair to maintain that some theologies rise as quickly as a passion and then as easily slip from presence and memory, that terms are often used casually and emotively, that hard evidence is often wanting or mingled indiscriminately with conclusions, that historical assertions are oversimplified to the point of parody, that current prejudices are rhetorically presented, and that sweeping generalizations are made whose warrant seems slender upon analysis? Where this does occur, what passes for theology is pathetically soft and there is little to wonder that it has not achieved the respect due a serious intellectual discipline.

In the Middle Ages, the development and application of the liberal arts—exegetical grammar, judicative rhetoric, with logic or dialectic—led to the formation of a theology, moving from the resolutions of discordant canons to the elaboration of *sententiae*, initially through the simple dialectic of the *Sic et non* and then through the learned compilations of Peter Lombard. Contemporary theology could well take a leaf from this history. Discussions of methodological reform within theology might learn from the development of those hundreds of years in which systematic theology was emerging in the Middle Ages. A new articulation and application of liberal arts to theology in the form of "theological arts" could perhaps steady and strengthen a discipline which often seems vague and inconsequential. This would not be to impose an a priori procedure upon theology, but to induce from current usages and to generalize what are already pervasive skills in the workings of the better theologians. These better practices need to be articulated, specified, established, regulated, and interrelated if theology is to deal in a careful, productive manner with serious meaning and truth.[17] One could list at least four such theological skills.

First, hermeneutics or semantics—what the Middle Ages often called grammar and what Marius Victorinus followed by Rabanus Maurus defined as the *scientia interpretandi*.[18] It is the primary ability to deal with structures of meaning, of symbols within their own context as well as within their effective histories and successive applications, and of literary form, so that poetic statement is not physics and mathematics is not theology. It is both the ability to receive and the ability to author, to read and to speak (write), in such a way that the symbols deliver meaning, that what is read or what is said "makes sense." This skill in interpretation is imperative not only for biblical criticism as *Formgeschichte* or *Redaktionsgeschichte*, but also for the writings of Fathers or councils and, through philosophical semantics, in the history of philosophic thought.[19] It is not a mastery of each of these fields, but a theological discipline which enables one to move through these texts with sensitivity and insight, looking for clues and pluralistic meanings within the abiding richness of statements, without simple-minded reduction of assertions to a single series of meanings or nonsense.

Second, methodology or argumentation. In the second book of his *Eruditio didascalica* or *Didascalicon*, Hugh of St. Victor collapses the distinction between rhetoric and dialectic to allow the former, Ciceronian understanding of rhetoric to emerge: an ability to investigate either by discovery or invention of arguments and to articulate, order, and revise what has been obtained.[20] In both Bonaventure and Aquinas, argumentation and its evidential basis are precise, and the question to be treated is carefully determined. Thus, each resolution is open to counter-argument on either the meaning of terms, the adequacy of evidence, or the movement of thought. Methodology as a pervasive art within theology should include, similarly, the ability to formulate appropriate questions, to establish or discover evidence, inquire into the implications and entailments of principles, evidence, and conclusions. In its better uses, it provides for a precision or modesty about what is asserted in consequence of the data given or the facts formulated.[21] Methodology as an art would not set out the various procedures of the diverse divisions within theology; that should be the function of the subject and problems of each. Nor does it indicate a mastery of each of these methods. It is, rather, a pervasive skill or a sensitivity to argument and to evidence, to the strength of conclusions and their warrants within data, and, negatively, to the substitutions of sophistry, pretensions, and empty claims.

Third, philosophy. Philosophy became in the Middle Ages the "art of arts and discipline of disciplines," and as a theological art it can still serve this analytic function of searching out the basic principles and assertions about reality which are presupposed whenever one puts a predicate upon a subject or engages in an action of freedom.[22] Theology, as any human enterprise, is ineluctably involved in philosophic commitments: in an ontology which distinguishes the real from the unreal or in an ethics which involves motive and value. The choice before the reflective mind is not whether such philosophic commitments will be present. They will always be present. Every human project has at least an implicit ontology and an implicit ethics. The choice is whether this abiding presence, this implicit ontology and ethics, will be attended to and articulated and open to education and correction. Philosophy, precisely as a skill, as an ability brought to bear upon significant discourse or valued action, is a disciplined ability to perceive and to investigate the ultimate dimensions of experience and things, of thought and intention, or of terms and categories either admitted or assumed.

And, finally, history: the ability to deal with change and sequence in human development, whether it be the history of a people or a church, the evolution of a concept like "person" or "substance," or the maturation of personal religious experience.[23] History as an art is not a mastery of one particular field or series of narrations, though it may be learned through such a mastery. It is, rather, a kind of consciousness which studies things, thoughts, and words in their development and possesses the skills and knowledge necessary to trace out that development. With such historical consciousness, one deals much more sensitively with themes, figures, and institutions in their complex and messy meanings as these work their way through diverse patterns of development and decline. It resists the inclination to take statements similarly framed as univocal and actions as simply repeated.

These basic four skills, taken in their generality from the liberal arts and particularized for theology, should obviously inform or be part of every theologian's work. They are not simply functional specialties which spell each other off in a concatenated progression of a single work, "successive stages in the process from data to results."[24] Not that they contradict the division of theology into functional specialties. What they attempt is quite different. They are skills employed simultaneously and in mutual involvement within inquiry that is significantly theological. As the prolonged schooling of Western Europe in the liberal arts led to the formulation of such theologies as one finds among medieval theologians, perhaps a careful formulation and adoption of theological arts could have a similar strengthening effect upon contemporary theology and, especially, on the introduction of students, both graduate and even undergraduate, to the doing of theology.[25]

Part Three: The Religious Question

Besides the implications of theology as a wisdom among other knowledges and the internal energizing of theology with carefully disciplined theological skills, there remain the context, the sensibilities and intentions, the inspiration and questions out of which theology arises. For Bonaventure and Aquinas, these were deeply religious: the desire of human beings to be with God, the human movement toward the ecstatic possession of God in contemplative love, and, in that love, to find and be in community with one another. One cannot help but note Bonaventure's way of affectivity, which Bonaventure himself contrasted to the speculative indifference of geometry: "Such is the knowledge which is taught in this book [Peter Lombard's *Liber sententiarum*]. For this knowledge aids faith, and faith is in the intellect in such a way that by its very nature it is oriented to move affectivity. And this is obvious. For the knowledge that Christ has died for us and similar knowledge moves a human being to love unless he is unmovable in his sins. This is not knowledge like that other, that the diameter is incommensurate with a side."[26]

Saint Thomas's answer reads differently, but it also placed *sacra doctrina*—God's teaching of human beings—within the context of the human religious orientation, the salvific movement of human beings toward God. Aquinas assigns the very necessity of this teaching to that graced orientation.[27] The focus of theology was principally upon God and only those aspects of human activity "through which a human being is ordered to the perfect knowledge of God, in which eternal happiness consists."[28]

Again, this is a focus that could well be redressed, not returned to the religious questions of the thirteenth century but integrated with the religious problematic of our own times, the contemporary search for God: "Where are you, my God? How shall we find you? How shall we find each other in you?" These searching questions, so characteristic of this century, may arise from different sources: the profound sense of exploitation and hopelessness worked in so many lives by economic injustice, the history of slaughter which this bloody century has written, the expanding possibilities raised by the biological, behavioral, and physical sciences, reflections upon the value of community and the experienced joy of living, etc. Life done in any depth spontaneously raises theological issues, but perhaps the religious inquiry that characterizes our age in the Western world is the quest for the silent, for the absent God. It embodies a longing that moves from early stages of religious interest and conversion to a dark and hidden contemplation that is deeper than human experience. It ranges over all religious mystery, from problems of faith through those of anguish and to the fulfillments of community and sanctity. This is the religious problematic that has elicited such interest in the study of religious experience and has retrieved the trinitarian dogma in order to appropriate God's self-giving in the communication that is part of human history and in the Spirit which transforms human interiority and forms the Christian community. The vocation of theology is not only to address such religious questions; it is to discover what they are.

*   *   *

Contemporary Catholic theology can find in the academic world and in the theological achievements of Bonaventure and Aquinas suggestions for the construction of theology today, an enterprise for which the Catholic university is peculiarly and uniquely suited: a theology that is in vital contact with the knowledges and works that human beings are about and so able to give integration to the university subjects in which these are represented, that is strengthened and energized through the disciplined employment of such permeating skills or theological arts as hermeneutics, methodology, philosophy, and history, and that would emerge from the religious sensibilities and issues of our own time, rising both to assimilate the richness and to meet the religious challenge that modernity and postmodernity present.

Notes

Preface

1. For the day of entrance, 31 August 1854, see Ernest Samuels, *The Young Henry Adams* (London: Oxford University Press, 1948), p. 8. Samuels records that such "noted alumni of that period as Charles W. Eliot, Phillips Brooks, and George Herbert Palmer have each claimed the distinction of having studied at Harvard during the feeblest moments of its history." For Adams' conditions of entrance, see Henry Adams, *The Education of Henry Adams*, ed. Ernest Samuels (Boston: Houghton Mifflin Company, 1973), ch. 4, pp. 54–55.

2. Adams, *Education,* ch. 20, pp. 299ff.

3. Ian Ker, *John Henry Newman: A Biography* (Oxford: Oxford University Press, 1990), p. 412.

4. Adams, *Education,* ch. 4, p. 55. Nor did his years as a professor—some twenty years later—lighten his judgment: "On the whole, he was content neither with what he had taught nor with the way he had taught it. The seven years he passed in teaching seemed to him lost." Ibid., ch. 20, p. 304.

5. Ibid., ch. 4, p. 64. "All went there because their friends went there, and the College was their ideal of social self-respect." Ibid., ch. 4, p. 54.

6. Ibid., ch. 4, p. 68.

7. Ibid., ch. 4, p. 63.

8. Ibid., ch. 4, pp. 56–58.

9. For a brief, summary history of those years in Ireland, see Martin J. Svaglic, "Introduction," in John Henry Newman, *The Idea of a University, Defined and Illustrated in Nine Discourses Delivered to the Catholics of Dublin, In Occasional Lectures and Essays Addressed to the Members of the Catholic University*, edited with an Introduction and Notes by Martin J. Svaglic (New York: Holt, Rinehart and Winston, 1966), pp. xii–xiv. The first edition of the *Idea of a University*, entitled *Discourses on the Scope and Nature of University Education, Addressed to the Catholics of Dublin*, appeared on 2 February 1853; the second edition, now entitled *The Scope and Nature of University Education*, appeared with significant editorial changes in 1859. Svaglic notes his indebtedness to two standard works on this subject: Fergal McGrath, S.J., *Newman's University: Idea and Reality* (London: Longmans, Green and Co., 1951) and A. Dwight Culler, *The Imperial Intellect* (New Haven: Yale University Press, 1955). For the critical edition of *The Idea of a University*, see I. T. Ker ed., *The Idea of a University* by John Henry Newman. (Oxford: Clarendon Press, 1976). References to *The Idea of a University* throughout this volume will be made from this critical edition. For the subsequent history of Newman's *University*, see this critical edition, p. xxvii-xxix and McGrath, pp. 490ff.

10. See Ker, ed., *The Idea of a University* by John Henry Newman, "Introduction," p. xxiv.

11. Adams, *Education*, ch. 29, pp. 429–430.

12. Newman, *The Idea of a University*, "Preface," p. 10.

13. Newman, *The Idea of a University*, Discourse II, #1, p. 33.

14. Steven Muller, "Universities Are Turning Out Highly Skilled Barbarians," *U.S. News and World Report*, 10 November 1980, p. 57.

15. Alexis de Tocqueville, *Democracy in America*, trans. Henry Reeve, translation revised by Francis Bowen, ed. Phillips Bradley (New York: Vintage, 1990), I: p. 317.

16. Georg Wilhelm Friedrich Hegel, *Phänomenologie des Geistes*, ed. Johannes Hoffmeister (Hamburg: Verlag von Felix Meiner, 1952), "Vorrede," p. 48.

17. The description of this kind of reflection belongs to Karl Rahner, *Foundations of Christian Faith*, trans. William V. Dych (New York: Crossroad, 1982), p. 1.

18. *Alexandrian Christianity*, selected translations of Clement and Origin with introduction and notes by John Ernest Leonard Oulton and Henry Chadwick (Philadelphia: Westminster Press, 1954), "General Introduction," pp. 16–17.

19. M.-D. Chenu, O.P., *Toward Understanding Saint Thomas*, translated with authorized corrections and bibliographical additions by A. M. Landry, O.P. and D. Hughes, O.P. (Chicago: Henry Regnery Company, 1964), pp. 91–92.

20. S. Thomae Aquinatis, *Quaestiones quodlibetales*, ed. Raymundo Spiazzi, O.P., (Taurini: Marietti, 1942): *Quodlibet* VI. *Quaestio* X. *"Utrum scilicet aliquis possit esse naturaliter vel miraculose simul virgo et pater,"* pp. 129–130; *Quodlibet* XII, *Quaestio* XIV. *"Utrum veritas sit fortior inter vinum et regem et mulierem,"* p. 238.

Chapter One: The Catholic University and the promise inherent in its Identity

1. This statement was found in Maclean's files after his death along with other notes that he had written for a preface; see "Publisher's Note," *Young Men and Fire* (Chicago: The University of Chicago Press, 1992), p. xiii.

2. Hastings Rashdall, *The Universities of Europe in the Middle Ages*, new edition edited by F.M. Powicke and A.B. Emden (Oxford: Clarendon Press, 1936), I: 219.

3. David R. Carlin Jr., "From Ghetto to Hilltop: Our Colleges, Our Selves," *Commonweal* 2 February 1993, p. 7.

4. For David O'Brien's diagnosis, see his *From the Heart of the American Church* (Maryknoll: Orbis, 1994) as well as chapter 3 of this present volume.

Among those whom O'Brien crowds together into—what one might call—a camp of critical concern are Philip Gleason, James Burtchaell, C.S.C., Peter Steinfels, Avery Dulles, S.J., Kenneth J. Woodward, and Michael J. Buckley, S.J., however differently the constituents of this group line up in the contemporary discussions within the church and the academy. The third chapter hopes to bring into some precision what disagreement lies among them.

5. The magisterial study of this decline in the denominationally affiliated universities in the United States is, of course, found in George M. Marsden, *The Soul of the American University: From Protestant Establishment to Established Nonbelief* (New York: Oxford University Press, 1994).

6. Friedrich Nietzsche, *Die Fröhliche Wissenschaft* iii. 125. in *Nietzsche Werke*. Kritische Gesamtausgabe, herausgegeben von Giorgio Colli und Mazzino Montinari, Fünfte Abteilung, Zweiter Band (Berlin: Walter de Gruyter, 1973), p. 160. ET: *The Gay Science*, trans. by Walter Kaufman (New York: Random House, 1974), p. 182.

7. Robert M. Hutchins, "The Integrating Principle of Catholic Higher Education," address delivered at the Midwest Regional Unit of the College and University Department of the National Catholic Educational Association, 7 April 1937, *College Newsletter, Midwest Regional Unit, N.C.E.A.* (May 1937), pp. 1, 4. Hutchins' description of collegiatism runs "the production of well-tubbed young Americans. They don't have much in their heads, but are acceptable as decoration of at least one political party and make good additions to a house-party."

8. Sigmund Freud, *The Future of an Illusion*, trans. James Strachey (New York: W.W. Norton and Company, Inc., 1961), p. 6.

9. Ignatius of Loyola used this metaphor—"*como gota de agua que entra en una esponja*"—to denote the gradual, almost unnoticeable progress of either disintegration or of development. See "Rules for Discernment of Spirits for the Second Week," II.7. #335 in *The Spiritual Exercises*. The Spanish text of the *Exercises* referenced in this volume by paragraph numbers is the "Autograph" [A] as found in *Monumenta Historica Societatis Iesu* (vol. 100), *Monumenta Ignatiana*, series secunda, nova editio, tomus I, *Exercitia spiritualia*, ed. Joseph Calveras, S.I. and Candidus de Dalmases, S.I. (Romae: Institutum Historicum Societatis Iesu, 1969) [Henceforth: *SpEx*]; ET: *The Spiritual Exercises of St. Ignatius*, translation and commentary by George E. Ganss, S.J. (St. Louis: The Institute of Jesuit Sources, 1992). Throughout the following book, when any cited English translation is changed, this modification will be indicated by (m).

10. John Paul II, *Ex corde Ecclesiae*, Part II ("General Norms"), Article 2, #3. The Latin text of this Apostolic Constitution can be found in the *Acta Apostolicae Sedis* vol. 82: no. 13 (3 Decembris 1990): pp. 1475–1509. ET: *Origins* 20, no.17 (4 October, 1990): pp. 265–276.

11. See "Jesuits Today," decree 2 of the Thirty-Second General Congregation of the Society of Jesus, #1–3; "Our Mission Today," decree 4 of the Thirty-Second General Congregation, passim, in *Documents of the 31st and 32nd*

General Congregations of the Society of Jesus, An English Translation. Prepared by the Jesuit Conference and edited by John W. Padberg, S.J. (St. Louis: The Institute of Jesuit Sources, 1977).

12. William P. Leahy, S.J., *Adapting to America: Catholics, Jesuits, and Higher Education in the Twentieth Century* (Washington, D.C.: Georgetown University Press, 1991), p. 16.

13. William B. Neenan, S.J., "A Catholic/Jesuit University?" in *Finding God in All Things*, ed. Michael J. Himes and Stephen J. Pope (New York: Crossroad, 1996), p. 305. Neenan is referring to the analysis conducted by Marsden, *The Soul of the American University.*

14. Timothy Healy, S.J., "Belief and Teaching," *Georgetown Magazine* (January–February 1982): p. 3 [emphasis added].

15. "Belief and Teaching," pp. 4–5. One of the five ways the Church can shape the university is through the presence of theology, but the value of theology seems mostly therapeutic: academic theology challenges absolute science, absolute art, absolute athletics, etc., and denies the completeness of any of kinds and subsets of learning. See pp. 6–7.

16. Charles F. Donovan, S.J., "Rev. Timothy Brosnahan, S.J., Boston College President, 1894–1898, National Spokesman for Jesuit Liberal Education," *Occasional Papers on the History of Boston College,* (September 1996) pp. 7–9.

17. Charles F. Donovan, S.J., David R. Dunigan, S.J., Paul A. FitzGerald, S.J., *History of Boston College From the Beginnings to 1990* (Chestnut Hill, Mass: The University Press of Boston College, 1990), p. 99.

18. O'Brien, *From the Heart of the American Church*, p. 97.

19. Another such positive vector is the growing commitment to the service of the oppressed and marginated within this nation and the world by the number of students who give some years after graduation to religious volunteer groups. For the need to include within the liberal or humanistic education of the student a "disciplined sensitivity to human life in its very ordinary or even wretched forms," as a foundational stage towards a sense of human solidarity, see chapter 6.

20. For this "nominal" definition of God, see Thomas Aquinas, *Summa theologiae* I.2.3.

21. John Paul II, "The Church Needs the University," 8 March, 1982 *L'Osservatore Romano*, English edition, 3 May 1982, p. 6. ET: modified.

22. *Gravissimum educationis* #8. The actual Latin of this text from the decree of Vatican II that gives the finality of all Catholic education reads: "*universam culturam humanam ad nuntium salutis postremo ordinare.*" Joseph Alberigo et al., ed., *Conciliorum oecumenicorum decreta*, editio 3 (Bologna: Instituto per le scienze religose, 1973), p. 964, lines 28–29. ET: Norman P. Tanner, S.J., ed., *Decrees of the Ecumenical Councils* (Washington, D.C.: Georgetown University Press, 1990), II: pp. 963–964 (m).

23. Blaise Pascal, *Pensées*, #548, ed. L. Brunschvieg (Paris: Librairie Hachette, 1920), p. 572. Cited and translated by Étienne Gilson, "The Intelligence in the Service of Christ the King," in *A Gilson Reader: Selections from the Writings of Étienne Gilson*, edited with an introduction by Anton C. Pegis (Garden City, New York: Image Books, 1957), pp. 34–35.

24. For the normative text of the Council of Chalcedon, see Denzinger-Schönmetzer, *Enchiridion Symbolorum*, editio xxxv (Friburgi: Herder, 1973), #302.

25. Gerard Manley Hopkins, S.J., "The Wreck of the Deutschland," in *The Hopkins Reader*, ed. John Pick (New York: Oxford University Press, 1953), xxix, p. 11.

26. Porphyry of Tyre, *On the Life of Plotinus and the Arrangement of His Work, #8. GT: Plotin*, texte établi et traduit par Émile Bréhier, troisième édition (Paris: Société d'édition "Les Belles Lettres," 1960), p. 11; ET (m): *Plotinus, The Enneads*, trans. Stephen MacKenna, ed. B.S. Page (New York: Pantheon Books Inc., 1957), p. 7. It should be noted that Porphyry is descibing Plotinus' mental concentration, not his social, ethical or religious commitments.

27. D. Iunii Iuvenalis, *Satirae*, with a literal English prose translation and notes by John Delaware Lewis (London: Trübner and Co., 1873), Satira X, linea 356: "*Orandum est ut sit mens sana in corpore sano.*" Horace, Liber II, Sermo 7, 1. ll. 85–86 in Horace's *Complete Works*, ed. Charles Bennett and John C. Rolfe (Boston: Allyn and Bacon, 1934), II. 60. For the reference to the *Iliad*, cf. bk. VI, line 208; bk xi line 784.

28. This is a slightly reworked statement from Buckley, "The Catholic University as Pluralistic Forum," *Thought* 46 (June 1971): p. 208. This statement is also repeated in "Jesuit, Catholic Higher Education: Some Tentative Theses," *Review for Religious* 42 (May–June 1983): p. 343 as well as in a report on the nature of a Catholic university, given to the members of the Academic and Faculty Affairs Committee of the Board of Trustees of the University of Notre Dame on 2 May 1991. For the conjunction of this with some of the areas in which this purpose is obtained, see the first draft of the Mission Statement of the University of Notre Dame as printed in *The Observer*, Monday, 7 September 1992, pp. 6–7.

29. See Buckley, "Jesuit Catholic Higher Education: Some Tentative Theses," pp. 343–344.

30. See note #9. The Apostolic Constitution, *Ex corde Ecclesiae*, has an Introduction and two major divisions. The Introduction, composed of paragraphs 1 to 11, can be cited by simple reference to these numbered paragraphs; Part I, "Identity and Mission," composed of paragraphs 12 to 49, can be similarly cited by reference to these numbered paragraph; Part II, "General Norms," must be cited by Article and numbered paragraph, e.g. [GN. Art 1. #2]. Because the references to the Apostolic Constitution are so numerous in this section of chapter 1, these references are placed in square brackets directly in the text.

31. This chapter does not touch upon the canonical declarations and norms of *Ex corde Ecclesia*. For a fine analysis of these, see James H. Provost, "The

Canonical Aspects of Catholic Identity in the Light of *Ex corde Ecclesiae*," *Studia canonica* 25 (1991), pp. 155–191.

32. Leahy, *Adapting to America*, p. 156.

Chapter Two: The Church and its Responsibility to Foster Knowledge

1. John Paul II, "The Church Needs the University," 8 March 1982, *L'Osservatore Romano*, English edition (3 May 1982), p. 6.

2. See the remarks of Ian G. Barbour, *Issues in Science and Religion* (Englewood Cliffs, New Jersey: Prentice-Hall, 1966), pp. 44–48. The matter can be framed through a simple parable of the late Joseph Wall: If a young man loves a woman, he may show his love by giving her a ring. Now there are many things that the woman can do. The most vicious would be to take the ring and forget the love that is behind it. That would be the most vicious—but it would not be the most stupid. The most stupid thing she could do would be to think that the ring and the man were in competition—that it was not a sacrament of his love but its competition—and that somehow or other she could show her love for him by denigrating the ring: "What a lousy piece of metal—only an eight carat diamond—how little worth it has compared with you, honey!" One does not enhance one's relationship with God by despising or ignoring the gifts that God has given as a pledge of an eternal love.

3. R.S. Crane, "Criticism as Inquiry; or The Perils of the 'High Priori Road,'" *The Idea of the Humanities* (Chicago: The University of Chicago Press, 1967), vol. II, p. 30.

4. Constantin James was the author of a number of books against Darwin. Pius IX wrote to thank the author for the gift of one of these and to congratulate him on "the work in which you refute so well the aberrations of Darwinism." James published this letter in *L'Hypnotisme expliqué dans sa nature et dan ses actes et Mes Entretiens avec S. M. L'Empereur Don Pédro sur le Darwinisme* (Paris: Librairie de la Société Bibliographique, 1888), pp. 84–85. These two works are published together and under the combined title indicated here. This text is translated and included in Philip Appleman, ed., *Darwin: A Norton Critical Edition* (New York: W.W. Norton and Company, Inc., 1970), p. 536n2. This book of James', very difficult to track down, was finally located in the Cornell University Library. It is interesting to record that the bookplate inside the inner cover indicates its prior ownership by President Andrew Dickson White—he of *A History of the Warfare of Science with Theology in Christendom* (New York: D. Appleton and Company, 1896) fame. White deals with this letter extensively on page 75 of the first volume of this polemic against theology. Despite the negative evaluation by the Pope, Darwin's work was never placed on the Index, though one of his followers, Emile Ferrière, managed to secure a place for seven of his books in 1892. See the decree of the Sacred Congregation of the Index dated 7 April 1892, in the *Acta Sanctae Sedis*, studio et cura Victorii

Piazzesi, vol. XXIV (Romae: S. Cong. de Propaganda Fide, 1891–1892), pp. 575–576.

5. *De revolutionibus orbium* simply disappeared from the list when the revised edition of the Index was published by Benedict XIV in 1758, while Galileo had to wait until after the French Revolution and the book lost this censure only in 1822. See articles on Copernicus and Galileo in *The New Catholic Encyclopedia* (Washington, D.C.: The Catholic University of America, 1967), vols. 4 and 6.

6. *"Monitum,"* 30 June 1962, in *Acta SS. Congregation. Suprema Sacra Congregatio S. Officii,* in *Acta Apostolicae Sedis* vol. LIV. (Ser. III, v. IV). N.1 (31 January 1962), p. 526. It is ironic to note that the same fasicule of *AAS* that carried this *monitum* from the Holy Office bore the Apostolic Constitution of John XXIII, *Humanae salutis,* calling for the Second Vatican Council.

7. See Richard J. Blackwell, *Galileo, Bellarmine, and the Bible* (Notre Dame: University of Notre Dame Press, 1991), pp. 234f. and 68. The scriptural reference is Joshua 10:12–13.

8. Henry Edward Cardinal Manning, "On the Subjects Proper to the Academia," in *Essays on Religion and Literature,* ed. H. E. Manning (London: Longman, Green, Longman, Roberts, & Green, 1865), p. 51; cited by Andrew Dickson White in *Warfare* (p. 71) and this is excerpted in *Darwin*, p. 364n1, but both are without adequate information. This set of essays, edited by Manning, should not be confused with the second volume that appeared in 1867.

9. Newman to E.B. Pusey 5 June 1870, *The Letters and Diaries of John Henry Newman,* edited with notes and an introduction by Charles Stephen Dessain and Thomas Gornall, S.J., *The Vatican Council, January 1870 to December 1871,* vol. XXV (Oxford: Clarendon Press, 1973), pp. 137–138.

10. *Stromateis* VI. 89 as cited in *Alexandrian Christianity,* p. 19. Clement compares them to the companions of Odysseus as they passed the Sirens, "they stop up their ears because they know that if they once allow themselves to listen to Greek learning they will not be able afterwards to find their way home again." (*Stromateis* VI. 89) Ibid.

11. Gita May, *Madame Roland and the Age of Revolution* (New York: Columbia University Press, 1970), p. 288.

12. John Searle, in his "The Battle over the University," noted the general lack of a coherent theory of undergraduate education and spoke with amazement of one of the most recent and best attempts to build such a theory, *The Voice of Liberal Learning* by the English philosopher Michael Oakeshott, ed., Timothy Fuller (New Haven: Yale University Press, 1989):

Perhaps the biggest single weakness of his conception of education is in the peripheral status it assigns to the natural sciences. The natural sciences do not fit his model, because, for the most part, the world of the natural sciences is not a world of meanings. It is a world of things; it is a world of entities, such as molecules or quarks, and forces, such as gravitational attraction or electromagnetic radiation. . . . But, like it or not, the natural sciences are perhaps our greatest single intellectual achievement as human beings, and any education that neglects this fact is to that extent defective. [*The New York Review of Books* 37, no. 19 (6 December 1990): p. 41.]

13. For this and the previous paragraph, see Michael J. Buckley, S.J., *At the Origins of Modern Atheism* (New Haven: Yale University Press, 1987), p. 325.

14. Quoted from Andrew Dickson White, "The Final Effort of Theology," in Appleman, ed., *Darwin* p. 364.

15. Werner Heisenberg, *Physics and Beyond: Encounters and Conversations* (New York: Harper and Row, 1971), p. 82. See Michael J. Buckley, S.J., "Religion and Science: Paul Davies and John Paul II," *Theological Studies,* 51, no. 2 (June 1990): pp. 311–312.

16. Paul Davies, *God and the New Physics* (New York: Simon and Schuster, 1983), p. ix. See Dan Wakefield, "And Now, a Word from our Creator," *New York Times Book Review* Feb. 12, 1989, pp. 1 and 28–29.

17. Stephen W. Hawking, *A Brief History of Time* (Toronto: Bantam Books, 1988), pp. 121–122. See Ian Barbour, *Religion in an Age of Science* (San Francisco: Harper and Row, 1990), p. 135.

18. Colossians 1:16–17.

19. Thomas Aquinas, *Summa theologiae* II–II. 1.1.

20. Ibid., II–II. 1.4. ad 2.

21. Ibid., II–II. 1. 4. ad 3. "*Lumen fidei facit videre ea quae creduntur.*"

22. Ibid., II–II. 1. 3.

23. Ibid., II–II. 1.3. ad 1: "*Cum fides perficiat intellectum . . .*"

24. 2 Thessalonians 2: 10.

25. William James, *The Varieties of Religious Experience* (New York: Penguin, 1987—reprinted from the standard edition of Longmans, Green, and Co., 1902), lecture II, p. 34.

26. Simone Weil, "Spiritual Autobiography," *Waiting for God* (1902; reprint, New York: Harper and Row, 1973), p. 69.

27. John Henry Newman, "Christianity and Scientific Investigation," *The Idea of a University*, p. 375.

28. See Karl Rahner, *Foundations of Christian Faith: An Introduction to the Idea of Christianity*, trans. by William V. Dych (New York: Crossroad, 1982), p. 152.

Chapter Three: A Conversation with a Friend

1. Geoffrey H. Hartman, *The Fateful Question of Culture* (New York: Columbia University Press, 1997), p. 173.

2. T. S. Eliot, "Ash Wednesday," IV, in T. S. Eliot, *The Complete Poems and Plays 1909–1950* (New York: Harcourt Brace & World, Inc., 1952), p. 64.

3. Peter Steinfels, "Commencement Address," Fordham University, 1992.

4. See Matthew 13:47–50.

5. "*Amicitia vera desiderat videre amicum, et colloquiis mutuis gaudere facit, ad quem principaliter est amicitia.*" *In III sent.* 27. 2. 1. ad 11.

Chapter Four: Ignatius' Understanding of the Jesuit University

1. *Constitutiones* IV. 11. 1. #440. The text of the *Constitutions* and of the *General Examen* is taken from the three-volume edition found in the *Monumenta Historica Societatis Iesu, Monumenta Ignatiana*, series tertia, Sancti Ignatii de Loyola, *Constitutiones Societatis Iesu* (Roma: Gregoriana, 1934, 1936, 1938). The Spanish text ["D"] is found in the second volume (64), and the Latin text in the third volume (65). In general, when the Spanish or Latin text of the *Constitutions* is cited, the reference for this citation is indicated by *"Constitutiones"* with the language indicated in the text; when the English translation is cited or when reference is made to the *Constitutions* without citation, this is indicated by *"Constitutions"*. When it is necessary to refer to a volume of the *Monumenta's* edition of the *Constitutions*, the Spanish volume is referenced as *ConsMHSI*, II and the Latin volume as *ConsMHSI*, III. ET: *The Constitutions of the Society of Jesus*, translated with an introduction and commentary by George E. Ganss, S.J. (St. Louis: Institute of Jesuit Sources, 1970). The paragraph enumeration in this edition has become standard since 1949 and is found in the *Societatis Iesu Constitutiones et Epitome Instituti* (Roma: Apud curia Praepositi Generalis, 1949). See Ganss, *Constitutions*, p. 39.

2. Hans-Georg Gadamer, *Truth and Method*, second revised edition, translation revised by Joel Weinsheimer and Donald G. Marshall (New York: Crossroad, 1989), pp. 306–307, 369–379.

3. Ibid., p. 290.

4. *Project 1: The Jesuit Apostolate of Education in the United States*, published by the staff of the Jesuit Conference (St. Louis: American Assistancy Seminar, 1975), volume #5, pp. 194–195.

5. The *Ratio studiorum* is the successively revised Jesuit plan of studies, an organization of curricula and of instructional methods rather than an exposition of educational theory. The central redaction is that of 1599. For the nature and history of this massively influential work, see Allan P. Farrell, S.J., *The Jesuit Code of Liberal Education: Development and Scope of the Ratio Studiorum* (Milwaukee: The Bruce Publishing Company, 1938).

6. Paul F. Grendler, *Schooling in Renaissance Italy: Literacy and Learning, 1300–1600* (Baltimore: The Johns Hopkins University Press, 1989), p. 363.

7. Ibid., p. 379. For a splendid history of this development, to which this chapter is much indebted, see John W. O'Malley, S.J., *The First Jesuits* (Cambridge, Mass.: Harvard University Press, 1993), pp. 200–242.

8. O'Malley, *First Jesuits*, pp. 206–208.

9. See O'Malley, *First Jesuits*, p. 203; Grendler, *Schooling*, p. 363–364.

10. O'Malley, *First Jesuits*, pp. 205, 233–234; Grendler, *Schooling*, pp. 79–80. Grendler speaks of the Roman College as "the famous school that became the heart of Catholic intellectual renewal."

11. *Constitutions* IV. 5. 1. #351–353. It is interesting to note the change from this subsumption of humane letters under "grammar" and "rhetoric" to that given in the provisions for the universities. For the nature of "positive theology," see pp. 98–99.

12. *Constitutiones* IV. 5. 1. #351.

13. *Constitutiones* IV. 7. 1. #392.

14. *Constitutions* IV. 7. B. #394. For the phrase, "the universities of the Society," see also *Constitutions* IV. 11. 1. #440; IV. 12. 1. #446; IV.15. D. #477, IV. 16. 1. #481.

15. O'Malley, *First Jesuits*, p. 205; Grendler, *Schooling*, pp. 79–80. The *"gratis"* indicated that this school, like every other Jesuit school of the time, charged no tuition. It was this provision that would allow them to serve all classes within society and which won for them a good deal of trouble.

16. Grendler, *Schooling*, pp. 377–381.

17. See Ganss, *Constitutions*, p. 210n1. For the history of the composition of these sections and their insertion into *Constitutions*, see *ConsMHSI*, II, pp. lxv–lxxiii.

18. *ConsMHSI*, II. clxiv.

19. *ConsMHSI*, II. clxv.

20. *SpEx*, p. 118; Pietro Tacchi Venturi, S.J., *Storia della Compañia di Gesù in Italia* (Roma: Civiltà Cattolica, 1950) II. 2: p. 272; James Brodrick, S.J., *Saint Peter Canisius*, (Chicago: Loyola University Press, 1962), p. 118; Georg Schurhammer, *Francis Xavier: His Life, His Times*, trans. Joseph Costelloe (Rome: The Jesuit Historical Institute, 1973), I: p. 239; Riccardo G. Villoslada, S.J., *Storia del Collegio Romano dal suo inizio (1551) alla soppressione della Compagnia di Gesù (1773)* (Roma: Gregoriana, 1954), passim. For a judicious estimation of the influence of Polanco, see O'Malley, *First Jesuits;* pp. 7, 335, 352, and 360.

21. Cited in O'Malley, *First Jesuits*, p. 209. O'Malley indicates that at the origins of this commitment, many pragmatic motives mingled with this conviction expressed by Ribadeneira, but that as the Jesuit program progressed "it increasingly subscribed to the educational faith enunciated so forcefully by Ribadeneira," p. 210.

22. *Constitutions* IV. 11. 1. #440 (m).

23. *Constitutiones* VII. 2. D #622d: *"Porque el bien quanto más vniuersal es más diuino."* cf. Ibid., #622a, #623a, #623f.

24. *Constitutions* IV 11.1. #440.

25. *Constitutions* IV. "Preamble," #307(m). One should compare this with Augustine's emphasis upon grammar and rhetoric in *De Doctrina Christiana*.

26. John O'Malley, S.J., "The Jesuit Educational Enterprise in Historical Perspective," *Jesuit Higher Education: Essays on an American Tradition of Excellence*, ed. Rolando E. Bonachea (Pittsburgh: Duquesne University Press, 1989), p. 15.

27. For the origin and meaning of *universitas*, see Rashdall, *Universities of Europe*, I: pp. 4–7. As Rashdall remarks: "Paris and Bologna are the two archetypal—it might almost be said the only *original* universities: Paris supplied the model for the universities of masters, Bologna for the universities of students."

Ibid., p. 17. For Newman's use of that term, see Newman, *Idea of a University*, Discourse II, p. 15.

28. *Constitutions* IV. 12. George Ganss explains: "'The arts' is Ignatius' term to designate the branches taught in his higher faculty of philosophy: logic, physics, metaphyhsics, moral philosophy, and some mathematics." *Constitutions*, p. 191n5.

29. Ganss, *Saint Ignatius' Idea of a Jesuit University*, 2nd edition, rev. (Milwaukee: Marquette University Press, 1956) pp. 46–51, 68–73; Ganss, *Constitutions*, p. 214n5.

30. *Constitutions* IV. 15. 1-A. #471–472.

31. *Constitutions* IV. 15. 2. #473.

32. *Constitutions* IV. 15. 3. #476.

33. Mario Scaduto, S.J., *L' epoca di Giacomo Lainez–L'azione* (Roma: La Civilitá Cattolica, 1974), pp. 280–281. Each of these initial years registered a significant increase in students, but the proportions in the various faculties did not change that much. Scaduto notes, for example, that in the previous academic year, the entire student body had numbered six hundred with fifty in theology, two hundred in philosophy, and the remaining students in humane letters.

34. James K. Farge, *Orthodoxy and Reform in Early Reformation France: The Faculty of Theology of Paris 1500–1543* (Leiden: E. J. Brill, 1985), pp. 11–16.

35. Ibid., pp. 34–36.

36. Ibid., p. 37.

37. Ibid., p. 37.

38. Pierre Imbart de La Tour, *Les origines de la Réforme*, 3 (Paris, 1914), p. 206. As cited in Farge, *Orthodoxy and Reform*, p. 1.

39. Jean Bochard is quoted in César-Egasse Du Boulay, *Historia Universitatis Parisiensis* 6 (Paris, 1673; reprint Frankfurt-am-Main, 1966), p. 179. Cited by Farge, *Orthodoxy and Reform*, p. 1.

40. *Constitutions* IV. 12. 4. #452.

41. Ganss, *Constitutions*, p. 215n6.

42. *Constitutions* IV. 12. 1. #446.

43. *Constitutions* IV. 5. A & B. #352–353: Referring to these colleges, Ignatius wrote: "In addition to grammar, rhetoric is understood to be under the classification of humane letters." For the changes wrought on grammar and rhetoric as they passed from the Middle Ages into the Quatrocento beginnings of the Renaissance, see Grendler, pp. 162–193, 203–234.

44. *Constitutions* IV. 12. 2. #447–448 (m).

45. See Grendler, *Schooling*, pp. 117–141.

46. *Constitutions* IV. 12. A. #448. I am grateful to John O'Malley, S.J., for pointing out that inclusive nature of grammar and rhetoric in the designation of the curriculum of the colleges.

47. O'Malley, *First Jesuits*, p. 210

48. *Constitutions* IV. 12. C. #451.

49. *Constitutions* IV. 12. 3. #450.

50. O'Malley, *First Jesuits*, p. 226.

51. *Constitutiones* IV. 12. 1. #446.

52. *Constitutiones* IV. 12. 2. #447.

53. *Constitutiones* IV. 12. 3. #450.

54. The "Spiritual Exercises" can denote either a thirty-day structured period of solitary prayer, meditation, and contemplation on the mysteries of the life of Christ, made in order to find the direction of God in one's life, or the book in which this structure is delineated. The *Exercises* came out of Ignatius' own religious development and articulate that experience programmatically. Both the *Exercises* and the themes that emerge from it have exercised a profound influence upon the members of the Society of Jesus. For the text of the *Spiritual Exercises*, p. 185n9.

55. *Constitutions* IV. 11. 1. #440; IV. 12. 1. #446.

56. *Constitutions* IV. 12. 1. #446; IV. 14. 1. #464; IV. 14. C. #467.

57. *Constitutions* IV. 14. B. #466.

58. *Constitutiones* IV. 12. 1. #446.

59. *Constitutions* IV. 12. 1. #446.

60. Aristotle, *Metaphysics*, V, 1, 1013a14; *Ethics*, I, 1, 1094a14, 27; VI, 8, 1141b22, 25; *Physics*, II, 2, 194b2; *Politics*, III, 11, 1282a3; *Poetics*, 19, 1456b11. Immanuel Kant, *The Critique of Pure Reason*, II, "Transcendental Doctrine of Method," chap. 3, "The Architectonic of Pure Reason," A 832/B 860.

61. John Keats, "On First Looking into Chapman's Homer," and "Ode to a Nightingale." *The Poetical Works of John Keats*, ed. H. Buxton Forman (New York: Thomas Y. Crowell & Co., 1895), pp. 47, 295.

Chapter Five: Humanism and Jesuit Theology

1. *Constitutiones* X. para 3. #814.

2. Paul O. Kristeller, "The Humanist Movement," in *Renaissance Thought and Its Sources*, ed. Michael Mooney (New York: Columbia University Press, 1979), pp. 21–22.

3. Paul O. Kristeller, "Humanism and Scholasticism in the Italian Renaissance," in *Renaissance Thought and Its Souces*, p. 99. "Renaissance humanism was not as such a philosophical tendency or system, but rather a cultural and educational program which emphasized and developed an important but limited area of studies. This area had for its center a group of subjects that was concerned essentially neither with the classics nor with philosophy, but might be roughly described as literature. It was to this peculiar literary preoccupation that the very intensive and extensive study which the humanists devoted to the Greek and especially to the Latin classics owed its peculiar character, which differentiates it from that of modern classical scholars since the second half of the eighteenth century." Kristeller, "The Humanist Movement," pp. 22–23.

4. Kristeller, "Humanism and Scholasticism in the Italian Renaissance," p. 91.

5. Kristeller, "The Humanist Movement," p. 22.

6. The first English translation of this work, done by Margot Adamson, was published as *True Humanism* (New York: Charles Scribner's Sons, 1938). Maritain professed himself "pleased neither with this title nor with the translation" [*Reflections on America* (New York: Charles Scribner's Sons, 1958), p. 174n2]. A second English translation was done by Joseph W. Evans in 1973 and published as *Integral Humanism* (Notre Dame: University of Notre Dame Press, 1973). In the second publication of this work, Maritain took the occasion to respond to the criticism of Louis Mercier and to make a "small number of corrections of detail" p. xi. This translation was revised by Otto Bird and published as volume 11 in *The Collected Works of Jacques Maritain* (Notre Dame: University of Notre Dame Press, 1996). The citations to this work are taken from this edition.

Humanisme intégral has been cited frequently as a major source for the Christian Democratic Movement in South America and figures as an important source of the social doctrine of Paul VI. Whatever disagreement is expressed in this book with Maritain's reading of Jesuit theology in no way equals the profound respect that the author has for so great a philosopher and for this very important book.

7. Maritain, *Integral Humanism*, p. 163.

8. Ibid., pp. 163–164.

9. Ibid., pp. 164–165.

10. Ibid., p. 166.

11. Ibid., p. 250.

12. Ibid., p. 250 [emphasis added].

13. Ibid., p. 250.

14. Ibid., p. 250.

15. For the origins and development of this aphorism, reaching absolutely contradictory statements, see C. A. Kneller, S.J., "Ein Wort des hl. Ignatius von Loyola," *Zeitschrift für Aszese u. Mystik* (1928): pp. 253–257; Augustine G. Ellard, S.J., "So Trust in God as if . . . ," *Review for Religious* 12 (1953), pp. 9–14.

16. Maritain, *Integral Humanism*, p. 169. [emphasis added].

17. The *De Auxiliis* controversy denotes a series of debates between the followers of Dominco Bañez, O.P., and the defenders of the orthodoxy of Luis de Molina. It dealt with the relationship between divine grace and human freedom. It began in Spain but was moved to Rome to liven up the pontificates of Clement VIII and Paul V.

18. Georg Schurhammer, *Francis Xavier: His Life, His Times*, vol. I: p. 411. It is interesting that Ignatius reports this as Favre teaching "*teología positiva*," while Laínez was treating "*escolástica*." Laínez himself reports their division of labor as "*uno cosas de Escritura, y otro cosas escolásticas*." *MHSI, Fontes Narrativi* I., pp. 7 and 122. Salmerón gives the additional information that Laínez was commenting upon Biel's *super Canone Missae. MHSI. Epistolae Salmerónis* II. The use of "positive" and "scholastic theology" is interesting, as well as the inclusion of Scripture under the former. Tacchi Venturi comments that at the Sapienza at that time, with Rome still recovering from the sack of 1527, there was no special chair for Scripture and opines that Favre in teaching positive

theology gave a considerable place to the interpretation of Scripture. Pietro Tacchi Venturi, *Storia della Compagnia di Gesu* (Roma: Civiltà Cattolica, 1950) II. 1. 93n.

19. Brodrick, *Saint Peter Canisius*, p. 133. See William V. Bangert, *Claude Jay and Alfonso Salmerón: Two Early Jesuits* (Chicago: Loyola University Press, 1985), pp. 112–115.

20. Riccardo G. Villoslada, *Storia del Collegio Romano dal suo inizio (1551) alla soppressione della Compangnia di Gesu (1773)* (Roma: Gregoriana, 1954), pp. 323–326. Ignatius seems to have emphasized "cases" to those who would learn a bit of Latin and a smattering of other subjects "as is necessary to hear confessions and *conuersar* with his neighbor. Of this type, perhaps, will be some of those who have a curacy of soul and are not capable of *mucha erudición.*" *Constitutions* IV. 13.E. #461. But see provisions for education in cases of consciences also in *Constitutions* IV. 5.D. #356; IV. 7.B. #394. In Part Four 8. D.#407, Ignatius elaborates further on what an education in "cases" would include.

21. Villoslada, *Collegio Romano*, pp. 30, 75.

22. Villoslada, *Collegio Romano*, pp. 323–325; p. 30. See *SpEx, "Para el sentido verdadero que en la Yglesia,"* #363; see also *Constitutions* IV. 12. 1. #446; IV. 14. 1. #464.

23. If this chapter were on Luis de Molina rather than on humanism in Jesuit theology, it would explore whether his primary concern has not been radically misunderstood, i.e., whether Molina's principal interest is not primarily the freedom of the human person, but rather the goodness and compassion of God. Molina, in a pronounced minority among theologians at that time, defended a far more humane doctrine on predestination, namely that if some human beings are damned, God does not predestine them *"ante praevisa merita,"* i.e., before assessing how they have lived. In this he was responding to Domingo Báñez, who argued that divine sovereignty implied that God included or excluded human beings from salvation according to his absolutely prior and independent decrees with no antecedent regard for the manner in which they had or were to live their lives—otherwise the divine action of salvation and knowledge would be conditioned by human beings, and God would be in some way a caused cause. Whatever impossible metaphysics Molina would generate or borrow from Pedro da Fonseca in his formulation of *scientia media* or whatever arguments Leonard Lessius would subsequently enter to bolster this position, it would repay exploration whether these efforts were actually to defend the goodness of God against a doctrine of divine power that seemed monstrous. In sharp contrast to what Maritain so lightly refers to as "a certain theological inhumanity," there was a deeply humane concern within the theology of Lessius, and one wonders if this might not be true also of Molina. For this reason, Francis de Sales—who had struggled so personally and so terribly with this issue for many years—would write to Lessius on this position of Molina and Lessius: *"J'ai toujours regardé cette opinion comme plus vraie et plus aimable en tant que plus digne della grâce et della miséricorde divine."* For Francis de Sales, Lessius, and perhaps Molina, what was at stake is the *misericordia Dei*, the compassion of God. For Francis de Sales and Lessius on this point, see X. M. Le Bachelet, "Le Décret d' Aquaviva sur la Grâce Efficace," in *Recherches de Science Religieuse* (Paris: Bureaux de la revue, 1924), 11B, pp. 46–60, 134–159.

Molina did not introduce this doctrine of predestination to salvation *post praevisa merita* into the theology of the Society, however. For this, the palm goes to the formidable Francisco de Toledo. However much this doctrine would later come to characterize the theology of Jesuits, it was initially resisted and Toledo was denounced to the then General Diego Laínez. Laínez, no shabby theologian himself, responded that the doctrine taught by Toledo had also been defended by such theologians as Albert Pighi and Johann Eck and that although he personally was in disagreement with it, it would not do to impose more limitations upon Jesuit theologians than those imposed by the church itself. In fact, the Order had to wait until Francis Borgia for the imposition of "Society doctrine," a most dangerous practice that has been discontinued. See Villoslada, *Collegio Romano*, p. 76.

24. For the four texts of the *Contemplatio ad amorem*, see *SpEx*, pp. 306–311. For an extensive analysis of the *Contemplatio*, see Michael J. Buckley, S.J., "The Contemplation to Attain Love," *The Way*, Supplement No. 24 (Spring 1975), pp. 92–104.

25. "Contemplation for Attaining Love," #234.

26. "Contemplation," #235.

27. "Contemplation," #236

28. "What attracted Ignatius *most* in the Divine Nature was its *providence*, above all as exercised in the souls of men, and even more especially in their free actions. . . . The Ignatian emphasis is rather on the realization of the larger design of the salvation of all men and the glory of God, brought about by God Himself through His action on individual souls." Joseph B. Wall, *The Providence of God in the Letters of Saint Ignatius* (San Jose: Smith-McKay, 1958), p. 2 [Italics added]. For an expansion of this point, see Michael J. Buckley, S.J., "'Always Growing in Devotion . . .': Jesuit Spirituality as Stimulus to Ecumenism," The Chancellor's Lecture at Regis College (Toronto: Regis College, 1987).

29. "Contemplation," #237.

30. "Contemplation," #237.

31. Hugo Rahner, *Ignatius the Theologian*, trans. Michael Barry (New York: Herder and Herder, 1968), p. 4.

32. "The Second Method for Making a Sound and Good Election," *SpEx* #184. See also the first rule in the distribution of alms: "*La primera es, que aquel amor que me mueve y me haze dar la limosna, descienda de arriba, del amor de Dios nuestro Señor . . .*" [*SpEx* #338]. The language in these two sections is almost identical.

33. *Spiritual Exercises*, "Third Week," *SpEx* #196.

34. *Constitutions* X. 2. #813. The doctrine of the instrument in the hands of God can be found throughout Ignatius' writings, cf. *Examen General* II. #30; *Constitutions* VII. 4. 3. #638. Compare this with Aquinas' doctrine that all human reality, even the humanity of Jesus, relates to God and the divine purpose instrumentally.

35. *Examen Generale* II. #30.

36. *Constitutions* VII. 4. 3. #638.

37. *Summa theologiae* III. 18. 1. ad 2: "Proprium est instrumenti quod moveatur a principali agente: diversimode tamen, secundum proprietatem naturae ipsius. Nam instrumentum inanimatum, sicut securis, aut serra, movetur ab artifice per motum solum corporalem. Instrumentum vero animatum anima sensibili movetur per appetitum sensitivum sicut equus a sessore. Instrumentum vero animatum anima rationali movetur per voluntatem eius, sicut per imperium domini movetur servus ad aliquid agendum; 'qui quidem servus est sicut instrumentum animatum,' ut Philosophus dicit in I. Politic." The translation is taken from the edition of the "Fathers of the English Dominican Province" (New York: Benzinger Brothers, Inc., 1947), II, p. 2126b. See *Summa contra gentiles* IV. 41; *In* III. *sent.* III. 18. 1; *De veritate* XX. 1; *De unione Verbi incarnati* 1, 4 and 5.

38. *Quaestiones quodlibetales, Quodlibet I. Quaestio IV.* a. 2 ad 2, p. 8.

39. Though Aquinas received the basic structure of his theory of instrumentality from influences that stretch from John Damascene to Aristotle, the highlighting of the difference between inanimate and animate instruments was his own invention as well as that between conjoined and separate. Ignaz Backes, *Die Christologie des hl. Thomas v. Aquin und die griechishcen Kirchenväter* (Paderborn: Schningh, 1931), p. 285. I am in great debt to Paul Crowley, S.J., for this discussion of instrumental causality, some of which is published in his article, "*Instrumentum Divinitatis* in Thomas Aquinas," *Theological Studies* 32, no. 3. (September 1991): pp. 451–475.

40. *In III. sent.* d. 18. 1.

41. *Constitutions* X. 1. #812 (m).

42. Ibid., X. 3. #814 (m). [emphasis added].

43. John Calvin, *Institutes of the Christian Religion*, trans. Henry Beveridge (Grand Rapids, Mich.: Eerdmans, 1962), bk. II, ch. 2. #1. [I: p. 223].

44. *The Didascalicon of Hugh of St. Victor*, trans. from the Latin with an Introduction and Notes by Jerome Taylor (New York: Columbia University Press, 1991), II. 20, p. 75. See Taylor's helpful Introduction, pp. 3ff. I am deeply indebted to the works, the lectures, and the conversations of Richard P. McKeon for the understanding presented here of the medieval liberal arts and the Renaissance humanities.

45. John of Salisbury, *The Metalogicon*, trans. Daniel D. McGarry (Berkeley: University of California Press, 1955), bk. 1, ch. 12, pp. 36–37 (m).

46. Ibid. For a discussion of the differences between the liberal arts of the Middle Ages and the humanities of the Renaissance, see chapter 6.

47. *Epistles* 88. 2 as cited by Grendler, *Schooling*, p. 118.

48. For a history of this understanding of grammar, see chapter 9.

49. Grendler, *Schooling*, pp. 115, 121.

50. R. S. Crane, "Shifting Definitions and Evaluations of the Humanities from the Renaissance to the Present," in *The Idea of the Humanities*, I: p. 30.

51. Kristeller, "Humanism and Scholasticism in the Italian Renaissance," p. 91.

52. Crane, "Shifting Definitions and Evaluations," I, pp. 31–35.

53. Richard P. McKeon, "The Transformation of the Liberal Arts in the Renaissance," in *Developments in the Early Renaissance*, ed. Bernard Levi (Albany: State University of New York Press, 1972), pp. 161–169.

54. " . . . *de studiis autem humanitatis quantum ad grammaticam, rhetoricam, historicam et poeticam spectat ac moralem* . . ." Kristeller, "Humanism and Scholasticism in the Italian Renaissance," p. 159n. See Ibid., pp. 10, 110.

55. H.I. Marrou, *A History of Education in Antiquity*, trans. George Lamb (New York: Sheed and Ward, 1956), pp. 98–99.

56. A. Gellii, *Noctes Atticae*, ed. P.K. Marshall. (Oxford: Clarendon Press, 1968), L. XIII. c. 17, II: pp. 399–400. So important is this text and influential in the understanding of the humanities and humanistic education, that it should be cited in its original here:

Qui uerba Latina fecerunt quique his probe usi sunt 'humanitatem' non id esse uoluerunt, quod uolgus existimat quodque a Graecis φιλανθροπία dicitur et significat dexteritatem quandam beneuolentiamque erga omnis homines promiscam, sed 'humanitatem' appellauerunt id propemodum, quod Graeci παιδείαν uocant, nos eruditionem institutionemque in bonas artis dicimus. Quas qui sinceriter cupiunt adpetuntque, hi sunt uel maxime humanissimi. Huius enim scientiae cura et disciplina ex uniuersis animantibus uni homini datast idcircoque 'humanitas' appellata est.

Sic igitur eo uerbo ueteres esse usos et cumprimis M. Varronem Marcumque Tullium omnes ferme libri declarant. Quamobrem satis habui unum interim exemplum promere. Itaque uerba posui Varronis e libro *rerum humanarum* primo, cuius principium hoc est: 'Praxiteles, qui propter artificium egregium nemini est paulum modo humaniori ignotus.' 'Humaniori,' inquit non ita, ut uulgo [*sic*] dicitur, facili et tractabili et beniuolo, tametsi rudis litterarum sit—hoc enim cum sententia nequaquam conuenit—, sed eruditiori doctiorique, qui Praxitelem, quid fuerit, et ex libris et ex historia cognouerit.

The Loeb edition of Gellius indicates that the references are to Cicero, *De oratore* I. 16, 71; II. 17, 72, etc., and to a fragment of Varro, Fr. 1, Mirsch. *The Attic Nights of Aulus Gellius*, edited with an English translation by John C. Rolfe, The Loeb Classical Library (London: William Heinemann, 1927), XIII. 17; II: pp. 456–457. R.S. Crane has pointed out the importance of this text, and given it extensive commentary. See Crane, "Shifting Definitions and Evaluations," pp. 23ff.

57. Aulus Gellius, *The Attic Nights* XIII. 17.1. Cf. R. S. Crane, "Shifting Definitions," pp. 23–24. The critical text used here is a later one than used by Crane, hence the discrepancy in spelling.

58. See Hans Baron, "Aulus Gellius and the Renaissance," in his *From Petrarch to Leonardo Bruni* (Chicago: The University of Chicago Press, 1968), pp. 196–197, n. 2. Baron follows Heinemann's opinion that Gellius' definition has unduly narrowed Cicero's original idea of *humanitas*, but that "it rather accurately foreshadowed the later humanistic usage." Leofranc Holford-Strevens advances a similar judgment of the narrowing of Cicero by Gellius contending that "Cicero freely employs the word in the sense denied him (e.g., *Sex. Rosc.* 46, Q. Fr. 1. 1. 27 . . .)," Leofranc Holford-Strevens, *Aulus Gellius* (Chapel Hill: The University of North Carolina Press, 1988), p. 130. Holford-Strevens maintains further that it was from this chapter of Gellius "sprang the Renaissance use of *humanitas* for classical studies." Ibid., n. 25. For a criticism of Gellius' restrictions on this term, see chapter 6.

59. These are not contradictory ideals, but they are not simply identifiable. Some of the confusion in contemporary undergraduate education has its origins in the confusion that does not appreciate the differences, in a conflation of two different educational ideals.

60. Pater Joannes de Polanco Patri Jacobo Lainio, 21 May 1547. *Monumenta Historica Societatis Iesu, Monumenta Ignatiana.* Series Prima. Tomus I. (Madrid: Gabriel Lopez del Horno, 1903), pp. 522–523. For the English translation (slightly modified here), cf. *Letters of Ignatius of Loyola,* selected and translated by William J. Young, S.J. (Chicago: Loyola University Press, 1959), pp. 133–134.

61. Polanco Patri Jacobo Lainio, *Letters of Ignatius,* p. 134.

62. Cf. Pedro Leturia, S.J., "Why the Society of Jesus Became a Teaching Order," trans. Victor R. Yanitelli, S.J., *Jesuit Educational Quarterly,* 4 (June 1941): p. 44n68. Leturia makes the very apposite point: "We propose to examine this question in the field of *humanities;* a theme, which, albeit more restricted, still remains peculiar in the history of the religious orders. For, in truth, the novelty was not that religious should teach scholastic philosophy and theology, but that they [the Jesuits] should found colleges of humane letters and dedicate themselves with apostolic zeal and thoroughness to the teaching of them." p. 33.

63. Crane, "Shifting Definitions and Evaluations," I: p. 21.

64. Ibid., I: p. 31 [Division of Vives' text added.] see I: 89ff.

65. Ibid., I: pp. 32–35. Crane fails to differentiate the comprehensive sense that Vives gave to the humanities from the more limited denotation among the earlier Italian humanists.

66. *Constitutions* IV. 12. 1. #446.

67. Paul O. Kristeller, "The Humanist Movement," *Renaissance Thought* (New York: Harper and Row, 1961), p. 7.

68. *Constitutions* IV. 12. 1. #446.

69. Robert Grudin, "Humanism," *The New Encyclopaedia Britannica,* Macropaedia. Fifteenth edition. (Chicago: The University of Chicago Press, 1986) 20: p. 728.

70. *Constitutions* IV. 12. 1. #446.

71. Yves Congar, O.P., *A History of Theology,* trans. and ed. Hunter Guthrie, S.J. (Garden City, N.Y.: Doubleday & Co., 1968), pp. 147–148.

72. Ibid., p. 171 [Emphasis his].

73. *SpEx* #363 (m). It is interesting to note that the phrase "or explain for our times" was added later in Ignatius' own hand. See David L. Fleming, *The Spiritual Exercises of St. Ignatius: A Literal Translation and a Contemporary Reading* (St. Louis: The Institute of Jesuit Sources, 1978), p. 234n. It is of interest to note that this particular rule, unlike many of these rules, did not come to Ignatius from the Council of Sens (1528).

74. Congar, *History of Theology*, pp. 170–172.

75. For further Ignatian provisions for positive theology, see *Constitutions* IV. 5. 1. #351; IV. 6. 4. #366; and IV. 14. 1. #464 with IV. 14. B. #466.

76. Congar, *History of Theology*, pp. 170–172.

77. *Constitutions* IV. 14. 1. #464.

78. See Buckley, *At the Origins of Modern Atheism*, p. 43.

79. Leonard E. Boyle, *The Setting of the Summa theologiae of Saint Thomas* (Toronto: The Pontifical Institute of Medieval Studies, 1982).

80. Villoslada, *Collegio Romano*, pp. 112–115.

81. *Constitutions* IV. 14. B. #466 (m).

82. Villoslada, *Collegio Romano*, pp. 103–104.

83. Ibid., pp. 114–115: "*Non ci sono altre cattedre di teologia scolastica che quelle per lo studio di S. Tommaso, e altro testo che la Somma del Dottor Angelico.*"

84. See chapter 4, p. 60–61.

85. Villoslada, *Collegio Romano*, p. 71; see the succession of positions by the same members of the faculty, pp. 322–336.

86. *Constitutions* X. 2. #813.

87. *Constitutions* X. 3. #814.

88. *Constitutions* X. 3. #814 (m).

89. *Constitutions* X. 3. #814 (m).

Chapter Six: The Search for a New Humanism: the University and the Concern for Justice

1. Paul VI, "On the Development of Peoples," (Washington, D.C.: United States Catholic Conference, 1967), paragraph 20, p. 16 (m): "*Quodsi ad progressionem promovendam necessarii sunt technici viri in dies numero crebriores, multo magis requiruntur viri sapientes, ad cogitandum acuti, qui ad novum humanismum investigandum se conferant, vi cuius nostrae aetatis homines . . . se ipsos quasi invenire possint.*" *AAS* LIX. No. 4 (15 Aprilis 1967), p. 267. Cf. paragraph 42, p. 29: "What must be aimed at is a complete humanism. And what is that if not the fully-rounded development of the whole man of all men."

2. "Better Off, But Not Much," *The Economist* (4 October 1997), p. 35.

3. From the ancient prayer, *Deus, qui humanae substantiae* found initially as a Nativity Oration in the Leonine Sacramentary, a compilation dating from about 540 A.D., and transferred to the prayer over the water being mixed with wine during the Carolingian period as indicated in the Ordo of Seez. It

remained in this position in the Roman Mass until 1969. The reform of 1969 continued to employ this prayer at this place in the Roman liturgy, but condensed it. Cf. Joseph A. Jungmann, S.J., *The Mass of the Roman Rite*, trans. Francis A. Brunner (New York: Benzinger Brothers, Inc., 1951), vol. 1, pp. 62 and 94; vol. II, pp. 62ff. Also, A. G. Martimort, *The Church at Prayer: The Eucharist* (New York: Herder and Herder, 1973), pp. 124–125. The actual prayer used over those centuries ran: "*Deus, qui humanae substantiae dignitatem mirabiliter condidisti, et mirabilius reformasti: da nobis per hujus aquae et vini mysterium, ejus divinitatis esse consortes, qui humanitatis nostrae fieri dignatus est particeps, Jesus Christus, Filius tuus Dominus noster: Qui tecum vivit et regnat in unitate Spiritus Sancti Deus: per omnia saecula saeculorum. Amen.*" For its employment as a question directed at economic exploitation and social oppression, cf., John Baptist Janssens, S.J., "*Instructio de apostolatu sociali,*" October 10, 1949, *Acta Romana Societatis Iesu.* XI:5 (1949), pp. 712–713; "*An ideo 'humanae substantiae dignitatem mirabiliter condidit Deus et mirabilius reformavit' ut pauci ditiores opes opibus addentes, plurimos fratres suos in Christo egestati addicant?*"

4. Paul VI, "On the Development of Peoples," paragraph 1, p. 3. [Italics added.]

5. "Justice in the World," Introduction, *Synod of Bishops: The Ministerial Priesthood and Justice in the World* (Washington, D.C.: National Conference of Catholic Bishops, 1972), p. 34.

6. *King Lear* III. iv. 28–33.

7. "Jesuits Today," #3–2. The phrase between the dashes is taken from paragraph #2. For the English of these decrees, see p. 185n11.

8. "Our Mission Today," #60 in *Documents of the 31st and 32nd General Congregations of the Society of Jesus.* [Hereafter cited as *Documents*].

9. "Jesuits Today," #9 *Documents*, p. 403; cf. "Our Mission Today," #2, #51, #76 in *Documents*, pp. 411, 429, 437.

10. "Our Mission Today," #60, *Documents*, p. 432; Ibid., #8 and #9, *Documents*, p. 413.

11. "Our Mission Today," #47–48, *Documents*, pp. 427–428.

12. Peter Rawlinson, *The Jesuit Factor* (London: Weidenfeld Nicolson, 1990); Michael Campbell-Johnston, "Not the Real Society of Jesus," *The Tablet* 244:7817 (12 May 1990), p. 587; Peter Rawlinson's response in "Letters," *The Tablet* 244:7819 (26 May 1990) p. 669.

13. Manfred Barthel, *The Jesuits: History and Legend of the Society of Jesus*, translated and adapted by Mark Howson (New York: William Morrow Co., Inc., 1984), p. 309. It should be noted that Barthel, unlike the previously mentioned sources, is basically sympathetic to the directions set by the Thirty-Second General Congregation.

14. Malachi Martin, *The Jesuits: The Society of Jesus and the Betrayal of the Roman Catholic Church* (New York: Simon & Schuster, 1987).

15. Richard Bernstein, "The Rising Hegemony of the Politically Correct," *New York Times*, The Week in Review (Sunday 28 October 1990), pp. 1 and 4;

Eugene D. Genovese, "Heresy, Yes—Sensitivity, No," *New Republic* (15 April 1991), pp. 30–35. Genovese's article is an extended review of *Illiberal Education: The Politics of Race and Sex on Campus* by Dinesh D'Souza.

16. This understanding of a university is expanded and defended in chapter 7.

17. See chapter 5.

18. Cf. Richard P. McKeon, "Character and the Arts and Disciplines," *Ethics* 78, no. 2 (January 1968): p. 118. This understanding of the development of education in the humanities is much indebted to Professor McKeon.

19. *Constitutions* IV, 12. A. #448. The Spanish which is being translated reads: *"Debaxo de letras de humanidad, sin la grammática se entiende lo que toca a rectórica, poesía y historia."*

20. For the contemporary embodiment of this idea, cf. Crane, "The Idea of the Humanities," pp. 8ff.

21. McKeon, "Character and the Arts and Disciplines," p. 112.

22. Dorothy Thompson, "The Lesson of Dachau," *Ladies Homes Journal* (September 1945), p. 6.

23. Aleksandr Pushkin, *Eugene Onegin*, trans. with commentary by Vladimir Nabokov (Princeton: Princeton University Press, 1975), bk. I, #18–#22.

24. Fyodor Dostoyevsky, *Notes from the Underground*, ed. Robert G. Durgy trans. Serge Shishkoff. The Crowell Critical Library (New York: Thomas Y. Crowell Company, 1969), p. 22–23. For these examples, see Michael Buckley, S.J., "The University and the Concern for Justice: The Search for a New Humanism," *Thought*, vol. 57, no. 225 (June 1982), p. 229.

25. Eric Maria Remarque, *All Quiet on the Western Front* (New York: Fawcett Crest, 1991), ch. 10, p. 263.

26. George Steiner, *Real Presences* (New Haven: Yale University Press, 1989), p. 144.

27. Paul VI, "On the Development of Peoples," paragraph 20, p. 16; cf. paragraph 42, p. 29: "What must be aimed at is a complete humanism. And what is that if not the fully-rounded development of the whole man and of all men."

28. *"Cum autem benignitas et humanitas apparuit Salvatoris nostri Dei."* Titus 3:4. The same translation is used for a humane kindness in Acts 28:2: "And the natives showed us unusual φιλανθρωπίαν *[humanitatem]*, for they kindled a fire and welcomed us all because it had begun to rain and was cold." For the settlement offered by Aulus Gellius, see chapter 5, pp. 93–94.

29. Giovanni Gioviano Pontano, *De sermone libri sex*, edited by S. Lupi and A. Risicato (Lungano, 1954), I.xxx.4. *"A comitate non uno modo differt humanitas. Etenim, qui aliorum moveatur damnis, incommodis, captivitate, orbitate, inopia, exilio malisque aliis, humanum hunc dicimus, nequaquam in hoc tamen comem. . . ."* Charles Trinkaus, *The Scope of Renaissance Humanism* (Ann Arbor: The University of Michigan Press, 1983), pp. 368 and 398n15.

30. Ibid., I.xxx.3. Trinkaus, pp. 368 and 398, n. 14.

31. "Our Mission Today," #20. (emphasis mine). For the Latin of this decree see *"De nostra missione hodierna: Diakonia fidei et iustitiae promotio,"* *Acta*

Romana Societatis Iesu xvi: ii (1974), *Decreta C. G. XXXII 1974–1975* (Romae: Ad Curiam Praepositi Generalis, 1975), d. 4.

32. Aristotle, *Poetics* ii. 1448a1; i. 1447a28; cf. iii. 1448a28; vi. 1449b36, 1450b3, 1450b9, 1451b29.

33. Cf. James J. Murphy, *Rhetoric in the Middle Ages* (Berkeley: The University of California Press, 1974), pp. 72, 136–140.

34. John Henry Newman, *An Essay in Aid of a Grammar of Assent*, (Garden City, New York: Doubleday and Company, Inc., 1955), Part I, Ch. 4, no. 2 p. 79. James Joyce, *A Portrait of the Artist as a Young Man*, text, criticism, and notes edited by Chester G. Anderson (New York: Penguin Books, 1977), Ch. 4, p. 164.

35. William Wordsworth, "Lines Written a Few Miles above Tintern Abbey," ll 89–92, in *Lyrical Ballads and Other Poems, 1797–1800*, ed., James Butler and Karen Green (Ithaca: Cornell University Press, 1992), p. 118.

36. Robert M. Hutchins, "The Great Conversation," in *Great Books of the Western World*, ed. Mortimer Adler (Chicago: Encyclopedia Britannica, 1952), vol. 1, pp. 3–5. The critically important issue of *praxis* within such an education is not being directly treated here, but not because it is a consideration of secondary importance. It is of crucial importance. However the relationship between humanistic education and *praxis* is so complicated that it would necessitate another essay of similar size.

37. Alfred North Whitehead, *The Aims of Education and Other Essays* (New York: Macmillan Publishing Co., Inc. 1949), pp. 31ff.

38. See note #36.

39. The original statement of Kant's reads: "Without sensibility no object would be given to us, without understanding no object would be thought. Thoughts without content are empty, intuitions without concepts are blind." Immanuel Kant, *Critique of Pure Reason*, trans. Norman Kemp Smith (London: Macmillan Publishers Ltd., 1963), A51; B75: p. 93.

40. Rainer Maria Rilke, "Archaïscher Torso Apollos," as in *Ahead of All Parting, The Selected Poetry and Prose of Rainer Maria Rilke*, ed. and translated by Stephen Mitchell (New York: The Modern Library, 1995), p. 67. The original reads: " . . .da ist keine Stelle/die dich nich sieht. Du mußt dein Leben ändern."

41. Steiner, *Real Presences*, p. 142.

42. Juan Luis Vives, *De disciplinis libri xx*, as cited in Crane, "The Idea of the Humanities," I, p. 5, and in "Shifting Definitions and Evaluations," I, pp. 31–32.

Chapter Seven: The Catholic University as Pluralistic Forum

1. Richard Hofstadter and W.P. Metzger, *The Development of Academic Freedom in the United States* (New York: Columbia University Press, 1955), p. 3, as cited in Frederick Crosson, "Two Faces of Academic Freedom" in *The Chal-*

lenge and Promise of a Catholic University, ed. Theodore M. Hesburgh, C.S.C. (Notre Dame: University of Notre Dame Press, 1994), p. 45.

2. John Dewey, *Art as Experience*, chs. i and iv (Capricorn Books, 1959), pp. 13–16, 58–60.

3. Aristotle, *Metaphysics*, A. 2. 982b12–20. Cf. Richard P. McKeon, "Philosophy and Method," *The Journal of Philosophy*, 48, no. 22 (25 October 1951): p. 664.

4. Robert J. Dwyer, "Freedom and Catholic U(u)niversity(ies)," as in syndicated column, "Under My Hat," *Twin Circle* (18 May 1969), p. 7.

5. John Foley, "Archbishop Foley Challenges Presidents," *National Jesuit News* (December 1985), p. 14.

6. "'Pay Any Price? Break Any Mold?' An Interchange Between Michael Heffron and William J. Richardson," *America* (29 April 1967), p. 624.

7. Josef Canon Salzbacher, *Meine Reise nach Nord-Amerika in Jahre 1842 mit satistischen Bemerkungen über die Züstande der katholischen Kirche bis auf die neuste Zeit*. Excerpted and translated in *Documents of American Catholic History*, ed. John Tracy Ellis (Milwaukee: The Bruce Publishing Company, 1956), p. 261.

8. This paragraph, describing the "custodial institution" is a direct quotation from Michael J. Buckley, S.J., "The Function of a Catholic University," *U.S. Catholic and Jubilee* (September 1969), p. 47. I am indebted to private conversations with the late Theodore Mackin for this distinction between the custodial institution and the universities of more recent and pluralistic character.

9. John Tracy Ellis, *The Life of James Cardinal Gibbons* (Milwaukee: The Bruce Publishing Company, 1952), vol. I, p. 418.

10. Robert M. Hutchins, *The University of Utopia*, 2nd edition (Chicago: The University of Chicago Press, 1964), pp. 78–81. For the differentiation between the medieval and the American tradition, cf. p. 75–78.

11. Buckley, "The Function of a Catholic University," p. 47.

12. Newman, *The Idea of a University*, Discourse II, #1, p. 33.

13. Newman, "Christianity and Scientific Investigation: A Lecture Written for the School of Science," in the *Idea of a University*, pp. 383.

14. *Gravissimum Educationis*, #8, in the *Documents of Vatican II*, ed. Walter M. Abbott, S.J (New York: Herder and Herder, 1966), p. 646.

15. See chapter 1, p. 20ff.

16. "The same motive of charity by which colleges are accepted and schools open to the public are maintained in them for the improvement in learning and in living not only of our own members, but even more especially of those from outside the Society. Through this same motive, the Society can extend itself to undertaking the work of universities, that through them this fruit sought in the colleges may be increased more universally [*mas uniuersalmente*] in the disciplines [*facultades*] that are taught and in the persons who attend...." *Constitutions IV. 11.1.#440 (m)*.

17. *Gaudium et spes*, #1, in Abbot, pp. 199–200.

18. William B. Neenan, S.J., "A Catholic/Jesuit University?" in *Finding God in All Things*, ed. Michael J. Himes and Stephen J. Pope (New York: Crossroad, 1996), p. 310.
19. John Henry Newman, *An Essay in Aid of a Grammar of Assent*, ed. I. T. Ker (Oxford: Clarendon Press, 1985), chapter VI, p. 129.
20. "Pay any Price? Break Any Mold," p. 625.

Chapter Eight: Philosophic Grammar and the Other Disciplines

1. Henry David Thoreau, *Walden; or, Life in the Woods*, ed. Philip van Doren Stern (New York: Bramhall House, 1970), "Economy," p. 155.
2. Sancti Bonaventurae, *In Librum I Sententiarum*, Prooemium, Quaestio II, ad 4: "*Quoniam ergo sacra Scriptura est de credibili, ut credibile, et hic est de credibili ut facto intelligibili.*" S.R.E. Cardinali S. Bonaventurae, *Opera omnia* (Paris; Ludovicus Vives, 1864), I, p. 18. The "*hic*" in Bonaventure's statement is referring to the *Liber Sententiarum* of Peter Lombard.
3. Richard Rorty, *Philosophy and the Mirror of Nature* (Princeton: Princeton University Press, 1979).
4. Arthur Schopenhauer, *The World as Will and Representation*, trans. E. F. J. Payne (New York: Dover, 1958), "Preface to the Second Edition," vol. I, p. xx. See Etienne Gilson: "It does not seem to have entered the minds of thirteenth-century theologians that one and the same man could be, at one and the same time, both a 'philosopher' and a 'saint'." *Elements of Christian Philosophy* (New York: Doubleday & Co., 1960), p. 12.
5. Martin Heidegger, *An Introduction to Metaphysics*, trans. Ralph Manheim (New York: Doubleday & Co., 1961), p. 9.
6. Norman Malcolm, *Ludwig Wittgenstein, A Memoir* (London: Oxford: 1958; reprint 1978), pp. 36–37 [emphasis his].
7. "We suppose, first, then, that the wise man knows all things, as far as possible, although he has not knowledge of each of them in detail." Aristotle, *Metaphysics* I. 2. 982a7–10. See Thomas Aquinas, *In Metaphysicorum Aristotelis Expositio*, I. lectio ii, #36 (Turini: Marietti, 1964), pp. 12–13. Contrast this with Socrates in Plato's *Apologia* 21d–23b. In the Socratic account, wisdom, as such, can only be predicated of the god, but in human wisdom lies the knowledge of one's own ignorance.
8. Samuel Eliot Morison, *Harvard College in the Seventeenth Century* (Cambridge, Mass.: Harvard University Press, 1936), I: p. 256; II: pp. 580 ff.
9. "*Philosophie wird durch Wissenschaftslogick, d.h. logische Analyse der Begriffe und Sätze der Wissenschaft ersetzt.*" Rudolf Carnap, *Logische Syntax der Sprache* (Wien: Julius Springer, 1934), p. iii.
10. Michael Dummett, *Origins of Analytical Philosophy* (Cambridge, Mass.: Harvard University Press, 1994), p. 4. "Widely as they differed from one another, the logical positivists, Wittgenstein in all phases of his career, Oxford 'ordinary

language' philosophy and post-Carnapian philosophy in the United States as represented by Quine and Davidson all adhered to these twin axioms." Ibid.

11. V. C. Chappell, ed., *Ordinary Language* (Englewood Cliffs, N. J.: Prentice-Hall, 1964), p. 2.

12. Maurice Merleau-Ponty, *In Praise of Philosophy*, trans. with a preface by John Wild and James M. Edie (Evanston: Northwestern University Press, 1963), p. 41.

13. Aristotle, *Metaphysics*, i.2. 982b14.

14. Niels Bohr, "Discussion with Einstein on Epistemological Problems in Atomic Physics," in *Albert Einstein, Philosopher-Scientist*, edited by Paul Arthur Schilpp (New York: Harper and Row, 1949), vol. I, p. 202. For the educational use and philosophic implications of this discussion, see Richard McKeon, "Philosophy as a Humanism," in *Philosophy Today*, 9, no. 314 (Fall 1965), pp. 163–164.

15. Thucydides, *History of the Peloponnesian War*, i. 22–24, 88–90, 118; ii. 8–9, 65; iii. 86.

16. "In the hundred years from Waterloo to Mons so gradually did the power of Germany grow—that combination of population, resources, technology, and will—that, like the growth of a child, those close to it were hardly aware of its extent. . . . A century later it was thought—erroneously, as it proved—that the combined power of Europe could stop the German bid. By 1917 it was clear that this could not be done; the United States intervened to prevent German domination of Europe." Dean Acheson, *Present at the Creation* (New York: Norton, 1969), p. 4. "The decision to intervene did not flow from a general principle of foreign policy, but as a specific distrust and fear of German intentions and ruthlessness. German miscalculation and stupidity fanned the fear." Ibid., note to page 4, p. 740. For Brüning, cf. Heinrich Brüning, "The Statesman," *The Works of the Mind*, ed. Robert B. Heywood (Chicago: The University of Chicago Press, 1966), pp. 93–118.

17. Samuel Taylor Coleridge, *Biographia Litteraria or Biographical Sketches of My Literary Life and Opinions*, ed. James Engell and W. Jackson Bate (Princeton: Princeton University Press, 1983), I: (chapters 10 and 13), pp. 168–170, 295–306.

18. Frank Lloyd Wright, "The Architect," in *The Works of the Mind*, p. 51.

19. Rudolf Bultmann, *Jesus Christ and Mythology* (New York: Charles Scribner's Sons, 1958), pp. 14–19.

20. Philip Frank, *Modern Science and Its Philosophy* (Cambridge: Harvard University Press, 1950), p. 265.

21. For an example, see Richard P. McKeon, *On Knowing—the Natural Sciences*, compiled by David. B. Owen, ed. David B. Owen and Zahava K. McKeon (Chicago: The University of Chicago Press, 1994).

22. Martianus Capella, *De nuptiis Philologiae et Mercurii*, ed. Adolf Dick (Leipzig: Teubner, 1925; rep. 1969). ET: *The Marriage of Philology and Mercury*, trans. William Harris Stahl and Richard Johnson with E. L. Burge, vol. II of *Martianus Capella and the Seven Liberal Arts*, trans. Stahl, Johnson, and

Burge (New York: Columbia University Press, 1977), bk. III, paragraph #230, p. 67.

23. Thomas Aquinas, *Summa theologiae* I. 29.

24. For the concept of "Christian philosophy," see Étienne Gilson, *The Spirit of Medieval Philosophy*, trans. A. H. C. Downes (1936; reprint, Notre Dame: University of Notre Dame Press, 1991) and Jacques Maritain, *An Essay on Christian Philosophy*, trans. Edward H. Flannery (New York: Philosophical Library, 1955).

Chapter Nine: Wisdom, Religion, and the Liberal Arts: Towards the Construction of Theology

1. George Steiner, *Real Presences* (New Haven: Yale University Press, 1989), p. 134.

2. Richard P. McKeon, "Philosophy and Theology, History and Science in the Thought of Bonaventura and Thomas Aquinas," *Journal of Religion* 58 Supplement (1978): pp. S24–S51.

3. "Philosophica scientia via est ad alias scientias; sed qui ibi vult stare cadit in tenebras." *De donis spiritus sancti* 4.12. [The edition of Bonaventure used throughout this chapter is that of the *Opera omnia* (Ad Clara Aquas [Quaracchi]: Ex Typographia Collegii S. Bonaventurae, 1882–1902); cited by volume number and page] (5:475b–476a). Cf. "Christus unus omnium magister," par. 14–15 (5:571). "Si ergo ad notitiam creaturae pervenire non potest nisi per id, per quod facta est; necesse est ut *verbum verax praecedat te*, in Ecclesiastico." *In hexaëmeron* 1.10 [5:331a. Cf. *Inhexaëm.* 1.17 (5:332), 4.1(5:349a); 6.2-4 (5:360b–361b); 7.1-14 (5:365a–367b). The third *Collatio* puts the position strongly and succinctly: "Unde omnes, qui non habent hanc fidem, manum habent amputatam." *In hexaëm.* 3.9 (5:345a).

4. "Et sic patet, quomodo *multiformis sapientia Dei* (Eph. 3:10), quae lucide traditur in sacra Scriptura, occultatur in omni cognitione et in omni natura. Patet etiam, quomodo omnes cognitiones famulantur theologiae; et ideo ipsa assumit exempla et utitur vocabulis pertinentibus ad omne genus cognitionis. Patet etiam, quam ampla sit via illuminativa, et quomodo in omni re, quae sentitur sive quae cognoscitur, interius lateat ipse Deus." *De reductione artium ad theologiam* 26 (5:325b); cf. Ibid., 7 (5:322a). "Reduction" can mean various things in Bonaventure: "reduci ad aliquid est dupliciter: aut sicut ad *principium*, aut sicut ad *terminum*." *In I sent.* 26.3, ad I (1:458). Fernando Gneo comments: "Anzitutto va ricordato che s. Bonaventura usa il termine *reductio* in contesti molto differenti (Gilson ne conta ben cinque). Ma, in fondo, la *reductio* è sempre propria di una realtà incapace di sussistenza assoluta e besognosa di un riferimento ad altro da cui, pertanto, è essenzialmente distinta. Quindi la *reductio* prende la dimensione di una vera e propria *mediazione* (fondazione e razionalizzazione) del *dato* che altrimenti resterebbe infondato: 'Verbum . . .est medium metaphysicum reducens, et haec est tota *nostra metaphysica . . .scilicet illuminari per radios spirituales et reduci ad summum.' In hexaëm.*, I .17." Fernando Gneo, "*La reductio artium ad theologiam secondo* S. Bonaventura," in *Arts libéraux et philosophie au moyen age*, Actes du Quatrième Congrès International de Philosophie Médiévale (Montréal: Institut d'Etudes Médiévales, 1969), pp. 634–35. [This volume is hereafter cited as ALPMA]. This same organic unity of the sciences moving toward the vision of God is the object of development in *De donis spiritus sancti* 4.2 ff. (5:474a ff.).

5. *De reductione artium ad theologiam* 5 (5:321a).

6. "Horum ostium est intellectus *Verbi increati,* qui est radix intelligentiae omnium; unde qui non habet hoc ostium, intrare non potest. Philosophi autem habent pro impossibili quae sunt summe vera quia, ostium est eis clausum." *In hexaëm.* 3.4 (5:343b). Christ as the source of the illumination of the sciences entitles him alone to be called "teacher." "Merito igitur soli Christo et non alii attribuenda est auctoritas officii, ut singulariter *unus Magister* dicatur, eo quod ipse est fontale principium et origo cuiuslibet scientiae humanae. Unde sicut unus est sol, tamen multos radios emittit; sic ab uno Magistro, Christo, sole spirituali, multiformes et diversae scientiae procedunt; et quemadmodum multiplices et distincti rivuli ab uno fonte egrediuntur, unus tamen est fons, qui in tot rivulos sine sui defectibilitate (se) multiplicat; sic ab uno fonte aeterno, ab uno Magistro, Christo, sine sui defectibilitate egrediuntur rivuli diversarum scientiarum." *Sermo i, Dominica xxii post Pentecosten,* "Magister, scimus quia verax es et viam Dei in veritate doces." (9:442a); cf. "Christus, unus omnium magister" 7–9 (5:569a–b).

7. "Propositum igitur nostrum est ostendere, quod in Christo *sunt omnes thesauri sapientiae et scientiae Dei absconditi* (Col. 2:3), et ipse est medium omnium scientiarum." *In hexaëm.* 1.11 (5:331a). The remainder of this initial *collatio* is devoted to demonstrating that Christ is the medium for metaphysics, physics, mathematics, logic, ethics, politics, and theology.

8. "Secundo docet, ubi debet *incipere*: quia *a medio,* quod est Christus; quod medium si negligatur, nihil habetur." *In hexaëm.* 1.1 (5:329a).

9. "*Clavis* ergo contemplationis est intellectus triplex, scilicet intellectus *Verbi increati,* per quod omnia producuntur; intellectus *Verbi incarnati,* per quod omnia reparantur; intellectus *Verbi inspirati,* per quod omnia revelantur. Nisi enim quis possit considerare de rebus, qualiter originantur, qualiter in finem reducuntur, et qualiter in eis refulget Deus; intelligentiam habere non potest." *In hexaëm.* 3.2 (5:343a). For Christ as the integral subject of theology, cf. *In I Sent.*, Prooemium I (1:7a). For this reason, only theology or *sacra doctrina* was a *scientia perfecta,* "quia incipit *a primo,* quod est primum principium, et pervenit ad ultimum, quod est praemium aeternum . . ." It is as perfect wisdom that it completes what philosophy can only begin: "Ipsa etiam sola est *sapientia perfecta,* quae incipit a causa summa, ut est *principium* causatorum; ubi terminatur cognitio philosophica; et transit per eam, ut est *remedium* peccatorum; et reducit in eam, ut est *praemium* meritorum et finis desideriorum." *Breviloquim* 1.1 (5:210a–b).

10. "De quibus omnibus est theologia, id est scientia divina, quia praecipuum in ea cognitorum est deus, quae alio nomine dicitur metaphysica, id est trans physicam, quia post physicam discenda occurrit nobis, quibus ex sensibilibus oportet in insensibilia devenire. Dicitur etiam philosophia prima, in quantum aliae omnes scientiae ab ea sua principia accipientes eam consequuntur." *Expositio super librum Boethii de trinitate* 5.1. [This work is hereafter cited as *In de trin.*] (Leiden: E.J. Brill, 1959). See *In metaphysicam Aristotelis commentarium*, Prooemium; *ST* I. 1. 8; *In de trin.* 5.1, ad 6. Yet the sciences remain irreducibly distinct from each other and metaphysics. [Unless otherwise noted, the texts of Saint Thomas cited throughout this chapter are taken from the Leonine, still incomplete, edition of the *Opera omnia.*]

11. ". . . in sacra doctrina philosophia possumus tripliciter uti. Primo ad demonstrandum ea quae sunt praeambula fidei, quae necesse est in fide scire ut ea quae naturalibus rationibus de deo probantur, ut deum esse, deum esse unum et alia huiusmodi vel de deo vel de creaturis in philosophia probata, quae fides supponit. Secundo ad notificandum per aliquas similitudines ea quae sunt fidei, sicut Augustinus in libro *De trinitate* utitur multis similitudinibus ex doctrinis philosophicis sumptis ad manifestandum trinitatem. Tertio ad resistendum his quae contra fidem dicuntur sive ostendendo ea esse falsa sive ostendendo ea non esse necessaria" *In de trin.* 2.3.

12. Aquinas makes the contrast between the two ways of ordering the sciences explicitly: ". . . aliarum scientiarum principia vel sunt per se nota, et probari non possunt: vel per aliquam rationem naturalem probantur in aliqua alia scientia. Propria autem hujus scientiae cognitio est, quae est per revelationem: non autem quae est per naturalem rationem. Et ideo non pertinet ad eam probare principia aliarum scientiarum, sed solum iudicare de eis; quidquid enim in aliis scientiis invenitur veritati huius scientiae repugnans, totum condemnatur ut falsum: unde dicitur II *Cor.* 10 [4]: *consilia destruentes, et omnem altitudinem extollentem se adversus scientiam Dei.*" *ST* I. 1. 6. ad 2. The further and more positive relationship of *sacra doctrina* to secular knowledge is explained in a previous answer to an objection. ". . . haec scientia accipere potest aliquid a philosophicis disciplinis, non quod ex necessitate eis indigeat, sed *ad maiorem manifestationem eorum quae in hac scientia traduntur.* Non enim accipit sua principia ab aliis scientiis, sed immediate a Deo per revelationem. Et ideo non accipit ab aliis scientiis tanquam a superioribus, sed utitur eis tanquam inferioribus et ancillis: sicut architectonicae utuntur subministrantibus, ut civilis militari. Et hoc ipsum quod sic utitur eis, non est propter defectum vel insufficientiam eius, sed propter defectum intellectus nostri; qui ex his quae per naturalem rationem ex qua procedunt aliae scientiae cognoscuntur, facilius manuducitur in ea quae sunt supra rationem, quae in hac scientia traduntur." *ST* I. 1. 5. ad 2. [emphasis added]. Thus, *sacra doctrina* can engage philosophy as both praeamble and preliminary guide [I. 5. *sed contra* and ad 2]; it subsumes philosophic reflection, while respecting its intrinsic integrity, to make more manifest the realities that *sacra doctrina* treats, as faith moves to understanding [I. 1. 5. ad 2]; *sacra doctrina* positions philosophy in a new manner by comprehending and locating all reflections upon the reality of God within itself [I. 1. 6]; it enters into philosophy, finally, to understand, criticize, and judge other assumptions and conclusions as false if they contradict its own doctrine [I. 1. 6. ad 2].

13. "Cum enim sapientis sit ordinare et iudicare . . .*ST* I.1.6. Cf. *In meta.,* Prooemium. For the fundamental relationship between faith and truth, cf. *ST* II–II.1.1.

14. See the judgment of Charles E. Curran in his presidential address to the Catholic Theological Society of America, *Proceedings of the Twenty-Fifth Annual Convention of the Catholic Theological Society of America* (1970), pp. 219–220.

15. Michael J. Lacey, "The Backwardness of American Catholicism," *Proceedings of the Forty-Sixth Annual Convention of the Catholic Theological Society of America* (1991), p. 1.

16. It constituted much of the first thesis to be advanced in that chapter: that science, done with integrity, constitutes something of the problematic situation which confronts theology in the reflection, yes, and even the self-understanding of the church.

17. As indicated in previous chapters, it is critically important not to read into the medieval *artes liberales* the doctrines and practices of the twentieth century on humanistic education. In the Middle Ages, the liberal arts were universal skills or developed abilities or disciplines that could be brought to bear upon any subject matter. Aquinas agrees with Hugh of St. Victor that these arts must first be learned by anyone who wishes to do philosophic reflection (cf. *In de trin.* 5.1. ad 3). This approach contrasts and complements a more content-oriented approach. See Congar, *A History of Theology*, pp. 12–14.

18. Maximi (*sic*) Victorini, *De arte grammatica*, "Grammatica quid est? Scientia interpretandi poetas atque historicos et recte scribendi loquendique ratio." Heinrich Keil, ed., *Grammatici Latini* (Lipsiae: Teubner, 1855–80), 6:188. The attribution of *De arte grammatica* is notoriously problematic. For an identical definition, see Audacis, *De scauri et palladii libris exerpta per interrogationem et responsionem*, Ibid., 7:321. While Donatus himself does not define grammar, Sergius does, commenting upon Donatus: "Ars grammatica praecipue consistit in intellectu poetarum et in recte scribendi loquendive ratione." *Explanationum in artem donati*, Ibid., 4:486. Cf. also Aspri, *Grammatici ars*: "grammatica est scientia recte scribendi et enunciandi interpretandique poetas per historiam formatam ad usum rationemque verborum." Ibid., 5:547. Dosithei Magistri, *Ars grammatica*: "Ars grammatica est scientia emendati sermonis in loquendo et scribendo poematumque ac lectionis prudens praeceptum." Ibid., 7:376. It was this tradition that Rabanus Maurus recapitulates for the Middle Ages in the *De clericorum institutione*, in which he repeats the definition of Victorinus and applies this art to scriptural interpretation. The cleric must learn the figures such as "allegoria, aenigma, parabola. Quorum omnium cognitio propterea Scripturarum ambiguitatibus dissolvendis est necessaria, quia sensus ad propietatem verborum si accipiatur, absurdus est." *De clericorum institutione,*

3.18 (*PL* 107. 395b). Charles Baldwin maintains that *grammatica* dominated the trivium until a shift of emphasis began in the eleventh century; see his *Medieval Rhetoric and Poetic* (New York: Macmillan, 1928), p. 151. John of Salisbury urges grammatical studies in the model of Bernard of Chartres, which was the interpretations, imitation, and discussion of great writings. Cf. *Metalogicon* 1.24 (*PL* 199:853 ff.). For the subsequent history of the use of grammar in the Middle Ages, see J. Reginald O'Donnell, "The Liberal Arts in the Twelfth Century with Special Reference to Alexander Nequam," *ALPMA*, pp. 127–35, with the discussion which follows on pp. 148–56. See also, in the same volume, Heinrich Roos, "Le *Trivium* à l'université au XIIIe siècle," pp. 193–97, and the discussion which follows on pp. 198–203.

19. See Richard P. McKeon, "Philosophic Semantics and Philosophic Inquiry," *Freedom and History*, ed. Zahava K. McKeon (Chicago: The University of Chicago Press, 1990), pp. 242–256.

20. Hugonis de S. Victore, *Eruditionis didascalicae* 2.31. "Ratio disserendi integrales partes habet, inventionem et judicium; divisivas vero, demonstrationem, probabilem, sophisticam. Demonstratio est in necessariis argumentis, et pertinet ad philosophos. Probabilis pertinet ad dialecticos et ad rhetores. Sophistica ad sophistas et cavillatores. Probabilis dividitur in dialecticam et rhetoricam, quarum utraque integrales habet partes inventionem et judicium. Quia enim ipsum genus, id est *artem dissertivam*, integraliter constituunt, necesse est ut in compositione omnium specierum ejus simul inveniatur. Inventio est quae docet invenire argumenta et constituere argumentationes. Scientia judicandi, quae de utroque, judicare docet." (*PL* 176:764; emphasis mine.) It was this combination of rhetoric and dialectic which was the "dissertive art" and which with grammar formed the trivium, which Hugh called *logica*. Thus he can write: "Logica dividitur in grammaticam et disertivam [*sic*]. Dissertiva dividitur in demonstrationem probabilem et sophisticam. Probabilis dividitur in dialecticam et rhetoricam." *Eruditiones didascalicae* 3.1 (*PL* 176:765).

21. The formative influence of the liberal arts on Aquinas is interesting to trace through his studies at the University of Naples. Peter Calo notes that he was sent to Naples "ut esset grammatica, dyalectica, et rhetorica eruditus adprime." This purpose was somewhat aborted, as none of the early biographers mention any study of rhetoric. While they agree that Aquinas' studies in the trivium were confined to grammar and logic, they disagree about the division among instructors. Peter Calo: "Nam cum martinum praeceptorem in grammatica in brevi excederet, traditus est magistro petro ybernico, qui in logicalibus et naturalibus eum instruxit." *Vita 4, Fontes vitae S. Thomae Aquinatis*, curia et labore D. Prummer, O.Pr. (Saint Maximin [Var]: *Revue Thomiste*, 1911–1934 fasc. 1, p. 20. [This compilation is hereafter cited as *Fontes*]. William of Tocco: "Unde puer du utriusque parentis consilio Neapolim mittitur, ut sub Magistri Martini grammaticalibus et logicalibus, et Magisteri Petri de Ibernia studiis in naturalibus edocetur." *Vita 5, Fontes*, fasc. 2, p. 70. Bernardus Cuidonis: " . . . persuasit parentibus ejus ut neapolim mitteretur ad studium liberalibus artibus imbeundus . . . In brevi itque tempore cum in grammaticalibus et logicalibus ac in naturali philosphia plurimum profecisset . . ." *Vita 4, Fontes*, fasc. 3, p. 170. Why no study of rhetoric? Perhaps the clue lies with Peter of Ireland. There is an unedited manuscript in the Vatican library which may cast some light upon this absence: Peter's commentary upon the *Isagoge* and Aristotle's *On Interpretation* entitled *Scriptum super porfirium peremeneias magistri petri de ybernia conventus frarum minorum de Bononia*. Peter writes: "Amplius autem ad scientiam rationalem transire oportet. sed quia naturales scientie non sunt presentis intentionis omissis illis ad rationalem scientiam transeamus. est ergo notandum quod de signis oportuit haberi scientiam. signum enim idem est quod sermo, sed dicit plato in timeo quod sermones inventi sunt ut per ipsos presto sint mutue voluntatis iudicia. et dicit tullius in secunda rhetorica quod sapientia sine eloquentia est quasi gladius in manu paralitici. eloquentia vero sine sapientia est quasi gladius in manu turibundi. ideo non solum oportuit havere scientias reales ad sapientiam ordinatas ideo etiam scientias sermocinales ad eloquentiam ordinatas et sic includitur evidenter quod non sufficiunt scientie reales nisi habeamus sermocinales sive rationales. possunt autem sermocinales scientie distingui diversimode secundum diversas acceptationes sermonis. in sermone enim sunt tria subiecta sermonis: veritas, bonitas, sive decor. primo modo de sermone est grammatica; secundo modo, logica; tertio modo rhetorica. vel aliter quod sermonis proprietates quedam sumuntur a parte vocis sive significati generalis, ut congruum et incongruum; quedam vero ex parte specialis significati in complexione unius ad alterum, et huiusmodi est . . .; autem alia passio que significatur sequitur in respectu ad nos ut persuasio. primo modo, grammatica; secundo modo, logica; tertio rhetorica. nam rhetoris officium est persuadere iudici ut moveat ipsum ad partis adverse indignationem et ad sue partis favorem" (*Vat. lat.* 5988; punctuation added). For Peter, rhetoric dealt with beauty or ornamentation rather than with truth or goodness and not so much with the intrinsic meaning of the text, but rather with its effect upon an audience. Perhaps we can guess for these reasons that Saint Thomas was moved from dialectic or logic directly to the study of natural philosophy.

22. Hugh of St. Victor cites this as a standard understanding of philosophy: "Aliter: 'Philosophia est ars artium, et disciplina disciplinarum,' id est ad quam omnes artes et disciplinae spectant." *Eruditionis didascalicae* 2:1 (*PL* 176:751).

23. History as a liberal art did not emerge until the Renaissance transformed the liberal arts from a command of methods to a command of certain subject matters or fields. For this change, see McKeon, *Freedom and History* pp. 166 and 175. See Grendler's judgment that "the Renaissance's most original curriculum innovation was teaching history," Grendler, *Schooling*, p. 255.

24. Bernard Lonergan, *Method in Theology* (New York: Herder & Herder, 1972), p. 126.

25. One must not think that these four theological arts are abstract in theory and unreal in practice. As a matter of fact, they are not unlike those disciplines elaborated at the University of Chicago in the Division of the Humanities and studied in four interdepartmental committees. See Richard P. McKeon, "Auto-

biography," in *Thirteen Americans: Their Spiritual Autobiographies*, ed. Louis Finkelstein (New York: Harper & Bros., 1953), pp. 90 ff.

26. "Talis est cognitio tradita in hoc libro. Nam cognitio haec iuvat fidem, et fides sic est in intellectu, ut, quantum est de sui ratione, nata sit movere affectum. Et hoc patet. Nam haec cognitio, quod Christus pro nobis mortuus est, et consimiles, nisi sit homo peccator et durus, movet ad amorem; non sic ista: quod diameter est asymeter costae." *In I sent.*, Prooemii (1:13b); cf. *De reductione artium ad theologiam* 26 (5:325b).

27. *ST* I.1.1.

28. *ST* I.1.4.

Name Index

Subject Index